Lecture Notes in Computer Science 8100

Commenced Publication in 1973
Founding and Former Series Editors:
Gerhard Goos, Juris Hartmanis, and Jan van Leeuwen

Editorial Board

Maciej Koutny   Wil M.P. van der Aalst
Alex Yakovlev (Eds.)

Transactions on Petri Nets and Other Models of Concurrency VIII

Springer

Editor-in-Chief

Maciej Koutny
Newcastle University
School of Computing Science
Newcastle upon Tyne, NE1 7RU, UK
E-mail: maciej.koutny@ncl.ac.uk

Guest Editors

Wil M.P. van der Aalst
Eindhoven University of Technology
Department of Mathematics and Computer Science
5600 MB Eindhoven, The Netherlands
E-mail: w.m.p.v.d.aalst@tue.nl

Alex Yakovlev
Newcastle University
School of Electrical, Electronic and Computer Engineering
Newcastle upon Tyne, NE1 7RU, UK
E-mail: alex.yakovlev@ncl.ac.uk

ISSN 0302-9743 (LNCS)   e-ISSN 1611-3349 (LNCS)
ISSN 1867-7193 (ToPNoC)   e-ISSN 1867-7746 (ToPNoC)
ISBN 978-3-642-40464-1   e-ISBN 978-3-642-40465-8
DOI 10.1007/978-3-642-40465-8
Springer Heidelberg New York Dordrecht London

CR Subject Classification (1998): D.2, F.3, F.1, D.3, J.1, I.6, I.2

Typesetting: Camera-ready by author, data conversion by Scientific Publishing Services, Chennai, India

Printed on acid-free paper

Springer is part of Springer Science+Business Media (www.springer.com)

Preface by Editor-in-Chief

The 8th issue of the LNCS Transactions on Petri Nets and Other Models of Concurrency (ToPNoC) contains revised and extended versions of a selection of the best papers from the workshops and tutorials held at the 33rd International Conference on Application and Theory of Petri Nets and Other Models of Concurrency, Hamburg, Germany, 25–29 June 2012.

I would like to thank the two guest editors of this special issue: Wil van der Aalst and Alex Yakovlev. Moreover, I would like to thank all authors, reviewers, and the organizers of the Petri net conference satellite workshops, without whom this issue of ToPNoC would not have been possible.

June 2013

Maciej Koutny
Editor-in-Chief
LNCS Transactions on Petri Nets and Other Models of Concurrency (ToPNoC)

LNCS Transactions on Petri Nets and Other Models of Concurrency: Aims and Scope

ToPNoC aims to publish papers from all areas of Petri nets and other models of concurrency ranging from theoretical work to tool support and industrial applications. The foundations of Petri nets were laid by the pioneering work of Carl Adam Petri and his colleagues in the early 1960s. Since then, a huge volume of material has been developed and published in journals and books as well as presented at workshops and conferences.

The annual International Conference on Application and Theory of Petri Nets and Other Models of Concurrency started in 1980. The International Petri Net Bibliography maintained by the Petri Net Newsletter contains close to 10,000 different entries, and the International Petri Net Mailing List has 1,500 subscribers. For more information on the International Petri Net community, see: http://www.informatik.uni-hamburg.de/TGI/PetriNets/

All issues of ToPNoC are LNCS volumes. Hence they appear in all main libraries and are also accessible in LNCS Online (electronically). It is possible to subscribe to ToPNoC without subscribing to the rest of LNCS.

ToPNoC contains:

- revised versions of a selection of the best papers from workshops and tutorials concerned with Petri nets and concurrency;
- special issues related to particular subareas (similar to those published in the *Advances in Petri Nets* series);
- other papers invited for publication in ToPNoC; and
- papers submitted directly to ToPNoC by their authors.

Like all other journals, ToPNoC has an Editorial Board, which is responsible for the quality of the journal. The members of the board assist in the reviewing of papers submitted or invited for publication in ToPNoC. Moreover, they may make recommendations concerning collections of papers for special issues. The Editorial Board consists of prominent researchers within the Petri net community and in related fields.

Topics

System design and verification using nets; analysis and synthesis, structure and behavior of nets; relationships between net theory and other approaches; causality/partial order theory of concurrency; net-based semantical, logical and algebraic calculi; symbolic net representation (graphical or textual); computer tools for nets; experience with using nets, case studies; educational issues related to nets; higher level net models; timed and stochastic nets; and standardization of nets.

Applications of nets to: biological systems; defence systems; e-commerce and trading; embedded systems; environmental systems; flexible manufacturing systems; hardware structures; health and medical systems; office automation; operations research; performance evaluation; programming languages; protocols and networks; railway networks; real-time systems; supervisory control; telecommunications; cyber physical systems; and workflow.

For more information about ToPNoC see: www.springer.com/lncs/topnoc

Submission of Manuscripts

Manuscripts should follow LNCS formatting guidelines, and should be submitted as PDF or zipped PostScript files to ToPNoC@ncl.ac.uk. All queries should be addressed to the same e-mail address.

Preface by Guest Editors

This volume of ToPNoC contains revised and extended versions of a selection of the best workshop papers presented at the 33rd International Conference on Application and Theory of Petri Nets and Other Models of Concurrency (Petri Nets 2012).

We, Wil van der Aalst and Alex Yakovlev, are indebted to the program committees of the workshops and in particular their chairs. Without their enthusiastic work this volume would not have been possible. Many members of the program committees participated in reviewing the extended versions of the papers selected for this issue. The following workshops were asked for their strongest contributions:

- PNSE 2012: International Workshop on Petri Nets and Software Engineering (chairs: Lawrence Cabac, Michael Duvigneau, and Daniel Moldt),
- CompoNet 2012: International Workshop on Petri Nets Compositions (chairs: Hanna Klaudel and Franck Pommereau),
- LAM 2012: International Workshop on Logics, Agents, and Mobility (chairs: Berndt Müller and Michael Köhler-Bußmeier),
- BioPNN 2012: International Workshop on Biological Processes and Petri Nets (chairs: Monika Heiner and Hofestädt)

The best papers of these workshops were selected in close cooperation with their chairs. The authors were invited to improve and extend their results where possible, based on the comments received before and during the workshop. The resulting revised submissions were reviewed by three to five referees. We followed the principle of also asking for fresh reviews of the revised papers, i.e. from referees who had not been involved initially in reviewing the original workshop contribution. All papers went through the standard two-stage journal reviewing process and eventually ten were accepted after rigorous reviewing and revising. Presented are a variety of high-quality contributions, ranging from model checking and system verification to synthesis, and from work on Petri-net-based standards and frameworks to innovative applications of Petri nets and other models of concurrency.

The paper by Paolo Baldan, Nicoletta Cocco, Federica Giummol, and Marta Simeoni, *Comparing Metabolic Pathways through Reactions and Potential Fluxes* proposes a new method for comparing metabolic pathways of different organisms based on a similarity measure that considers both homology of reactions and functional aspects of the pathways. The paper relies on a Petri net representation of the pathways and compares the corresponding T-invariant bases. A prototype tool, CoMeta, was implemented and used for experimentation.

The paper *Modeling and Analyzing Wireless Sensor Networks with VeriSensor: An Integrated Workflow* by Yann Ben Maissa, Fabrice Kordon, Salma Mouline, and Yann Thierry-Mieg presents a Domain Specific Modeling Language

(DSML) for Wireless Sensor Networks (WSNs) offering support for formal verification. Descriptions in this language are automatically translated into a formal
specification for model checking. The authors present the language and its translation, and discuss a case study illustrating how several metrics and properties
relevant to the domain can be evaluated.

The paper *Local State Refinement on Elementary Net Systems: An Approach
Based on Morphisms* by Luca Bernardinello, Elisabetta Mangioni, and Lucia
Pomello presents a new kind of morphism for Elementary Net Systems for performing abstraction and refinement of local states in systems. These α-mor-
phisms formalize the relation between a refined net system and an abstract one,
by replacing local states of the target net system with subnets.The main results concern behavioral properties preserved and reflected by the morphisms.
In particular, the focus is on the conditions under which reachable markings are
preserved or reflected, and the conditions under which a morphism induces a
weak bisimulation between net systems.

The paper *From Code to Coloured Petri Nets: Modelling Guidelines* by Anna
Dedova and Laure Petrucci presents a method for designing a coloured Petri net
model of a system starting from its high-level object-oriented source code. The
entire process is divided into two parts: grounding and code analysis. For each
part detailed step-by-step guidelines are given. The approach is illustrated using
a case study based on the so-called NEO protocol.

The paper by Agata Janowska, Wojciech Penczek, Agata Półrola, and Andrzej Zbrzezny, *Using Integer Time Steps for Checking Branching Time Properties of Time Petri Nets* extends the result of Popova, which states that integer
time steps are sufficient to test reachability properties of time Petri nets. The
authors prove that the discrete-time semantics is also sufficient to verify properties of the existential and the universal version of CTL* for time Petri nets with
the dense semantics. They compare the results for SAT-based bounded model
checking of the universal version of CTL-X properties and the class of distributed
time Petri nets.

The paper *When Can We Trust a Third Party? – A Soundness Perspective*
by Kees M. van Hee, Natalia Sidorova, and Jan Martijn van der Werf explores
the validity of a system comprising two agents and a third-party notary, which
provides a communication interface between the agents, without any of them
getting knowledge of the actual implementation features of the other. This is
studied in a business-process setting, where the components are modelled as
communicating workflow nets. The paper shows that if the notary is an acyclic
state machine, or if it contains only single-entry-single-exit (SESE) loops, then
the notary ensures soundness if it is sound with each of the organizations individually.

The paper *Hybrid Petri Nets for Modelling the Eukaryotic Cell Cycle* by
Mostafa Herajy, Martin Schwarick, and Monika Heiner describes a model based
on Generalised Hybrid Petri Nets (GHPN) with extensions, and a corresponding
tool for modelling and simulating the eukaryotic cell cycle. Specific problems
encountered in studying such cycles call for the combination of stochastic and

deterministic approaches to modelling the different aspects of the process, and the "hybridization" also includes mixing continuous and discrete elements. The new model is implemented using Snoopy, a tool for animating and simulating Petri nets in various paradigms.

The paper *Simulative Model Checking of Steady-State and Time-Unbounded Temporal Operators* by Christian Rohr starts from the observation that large stochastic models can only be analyzed using simulation. Hence, the author advocates simulative model checking. While finite time horizon algorithms are well known for probabilistic linear-time temporal logic, Rohr provides an infinite time horizon procedure as well as steady state computation, based on exact stochastic simulation algorithms. The paper illustrates the applicability of this idea using the model checking tool MARCIE applied to models of the RKIP-inhibited ERK pathway and angiogenetic process.

The paper *Model-Driven Middleware Support for Team-Oriented Process Management* by Matthias Wester-Ebbinghaus and Michael Köhler-Bußmeier proposes a model for collaborative processes that provides a way to capture the whole context of team-oriented process management: from the underlying organizational structure over team formation up to process execution by the team. The model is based on Mulan, a multi-agent system framework, so as to benefit from the advantages of high-level Petri nets implementing a hierarchical organization described with place-transition nets (Sonar model) and subject to on-line dynamic changes. A running example provides an effective illustration of the model.

The paper *Grade/CPN: A Tool and Temporal Logic for Testing Colored Petri Net Models in Teaching* by Michael Westergaard, Dirk Fahland, and Christian Stahl proposes a semi-automatic tool for grading Petri net modelling assignments. It permits the teacher to describe the expected constraints of the model to be designed, as well as the properties that should be satisfied. The tool performs basic well-formedness checks, and simulates the model with the view to test some properties that are specified in Britney Temporal Logic developed by the authors. The tool is extensible by means of plugins.

As guest editors, we would like to thank all authors and referees who have contributed to this issue. Not only is the quality of this volume the result of the high scientific value of their work, but we would also like to acknowledge the excellent cooperation throughout the whole process that has made our work a pleasant task. Finally, we would like to pay special tribute to the work of Ine van der Ligt of Eindhoven University of Technology who has provided technical support for the composition of this volume, including interactions with the authors. We are also grateful to the Springer/ToPNoC team for the final production of this issue.

June 2013
Wil van der Aalst
Alex Yakovlev
Guest Editors, 8th Issue of ToPNoC

Organization of This Issue

Guest Editors

Wil van der Aalst, The Netherlands
Alex Yakovlev, UK

Co-chairs of the Workshops

Lawrence Cabac (Germany)
Michael Duvigneau (Germany)
Monika Heiner (Germany)
Ralf Hofestädt (Germany)
Hanna Klaudel (France)
Michael Köhler-Bußmeier (Germany)
Daniel Moldt (Germany)
Berndt Müller (UK)
Franck Pommereau (France)

Referees

Paolo Baldan
Kamel Barkaoui
Marco Beccuti
Liu Bing
Rainer Breitling
Claudine Chaouiya
Gianfranco Ciardo
José Manuel Colom
Raymond Devillers
David Gilbert
Luis Gomes
Stefan Haar
Vladimir Janousek
Agata Janowska
Radek Koci

Michael Köhler-Bußmeier
Victor Khomenko
Hiroshi Matsuno
Sucheendra Kumar Palaniappan
Wojciech Penczek
Laure Petrucci
Louchka Popova-Zeugmann
Hanna Klaudel
Radek Koci
Christian Rohr
Marta Simeoni
Maciej Szreter
Catherine Tessier
Walter Vogler
Fei Xia

Table of Contents

Comparing Metabolic Pathways through Reactions and Potential
Fluxes   1
    Paolo Baldan, Nicoletta Cocco, Federica Giummolè, and
    Marta Simeoni

Modeling and Analyzing Wireless Sensor Networks with VeriSensor:
An Integrated Workflow   24
    Yann Ben Maissa, Fabrice Kordon, Salma Mouline, and
    Yann Thierry-Mieg

Local State Refinement and Composition of Elementary Net Systems:
An Approach Based on Morphisms   48
    Luca Bernardinello, Elisabetta Mangioni, and Lucia Pomello

From Code to Coloured Petri Nets: Modelling Guidelines   71
    Anna Dedova and Laure Petrucci

Using Integer Time Steps for Checking Branching Time Properties of
Time Petri Nets   89
    Agata Janowska, Wojciech Penczek, Agata Półrola, and
    Andrzej Zbrzezny

When Can We Trust a Third Party?: A Soundness Perspective   106
    Kees M. van Hee, Natalia Sidorova, and
    Jan Martijn E.M. van der Werf

Hybrid Petri Nets for Modelling the Eukaryotic Cell Cycle   123
    Mostafa Herajy, Martin Schwarick, and Monika Heiner

Simulative Model Checking of Steady State and Time-Unbounded
Temporal Operators   142
    Christian Rohr

Model-Driven Middleware Support for Team-Oriented Process
Management   159
    Matthias Wester-Ebbinghaus and Michael Köhler-Bußmeier

Grade/CPN: A Tool and Temporal Logic for Testing Colored Petri Net
Models in Teaching   180
    Michael Westergaard, Dirk Fahland, and Christian Stahl

Author Index   203

Comparing Metabolic Pathways through Reactions and Potential Fluxes

Paolo Baldan[1], Nicoletta Cocco[2], Federica Giummolè[2], and Marta Simeoni[2]

[1] Dipartimento di Matematica, Università di Padova, Italy
[2] DAIS, Università Ca' Foscari Venezia, Italy

Abstract. Comparison of metabolic pathways is useful in phylogenetic analysis and for understanding metabolic functions when studying diseases and in drugs engineering. In the literature many techniques have been proposed to compare metabolic pathways. Most of them focus on structural aspects, while behavioural or functional aspects are generally not considered. In this paper we propose a new method for comparing metabolic pathways of different organisms based on a similarity measure which considers both homology of reactions and functional aspects of the pathways. The latter are captured by relying on a Petri net representation of the pathways and comparing the corresponding T-invariant bases, which represent minimal subsets of reactions that can operate at a steady state. A prototype tool, CoMETA, implements this approach and allows us to test and validate our proposal. Some experiments with CoMETA are presented.

1 Introduction

The life of an organism depends on its metabolism, the chemical system which generates the essential components - amino acids, sugars, lipids and nucleic acids - and the energy necessary to synthesise and use them. Subsystems of metabolism dealing with some specific functions are called metabolic pathways. An example is the *Glycolysis* pathway, a fundamental pathway common to most organisms which converts glucose into pyruvate and releases energy. Comparing metabolic pathways of different species yields interesting information on their evolution and it may help in understanding metabolic functions, which is important when studying diseases and for drugs design. Differences in metabolic functions may be interesting for industrial processes as well, for example some *Archaea* and *Bacteria*, because of environmental constraints, have developed alternative sugar metabolic pathways, which use and transform different compounds with respect to *Glycolysis* and as a result they may behave as methanogens or denitrifying.

In the recent literature many techniques have been proposed for comparing metabolic pathways of different organisms. Each approach chooses a representation of metabolic pathways which models the information of interest, proposes a similarity or a distance measure and possibly supplies a tool for performing the comparison.

M. Koutny et al. (Eds.): ToPNoC VIII, LNCS 8100, pp. 1–23, 2013.

Representations of metabolic pathways at different degrees of abstraction have been considered. A pathway can be simply viewed as a set of components of interest, which can be reactions, enzymes or chemical compounds. In other approaches pathways are decomposed into sets of paths, leading from an initial metabolite to a final one. The most detailed representations model a metabolic pathway as a graph. Clearly, more detailed models produce more accurate comparison results, in general at the price of being more complex.

The distance measures in the literature generally focus on static, topological information of the pathways, disregarding the fact that they represent dynamic processes. We propose to take into account behavioural aspects: we represent the pathways as Petri nets (PNs) and compare aspects related to their behaviour as captured by T-invariants. PNs seem to be particularly natural for representing and modelling metabolic pathways (see, e.g., [10] and references therein). The graphical representations used by biologists for metabolic pathways and the ones used in PNs are similar; the stoichiometric matrix of a metabolic pathway is analogous to the incidence matrix of a PN; the flux modes and the conservation relations for metabolites correspond to specific properties of PNs. In particular minimal (semi-positive) T-invariants correspond to elementary flux modes [51] of a metabolic pathway, i.e., minimal sets of reactions that can operate at a steady state. The space of semi-positive T-invariants has a unique basis of minimal T-invariants which is characteristic of the net and we use it in the comparison. The similarity measure between pathways that we propose considers both homology of reactions, represented either by the Sørensen or by the Tanimoto index on the multisets of enzymes in the pathways, and similarity of behavioural aspects as captured by the corresponding T-invariant bases.

We developed a prototype tool, CoMeta, implementing our proposal. A first version of CoMeta, with some experiments, was presented in [12]. In this paper we give a detailed description of the present extended version of the tool and report on further experiments for its validation. Given a set of organisms and a set of metabolic pathways, CoMeta automatically gets the corresponding data from the KEGG database, which collects metabolic pathways for different species. Then it builds the corresponding PNs, computes the T-invariants and the similarity measures and gives the results of the comparison among organisms as a distance matrix. Such matrix can be visualised as a phylogenetic tree.

The PNs corresponding to the metabolic pathways of an organism can be seen as subnets of the full metabolic network. They can be analysed either in isolation, focussing on the internal behaviour, or as open interactive subsystems of the full network. The first approach guarantees correctness, i.e., minimal T-invariants of the pathway are minimal T-invariants of the full network. The second approach, instead, guarantees completeness, i.e., the set of invariants includes all the projections of invariants of the full network over the pathway, but possibly more because of the assumption of having an arbitrary environment. Hence, in the open approach, we loose correctness, but, still, as shown in [41], minimal T-invariants of the full network can be obtained compositionally from those of the open subnetworks.

The tool CoMETA offers the possibility of representing a pathway either in isolation or as an interactive subnet. Several experiments with CoMETA have been performed and the approach viewing a pathway as an isolated subsystem, despite the fact that it excludes the input-output fluxes from the analysis, generally provides better results. This could be due to the fact that the completely automatised approach to open subnetworks, which consists in taking as input/output all metabolites which are either only produced or only consumed by the pathway and all metabolites linking the pathway to the rest of the network, is probably too rough and needs to be refined.

A further interesting development of CoMETA would be to compare organisms by considering their whole metabolic networks, thus identifying T-invariants corresponding to functional subunits in the entire metabolism. However, the complexity of determining the Hilbert basis and the average size of metabolic networks makes the computational cost of this approach prohibitive. We will further comment on this possibility along the paper and in the concluding section.

The paper is organised as follows. In Section 2 we introduce metabolic pathways and we provide a classification of various proposals for the comparison of metabolic pathways in the literature. In Section 3 we show how a PN can model a metabolic pathway and present our comparison technique. In Section 4 we briefly illustrate the tool CoMETA and we present some experiments. A short conclusion follows in Section 5.

2   Comparison of Metabolic Pathways

In this section we briefly introduce metabolic pathways and classify various proposals for the comparison of metabolic pathways in the literature.

2.1   Metabolic Pathways

Biologists usually represent a metabolic pathway as a network of *chemical reactions*, catalysed by one or more *enzymes*, where some molecules (*reactants* or *substrates*) are transformed into others (*products*). Enzymes are not consumed in a reaction, even if they are necessary and used while the reaction takes place. The product of a reaction is the substrate for other ones.

To characterise a metabolic pathway, it is necessary to identify its components (namely the reactions, enzymes, reactants and products) and their relations. Quantitative relations can be represented through a *stoichiometric matrix*, where rows represent molecular species and columns represent reactions. An element of the matrix, a *stoichiometric coefficient* n_{ij}, represents the degree to which the i-th chemical species participates in the j-th reaction. By convention, the coefficients for reactants are negative, while those for products are positive. The kinetics of a pathway is determined by the rate associated with each reaction. It is represented by a *rate equation*, which depends on the concentrations of the reactants and on a *reaction rate coefficient* (or *rate constant*) which includes all the other parameters (except for concentrations) affecting the rate.

Information on metabolic pathways are collected in databases. In particular the KEGG PATHWAY database [2] (KEGG stands for *Kyoto Encyclopedia of Genes and Genomes*) contains metabolic, regulatory and genetic pathways for different species whose data are derived by genome sequencing. It integrates genomic, chemical and systemic functional information [29]. The pathways are manually drawn, curated and continuously updated from published materials. They are represented as maps which are linked to additional information on reactions, enzymes and genes, which may be stored in other databases. Metabolic pathways are generally well conserved among most organisms. In KEGG a reference pathway is manually built as the union of the corresponding pathways in the various organisms. Then, from the reference pathway, it is possible to extract the specific pathway for each single organism. This provides a uniform view of the same pathway in different organisms, a fact that can be useful for comparison purposes. KEGG pathways are coded using KGML (*KEGG Markup Language*) [1], a language based on XML.

2.2   Comparison Techniques for Metabolic Pathways

Many proposals exist in the literature for comparing metabolic pathways and whole metabolic networks of different organisms. Each proposal is based on some simplified representation of a metabolic pathway and on a related definition of similarity score (or distance measure) between two pathways. Hence we can group the various approaches in three classes, according to the structures they use for representing and comparing metabolic pathways. Such structures are:

- *Sets.* Most of the proposals in the literature represent a metabolic pathway (or the entire metabolic network) as the set of its main components, which can be reactions, enzymes or chemical compounds (for some approaches in this class see, e.g., [20,21,35,27,17,16,13,59,40]). This representation is simple and efficient and very useful when entire metabolic networks are compared. The comparison is based on suitable set operations.
- *Sequences.* A metabolic pathway is sometimes represented as a set of sequences of reactions (enzymes, compounds), i.e., pathways are decomposed into a set of selected paths leading from an initial component to a final one (see, e.g., [60,36,14,33,61]). This representation may provide more information on the original pathways, but it can be computationally more expensive. It requires methods both for identifying a suitable set of paths and for comparing them.
- *Graphs.* In several approaches, a metabolic pathway is represented as a graph (see, e.g., [25,42,19,63,34,8,15,30,37,32,9,7]). This is the most informative representation in the classification, as it considers both the chemical components and their relations. A drawback can be the complexity of the comparison techniques. In fact, exact algorithms for graph comparison involves two complex problems: the graph and subgraph isomorphism problems, which are GI-complete (graph isomorphism complete) and NP-complete, respectively. For this reason efficient heuristics are normally used and simplifying assumptions are introduced, which produce further approximations.

The similarity measure (or distance) and the comparison technique strictly depend on the chosen representation. When using a set-based representation, the comparison between two pathways roughly consists in determining the number of common elements. A similarity measure commonly used in this case is the *Jacard index* [28] defined as:

$$J(X,Y) = \frac{|X \cap Y|}{|X \cup Y|}$$

where X and Y are the two sets to be compared. When pathways are represented by means of sequences, alignment techniques and sum of scores with gap penalty may be used for measuring similarity. In the case of graph representation, more complex algorithms for *graph homeomorphism* or *graph isomorphism* are used and some approximations are introduced to reduce the computational costs.

In any case the definition of a similarity measure between two metabolic pathways relies on a similarity measure between their components. Reactions are generally identified with the enzymes which catalyse them, and the most used similarity measures between two reactions/enzymes are based on:

- *Identity.* The simplest similarity measure is just a boolean value: two enzymes can either be identical (similarity $= 1$) or different (similarity $= 0$).
- *EC hierarchy.* The similarity measure is based on comparing the unique *EC number* (Enzyme Commission number) associated with each enzyme, which represents its catalytic activity.

  The EC number is a 4-level hierarchical scheme, $d_1.d_2.d_3.d_4$, developed by the International Union of Biochemistry and Molecular Biology (IUBMB) [62]. For instance, *arginase* is numbered by EC:3.5.3.1, which indicates that the enzyme is a hydrolase (EC:3.*.*.*), and acts on the "carbon nitrogen bonds, other than peptide bonds" (sub-class EC:3.5.*.*) in linear amidines (sub-sub-class EC:3.5.3.*). Enzymes with similar EC classifications are functional homologues, but do not necessarily have similar amino acid sequences.

  Given two enzymes $e = d_1.d_2.d_3.d_4$ and $e' = d'_1.d'_2.d'_3.d'_4$, their similarity $S(e, e')$ depends on the length of the common prefix of their EC numbers:

  $$S(e, e') = \max\{i : d_1.d_2 \ldots d_i = d'_1.d'_2.\ldots.d'_i\}/4$$

  For instance, the similarity between *arginase* ($e = 3.5.3.1$) and *creatinase* ($e' = 3.5.3.3$) is 0.75.
- *Information content.* The similarity measure is based on the EC numbers of enzymes together with the information content of the numbering scheme. This is intended to correct the large deviation in the distribution in the enzyme hierarchy. For example, the enzymes in the class 1.1.1 range from EC:1.1.1.1 to EC:1.1.1.254, whereas there is a single enzyme in the class 5.3.4. Given an enzyme class h, its information content can be defined as $I(h) = -log_2 C(h)$, where $C(h)$ denotes the number of enzymes in h (hence large classes have a low information content). The similarity between two enzymes e_i and e_j is then $I(h_{ij})$, where h_{ij} is their smallest common upper class.

— *Sequence alignment.* The similarity measure is obtained by aligning the genes
or the proteins corresponding to the two enzymes and by considering the
resulting alignment score.

3 Behavioural Aspects in Metabolic Pathways Comparison

In this section we briefly discuss how to represent a metabolic pathway as a PN.
Then we define a similarity measure between two metabolic pathways modelled
as PNs, which takes into account the behaviour of the pathways by comparing
their minimal T-invariants. Such measure is combined with a simpler one which
considers homology of reactions.

3.1 Metabolic Pathways as Petri Nets

PNs are a well known formalism originally introduced in computer science for
modelling discrete concurrent systems. PNs have a sound theory and many applications both in computer science and in real life systems (see [38] and [18]
for surveys on PNs and their properties). A large number of tools have been
developed for analysing properties of PNs. A quite comprehensive list can be
found at the *Petri Nets World* site [4].

In some seminal papers Reddy et al. [45,43,44] and Hofestädt [26] proposed
PNs for representing and analysing metabolic pathways. Since then, a wide
range of literature has grown on the topic [10]. The structural representation
of a metabolic pathway by means of a PN can be obtained by exploiting the
natural correspondence between PNs and biochemical networks. In fact places
are associated with molecular species, such as metabolites, proteins or enzymes;
transitions correspond to chemical reactions; input places represent the substrate
or reactants; output places represent reaction products. The incidence matrix of
the PN is identical to the stoichiometric matrix of the system of chemical reactions. The number of tokens in each place indicates the amount of substance
associated with that place. Quantitative data can be added to refine the representation of the behaviour of the pathway. In particular, extended PNs may
have an associated transition rate which depends on the kinetic law of the corresponding reaction. Large and complex networks can be greatly simplified by
avoiding an explicit representation of enzymes and by assuming that ubiquitous
substances are in a constant amount. In this way, however, processes involving
these substances, such as the energy balance, are not modelled.

Once metabolic pathways are represented as PNs, we may consider their behavioural aspects as captured by the T-invariants (transition invariants) of the
nets which, roughly, represent potential cyclic behaviours in the system. More
precisely a T-invariant is a (multi)set of transitions whose execution starting
from a state will bring the system back to the same state. Alternatively, the
components of a T-invariant may be interpreted as the relative firing rates
of transitions which occur permanently and concurrently, thus characterising

a steady state. Therefore the presence of T-invariants in a metabolic pathway is biologically of great interest as it can reveal the presence of steady states, in which concentrations of substances have reached a possibly dynamic equilibrium.

Although space limitations prevent us from a formal presentation of nets and invariants, it is useful to recall that the set of (semi-positive) T-invariants can be characterised finitely, by resorting to its Hilbert basis [48].

Remark 1. Unique basis The set of T-invariants of a (finite) PN N admits a unique basis which is given by the collection $\mathcal{B}(N)$ of minimal T-invariants.

The above means that any T-invariant can be obtained as a linear combination (with positive in teger coefficient) of minimal T-invariants. Uniqueness of the basis $\mathcal{B}(N)$ allows us to take it as a characteristic feature of the net.

In a PN model of a metabolic pathway, a minimal T-invariant corresponds to an elementary flux mode, a term introduced in [51] to refer to a minimal set of reactions that can operate at a steady state. It can be interpreted as a minimal self-sufficient subsystem which is associated with a function. By assuming both the fluxes and the pool sizes constants the stoichiometry of the network restricts the space of all possible net fluxes to a rather small linear subspace. Such subspace can be analysed in order to capture possible behaviours of the pathway and its functional subunits [46,47,49,50,51,52]. Minimal T-invariants have been used in Systems Biology as a fundamental tool in model validation techniques (see, e.g., [24,31]), moreover some analysis and decomposition techniques based on T-invariants have been proposed (see, e.g., [23,22]). In this paper we propose to use minimal T-invariants for metabolic pathways comparison.

The PNs corresponding to the metabolic pathways of an organism are subnets of a larger net representing its full metabolic network. The minimal T-invariants of these subnets have a clear relation with the (minimal) T-invariants of the full network. It can be easily seen that, considering the pathway as an isolated subsystem guarantees correctness: minimal T-invariant of the pathway are minimal T-invariant of the full network. If, instead, a pathway is considered as an interactive subsystem (i.e., its input/output metabolites are taken as open places, where the environment can freely put/remove substances) then completeness is guaranteed: any invariant of the full network, once projected onto the pathway, is an invariant of the open pathway. The converse does not hold, i.e., there can be invariants of the open pathway which do not correspond to invariants of the full network. Hence, in the open approach, we may loose correctness, but, still, as shown in [41], minimal T-invariants of the full network can be obtained compositionally from those of the subnetworks.

The problem of determining the Hilbert basis is EXPSPACE since the size of such basis can be exponential in the size of the net. Still, in our experience, the available tools like INA [57] or 4ti2 [6] work fine on PNs arising from metabolic pathways. On the contrary, the computational cost becomes prohibitive when dealing with full metabolic networks.

3.2   A Combined Similarity Measure between Pathways

Metabolic pathways are complex networks of biochemical reactions describing fluxes of substances. Such fluxes arise as the composition of elementary fluxes, i.e., cyclic fluxes which cannot be further decomposed. Most of the techniques briefly discussed in Section 2 compare pathways on the basis of homology of their reactions, that is they determine a point to point functional correspondence. Some proposals consider the topology of the network, but still most techniques are eminently static and ignore the flow of metabolites in the pathway.

Here we propose a comparison between metabolic pathways based on the combination of two similarity scores derived from their PN representations. More precisely, we consider a "static" score, R_score (reaction score), taking into account the homology of reactions occurring in the pathways and a "behavioural" score, I_score (invariant score), taking into account the dynamics of the pathway as expressed by the T-invariants.

Both R_score and I_score are based on a similarity index. We propose to use either the Sørensen index [56] or the Tanimoto index [58], in both cases extended to multisets. Let X_1 and X_2 be multisets and $\cap$ and $|\cdot|$ be intersection and cardinality generalised to multisets[1], then

- the *Sørensen index* is given by

$$S\_index(X_1, X_2) = \frac{2|X_1 \cap X_2|}{|X_1| + |X_2|}$$

- the *Tanimoto index (extended Jacard index)* is given by

$$T\_index(X_1, X_2) = \frac{|X_1 \cap X_2|}{|X_1| + |X_2| - |X_1 \cap X_2|}$$

Given two pathways represented by the PNs P_1 and P_2, the R_score is computed by comparing their reactions. Each reaction is actually represented by the EC numbers of the associated enzymes. More precisely, if X_1 and X_2 denotes the multisets of the EC numbers of the reactions in P_1 and P_2, respectively, we can define the R_score either as

$$R\_score(X_1, X_2) = S\_index(X_1, X_2)$$

if we select the Sørensen index or as

$$R\_score(X_1, X_2) = T\_index(X_1, X_2)$$

if we select the Tanimoto index. We adopt a multiset representation since an EC number may occur more than once in a pathway. The Tanimoto index was

---

[1] Formally, a multiset is a pair (X, m_X) where X is the *underlying set* and $m_X :$ $X \to \mathbb{N}^+$ is the *multiplicity function*, associating to each $x \in X$ a positive natural number indicating the number of its occurrences. Then $|(X, m_X)| = \sum_{z \in X} m_X(z)$ and $(X, m_X) \cap (Y, m_Y) = (X \cap Y, m_{X \cap Y})$ where $m_{X \cap Y}(z) = min(m_X(z), m_Y(z))$ for each $z \in X \cap Y$.

used, for example, in [59], it fits multisets and it is normalised. The Sørensen index, instead, was not used previously in the literature for pathway comparison. Intuitively it captures what two multisets have in common and it is normalised. In the experiments none of the indexes proved to be definitively better than the other. Hence both indexes are currently offered in CoMETA, which leaves the choice to the user.

Presently the similarity considered between enzymes is the identity, but finer similarity measures between enzymes, such as the one determined by the EC hierarchy, could be easily accommodated in this setting.

The distance based on reactions, or R-distance, is then defined as follows

$$d_R(P_1, P_2) = 1 - R\_score(X_1, X_2).$$

The behavioural component of the similarity is obtained by comparing the Hilbert bases of minimal T-invariants of the net representations, seen either as isolated or open subnets of the full metabolic network. Each invariant is represented by a multiset of EC numbers, corresponding to the reactions occurring in the invariant, and the similarity between two invariants is given, as before, by a similarity index, either the S_index or the T_index. Note that when T-invariants are sets of transitions (rather than proper multisets) they can be seen as subnets of the net at hand, and the similarity between two T-invariants coincides with the R_score of the corresponding subnets.

A heuristic match between the two bases $\mathcal{B}(P_1)$ and $\mathcal{B}(P_2)$ is performed and the similarity values corresponding to the indexes of the matching pairs are accumulated into I_SCORE(P_1, P_2) by the algorithm described in Fig. 1.

Again, the similarity between pathways based on minimal T-invariants induces a distance, the I-distance:

$$d_I(P_1, P_2) = 1 - I\_score(P_1, P_2)$$

The two distances are combined by taking a weighted sum, as shown below, where $\alpha \in [0, 1]$:

$$d_D(P_1, P_2) = \alpha\, d_R(P_1, P_2) + (1 - \alpha)\, d_I(P_1, P_2)$$

The parameter α allows the analyst to move the focus between homology of reactions and similarity of functional components as represented by the T-invariants.

Two organisms O_1 and O_2 can be compared by considering n metabolic pathways $P_1, \ldots, P_n$. In this case the distances between the two organisms with respect to the various metabolic pathways P_j, $j \in [1, n]$, need to be combined. The simplest solution consists in taking the average distance:

$$d_D(O_1, O_2) = \frac{\sum_{j=1}^{n} d_D(P_j^1, P_j^2)}{n}$$

When a pathway P_j occurs in one of the two organisms but not in the other, the corresponding pathway distance $d_D(P_j^1, P_j^2)$ in the formula above is assumed to be 1.

```
function I_SCORE(P_1, P_2);
    input:    two metabolic pathways P_1 and P_2;
    output:   the similarity measure between B(P_1) and B(P_2);
begin
    I_1 = B(P_1); I_2 = B(P_2);
    score = 0;
    card = max{|I_1|, |I_2|};
    while (I_1 ≠ ∅ ∧ I_2 ≠ ∅) do
    begin
        (X_1, X_2) = FIND_MAX_SIM(I_1, I_2);    {Returns a pair of T-invariants, (X_1, X_2),
                        in I_1 × I_2 such that Index(X_1, X_2) is maximum,
                        where Index(X_1, X_2) is the Sørensen or the Tanimoto index}
        score = score + Index(X_1, X_2);
        I_1 = I_1 - {X_1};
        I_2 = I_2 - {X_2};
    end;
    score = score / card;
    return score
end I_SCORE;
```

Fig. 1. Comparing bases of T-invariants

4   Experimenting with CoMeta

In this section we briefly illustrate the prototype tool CoMETA (Comparing METAbolic pathways) which implements our proposal, and we report on some experiments.

4.1   CoMeta

CoMETA is a user-friendly tool written in Java and running under Linux and Mac. It uses an external tool for computing the Hilbert basis called 4ti2 [6], a software package for algebraic, geometric and combinatorial problems on linear spaces[2].

CoMETA offers a set of integrated functionalities. We describe them with the help of the graphical user interface, pictured in Figure 2. Looking at the main window in Figure 2(a), we can distinguish an upper part, which allows for the selection of the desired KEGG organisms and pathways from the complete lists on top of the window, and a lower part where a tabbed panel indicates the various commands which can be performed. The first tab of the tabbed panel is shown in the main window, while the others are in Figure 2(b), 2(c), and 2(d), respectively.

The main functionalities of the tool are the following:

---

[2] A previous version of the tool uses INA (Integrated Tool Analyser) [57] as external tool for computing the Hilbert basis. It runs under Windows and Linux.

– *Select organisms and pathways:* CoMeta proposes the lists of KEGG organisms and pathways (see the two lists on top of the main window, Figure 2(a)) and allows the user to select the ones to be compared by double-clicking them. In Figure 2(a) six organisms and one pathway have been selected. Such lists can be saved and then recovered for further processing by using the "File" menu.

– *Retrieve KEGG information:* by clicking on the "Download KEGG files" button in the first tab of the tabbed panel shown in Figure 2(a), CoMeta downloads the information for the selected organisms and pathways from the KEGG database.

– *Translate into PNs:* by clicking the "Translate KEGG files into PNs" button in the second tab of the tabbed panel shown in Figure 2(b), CoMeta translates the selected organisms and pathways into corresponding PNs. Only pathways which are networks of biochemical reactions can be translated. The user can choose between a translation producing isolated or open networks. For this purpose, CoMeta resorts to the tool MPath2PN [11] which have been developed for transforming a metabolic pathway, expressed in one of the various existing DB formats, into a corresponding PN, expressed in one of the various PNs formats. In this case the translation is from KGML to PNML [3], a standard format for PNs tools. We refer to [11] for the detailed explanation of the translation. The resulting PNML files are available for further processing. Besides, CoMeta produces a text file representing the stoichiometric matrix of the net, which is the input of 4ti2.

– *Compute Distances:* by using the third tab of the tabbed panel shown in Figure 2(c), the R-distance and the I-distance as defined in Section 3.2 are computed. The user can select either the Sørensen or the Tanimoto index. CoMeta uses the tool 4ti2 to compute the bases of semi-positive T-invariants of the PN representations of the pathways. CoMeta allows the user to inspect the details of the comparison between any pair of organisms (T-invariants bases, invariants matches, reactions and invariants scores, etc.) by clicking on the "Show details" button.

– *Compute the combined distance:* by using the fourth tab of the tabbed panel shown in Figure 2(d), the user can specify the parameter α for computing the combined distance. By clicking on the "Export matrices" button, the R-distance, I-distance and the combined distance matrices can be exported as text files to be inspected and for further analyses. By clicking the "Show tree(s)" button CoMeta builds and visualises a phylogenetic tree corresponding to the chosen combined distance. Currently CoMeta offers the UPGMA [55,53] and Neighbour Joining [39,53] methods[3].

---

[3] UPGMA (Unweighted Pair Group Method with Arithmetic Mean) is a hierarchical clustering method which constructs a rooted tree (dendrogram) from a pairwise distance matrix. It assumes a constant rate of evolution (molecular clock hypothesis). Neighbour joining is a bottom-up clustering method and it produces an unrooted tree. CoMeta sets a root in the tree between the last joined two clusters. It is a polynomial-time algorithm, practical for analyzing large data sets.

(a) CoMeta main window

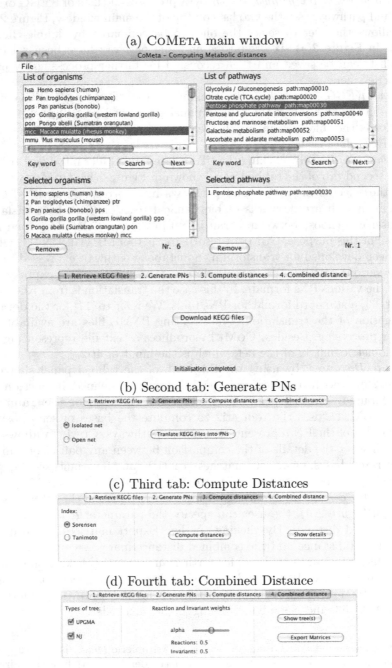

(b) Second tab: Generate PNs

(c) Third tab: Compute Distances

(d) Fourth tab: Combined Distance

Fig. 2. The CoMeta graphical user interface

4.2   Experiments

The comparison of metabolic pathways can be useful for studying some specific metabolic functions in a group of selected organisms. In this case the comparison will be conducted on a single or few metabolic pathways. Alternatively, in the literature metabolic pathways comparison has been applied to phylogenetic inference (see e.g. [20,21,25,27,16,13,19,32]). For this purpose it could be appropriate to compare all metabolic pathways (or, as mentioned in the introduction, the whole metabolic network) of the selected organisms. However, also in this context, it can be interesting to focus on the evolution of one or few relevant metabolic functions.

In order to validate our proposal we conducted various experiments with CoMETA, some of which are briefly reported below. First, with the aim of investigating the relationships between the R-distance and the I-distance and of getting insights on the more appropriate values for the parameter α, we studied extensively the distributions of the R-distance and I-distance on the organisms stored in KEGG with respect to a single well documented pathway, the *Glycolysis*. Then we used our distances for classifying the *Glycolysis* of heterogeneous groups of bacteria and archaea. A further set of experiments, some of which were presented in [12], consisted in building phylogenetic trees for groups of organisms on the basis of some selected pathways. This allows for some comparison with analogous work in the literature. The first set of experiments is conducted considering both the isolated and the open variants of the pathways. The second and third experiments focus on the isolated approach which, in our experience, produces better results.

Exploring KEGG Pathways with CoMeta. In this first set of experiments we explored the metabolic pathways of the organisms stored in KEGG with CoMETA, in order to analyse the significance of the proposed distances d_R and d_I and their relationship in both the open and isolated approaches. We considered different pathways and different classes of organisms[4]. For each class we studied the distribution of the values of the proposed distances for all the pairs of different organisms in the class. For brevity we report here only some results regarding the *Glycolysis* pathway and the Sørensen index.

Each row in Figure 3 corresponds to a class of organisms and shows the histograms for the I-distance (open and isolated approaches) and the R-distance. The continuous lines represent estimates of the density of the considered distances. Graphics with the same dimensions have been used for the same row, this makes it easier to compare histograms of the proposed distances for the same group of organisms.

---

[4] A class is a taxonomic group consisting of organisms that share some common attributes. Organisms in KEGG are classified hierarchically: at the very first level there are the three reigns *Eukaryotes*, *Prokaryotes* and *Archaea*, then three levels of categories (eg. *Animals*, *Vertebrates* and *Mammals* are three nested levels inside *Eukaryotes*) and the last level corresponds to species, eg. *Homo sapiens*.

The first row corresponds to experiments conducted on the class *Archaea*. The histograms show that the I-distance in the isolated approach and the R-distance behave in a rather similar way and that both their densities are mostly concentrated in $[0, 0.3]$. Instead, in the open approach the I-distance has a quite different distribution, ranging over the whole interval $[0, 1]$. This suggests that, within the class of the *Archaea*, the *Glycolysis* pathway greatly differs on the potential fluxes involving the boundaries.

The second row corresponds to experiments conducted on the class *Eukaryotes*. The histograms show that the I-distance and the R-distance exhibit different distributions. In fact, the I-distance, in both variants, shows a rather flat distribution ranging from 0 to 1 for the open approach and from 0 to 0.8 for the isolated approach, while the R-distance takes values only in the interval $[0, 0.6]$, with a unimodal distribution, mostly concentrated in $[0.05, 0.25]$. This suggests that, within the class of the *Eukaryotes* and with respect to the *Glycolysis* pathway, the I-distance, in both variants, discriminates more than the R-distance, for which most organisms are very similar.

Further experiments (rows three to five) focus on refinements of the class of *Eukaryotes* which, in KEGG, is rather heterogeneous. It contains 180 organisms organised in various subclasses. More precisely, the histograms in rows from three to five of Figure 3, represent respectively the subclasses *Animals*, *Vertebrates* and *Mammals*, each included in the previous one. Let us focus on the subclass *Animals*, which in KEGG contains 59 still very heterogeneous organisms. The R-distance has a narrower range varying from 0 to 0.3, while I-distance ranges in the larger intervals $[0, 1]$ for the open approach and $[0, 0.75]$ for the isolated one. The *Vertebrates* in KEGG are a rather homogeneous subclass of the *Animals*, consisting of 26 organisms. The range of the distances remarkably decreases, meaning that our distances view the *Vertebrates* as an homogeneous class within the *Animals*, with respect to the *Glycolysis* pathway. The R-distance considers most of the *Vertebrates* as equal (0 distance), while the I-distance, in particular in the open approach, is still able to discriminate between some of them. The *Mammals* stored in KEGG form a homogeneous subclass of 17 organisms among the *Vertebrates* and this is confirmed by the distribution of the distances which are mostly concentrated around 0.

This exploration seems to confirm that both the R-distance and the I-distance are meaningful and that, in some cases, the I-distance (especially in the open approach), is able to discriminate more than the R-distance.

Classifying Heterogeneous Organisms with Respect to Glycolysis. We present a classification among organisms produced by comparing a specific pathway. We consider the *Glycolysis* pathway in a set of organisms which differ greatly with respect to sugar metabolism, i.e., a mixed group of bacteria and archaea including nitrogen-fixing, sulfate-reducing and methanogen organisms. More precisely we consider the *Glycolysis* of the following organisms: *Desulfovibrio vulgaris Hildenborough* (dvu), *Syntrophobacter fumaroxidans* (sfu), *Rhodobacter sphaeroides 2.4.1* (rsp), *Clostridium difficile 630* (cdf), *Desulfotomaculum*

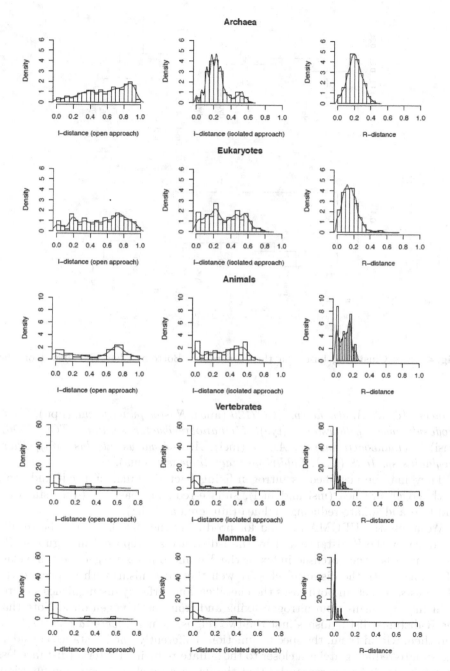

Fig. 3. Histograms of the I-distance (open and isolated approaches) and R-distance for the *Archaea, Eukaryotes, Animals, Vertebrates* and *Mammals* in KEGG wrt. the *Glycolysis* pathway

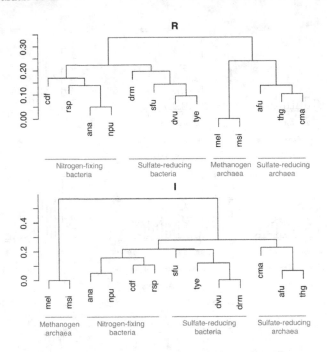

Fig. 4. Top: Clustering based on the R-distance. Bottom: Clustering based on the I-distance.

reducens (drm), *Anabaena sp. PCC7120* (ana), *Nostoc punctiforme* (npu), *Thermodesulfovibrio yellowstonii* (tye), *Methanobrevibacter smithii ATCC 35061* (msi), *Methanobacterium sp. AL-21* (mel), *Archaeoglobus fulgidus* (afu), *Thermogladius sp. 1633* (thg), *Caldivirga maquilingensis* (cma).

They may be classified as nitrogen-fixing bacteria (ana, npu, cdf and rsp), methanogen archaea (msi and mel), sulfate-reducing bacteria (dvu, sfu, drm and tye) and sulfate-reducing archaea (afu, cma and thg).

We apply the UPGMA method for producing the classification. The results obtained by the R-distance and by the I-distance are reported in Figure 4. By choosing either the Sørensen index or the Tanimoto index we get the same classifications. Both the distances classify well these organisms with respect to the *Glycolysis*. In fact, in both cases the classification perfectly distinguishes sulfate-reducing organisms from nitrogen-fixing and from methanogen ones. Note that the R-distance distinguishes first the two reigns, namely *Bacteria* and *Archaea*, and then, within them, the specific function. Differently, the I-distance considers the sulfate-reducing archaea closer to the sulfate-reducing bacteria (distance less than 0.3), i.e. it better recognises that the two groups share a common function.

Phylogenetic Reconstruction. This experiment considers a set of 16 organisms, mainly bacteria, and it builds a phylogenetic tree, showing the inferred evolutionary relationships among the various organisms, by comparing their

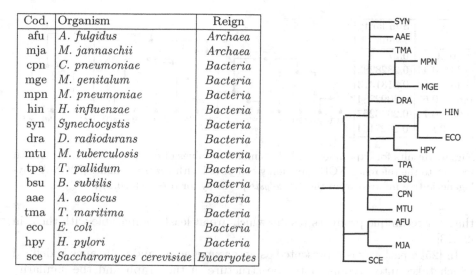

Cod.	Organism	Reign
afu	A. fulgidus	Archaea
mja	M. jannaschii	Archaea
cpn	C. pneumoniae	Bacteria
mge	M. genitalum	Bacteria
mpn	M. pneumoniae	Bacteria
hin	H. influenzae	Bacteria
syn	Synechocystis	Bacteria
dra	D. radiodurans	Bacteria
mtu	M. tuberculosis	Bacteria
tpa	T. pallidum	Bacteria
bsu	B. subtilis	Bacteria
aae	A. aeolicus	Bacteria
tma	T. maritima	Bacteria
eco	E. coli	Bacteria
hpy	H. pylori	Bacteria
sce	Saccharomyces cerevisiae	Eucaryotes

Fig. 5. Left: organisms for experiment 3. Right: reference NCBI taxonomy.

Glycolysis pathways. This experiment has been originally reported in [25] as a test case and then it has been considered in [13]. The organisms and their reference NCBI taxonomy [5] are show in Figure 5.

Focusing on an experiment already studied in the literature may help in comparing our technique with other proposals, although, as clarified below, a precise comparison is quite difficult for the variability of data sources and reference classifications.

We consider the Sørensen index, the value of α ranges in $[0, 1]$, phylogenetic trees are built using the UPGMA method and they are compared with the reference NCBI classification of the 16 organisms. Following [25,13], in order to perform such a comparison we use the *cousins* tool [64,54] with threshold 2. The tool compares unordered trees with labelled leaves by counting the sets of common cousin pairs up to a certain cousin distance[5]. The outcome is reported in the table in Figure 6 (left). Our best result, 0.3131313, corresponds to the phylogenetic tree in Figure 6 (right) and to our combined distance with $\alpha \in [0.45, 0.63]$. The same best result is obtained using the Tanimoto index, for $\alpha \in [0.40, 0.59]$.

Our results cannot be immediately compared with those in [25,13]. In fact, the reference NCBI classification of the 16 organisms and the corresponding KEGG data have been changing in the meantime. Nevertheless, the experiment suggests

---

[5] A *cousin pair* is a triple consisting of a pair of leaves and their cousin distance: 0 if they are siblings (same parent), 0.5 if the parent of one of them is the grandparent of the other, 1 if they are cousins (same grandparent but not same parent), 1.5 if their first common ancestor is the grandparent of one of them and the great-grandparent of the other one, 2 if they are second cousins (same great-grandparent but not same grandparent) and so on.

α	Similarity value
0.00	0.27
0.39 - 0.44	0.2828283
0.45 - 0.63	0.3131313
0.64 - 0.65	0.3092784
0.66 - 0.75	0.2673267
1.00	0.2427184

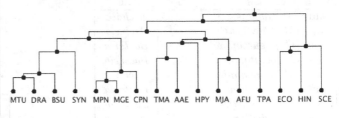

Fig. 6. Results for experiment 3. Left: similarity values of our phylogenetic trees with respect to the reference NCBI taxonomy computed with *cousins*. Right: UPGMA phylogenetic tree inferred from the *Glycolysis* pathway for $\alpha \in [0.45, 0.63]$.

that our technique produces results which are at least comparable with those in [25,13].

In [25] a pathway is represented as an *enzyme graph* and a distance is defined which takes into account both the structure of the graph and the similarity between corresponding nodes. A phylogenetic tree is built with the resulting distance matrix by using the Neighbour Joining method. The authors consider the 16 organisms wrt the *Glycolysis* pathway and *cousins* provides a similarity value of 0.26 between their phylogenetic tree and the reference NCBI taxonomy (this outperforms the results of the phylogenies obtained by NCE, 16SrRNA and [35]). As shown in Figure 6 our results improve those in [25]. Although space limitations prevent us to report the details here, this holds when we use Neighbour Joining trees too.

In [13] a heuristic comparison algorithm is proposed which computes the intersection and symmetric difference of the sets of compounds, enzymes, and reactions in the metabolic pathways of different organisms. Their similarity matrix is supplied to a fuzzy equivalence relations-based (FER) hierarchical clustering method to compute the classification tree. The authors say that they were not able to recompute the same results obtained by [25] on the experiment of the 16 organisms. In the *cousins* comparison with respect to the reference NCBI taxonomy their best result has a similarity value of 0.3195876, which is very close to our best result.

5   Conclusions

Biological questions related to evolution and to differences among organisms can be answered by comparing their metabolic pathways. In this paper we propose a new similarity measure for metabolic pathways which combines a similarity based on reactions and a similarity based on behavioural aspects as captured by minimal T-invariants of the PN representation of a pathway seen either as an isolated or an open subsystem.

We implemented a tool, COMETA, to experiment with our proposal. It is not easy to compare our results with those in the literature since no benchmark is available and the information in the databases are continuously updated. Nevertheless experiments made with CoMeta show that:

- Our combined measure produces meaningful classifications.
- Neither the comparison based on reactions nor the one based on T-invariants is always preferable. The refinement due to the introduction of the behavioural measure can be useful, but further investigations are necessary to determine how to combine properly the two measures.
- Measures based on more sophisticated representations of a pathway (e.g., using graphs rather than sets, or considering compounds besides enzymes) do not necessarily give better results than our combined measure, as our last experiment shows.

The above considerations apply to the comparison of the pathways seen as isolated subsystems of the full metabolic network and, indeed, the experiments mainly focus on this approach. Results obtained when representing the pathways as open, interactive, subsystems are less satisfactory. We believe this may be due to our completely automatised approach, which considers all metabolites which are only consumed or only produced by a pathway and all metabolites linking the pathway to the rest of the network as input/output places of the subnet. This is probably too rough and needs to be refined. In addition, it must be remarked that KEGG indicates the connections among pathways in a very abstract way and these information are not sufficiently precise and complete to be safely used for building the open subnet. We are currently extending CoMeta to grant to the user the possibility of choosing, among the metabolites in the border of the pathway, those which should be considered as input/output places. Such a choice can be guided by making explicit which metabolites are sources, which are sinks and which are indicated by KEGG as links between pathways.

We are considering also other improvements for CoMeta. We would like to give the possibility of a more general clustering of organisms based on the combined distance. We also plan to add more refined reactions/enzymes similarity measures based, e.g., on the hierarchical similarity of EC numbers. Moreover, although the simple greedy algorithm for matching invariants bases in the I_SCORE computation seems to provide good results at a very low computational cost, we plan to investigate possible refinements improving the quality of the match, while keeping a reasonable efficiency. A further extension could be to introduce the possibility to associate weights to the pathways when considering sets of pathways in the comparison. Weights could be decided by the user for putting more emphasis on some pathways of interest, or they could be derived on the basis of characteristics of the pathways, like their size.

Another interesting direction of development for CoMeta would be the comparison of different organisms by considering their whole metabolic networks. Unfortunately, this introduces several difficulties. KEGG does not provide an explicit detailed representation of full metabolic networks and, in general, obtaining a good quality complete network is a difficult task. In addition, the most serious obstacle in this direction seems to be its computational cost. The fact that the Hilbert basis can be exponential in the size of the network, combined with the average size of metabolic networks (more than 1000 compounds and 1500 reactions) suggests that the computation is unfeasible in practice and this was confirmed by our experiments.

Different solutions for guaranteeing the scalability of the approach can be explored:

- *incrementality:* Instead of comparing the full metabolic network, it could be interesting to compare smaller networks obtaining by merging, in an incremental fashion, a number of metabolic pathways of interest. This would allow to control the complexity growth. A difficulty consists in obtaining from KEGG precise information on how different pathways should be joined and in identifying possible overlaps.
- *network simplification:* Techniques for detecting portions of the network which are not active under some specific context conditions could be devised. This would allow to crop the network and to eliminate some potential fluxes. Clearly this requires some knowledge of quantitative information, which is not supplied by KEGG.

CoMETA is part of a larger project to integrate various tools for representing and analysing metabolic pathways through PNs. CoMETA is freely available at: http://www.dsi.unive.it/~biolab.

Acknowledgements. We are grateful to Paolo Besenzon, Silvio Alaimo and Alessandro Roncato for their contribution to the implementation of CoMETA. We are indebted to the anonymous reviewers for their comments on the paper.

References

1. Kegg Markup Language manual, http://www.genome.ad.jp/kegg/docs/xml
2. KEGG pathway database - Kyoto University Bioinformatics Centre, http://www.genome.jp/kegg/pathway.html
3. Petri Net Markup Language, http://www.pnml.org
4. Petri net tools, http://www.informatik.uni-hamburg.de/TGI/PetriNets/tools
5. Taxonomy - site guide - NCBI, http://www.ncbi.nlm.nih.gov/guide/taxonomy/
6. 4ti2 team. 4ti2—a software package for algebraic, geometric and combinatorial problems on linear spaces, http://www.4ti2.de
7. Ay, F., Dang, M., Kahveci, T.: Metabolic network alignment in large scale by network compression. BMC Bioinformatics 13(suppl. 3) (2012)
8. Ay, F., Kahveci, T., de Crecy-Lagard, V.: Consistent alignment of metabolic pathways without abstraction. In: Int. Conf. on Computational Systems Bioinformatics (CSB), pp. 237–248 (2008)
9. Ay, F., Kellis, M., Kahveci, T.: SubMAP: Aligning metabolic pathways with subnetwork mappings. Journal of Computational Biology 18(3), 219–235 (2011)
10. Baldan, P., Cocco, N., Marin, A.: M Simeoni. Petri nets for modelling metabolic pathways: a survey. Natural Computing 9(4), 955–989 (2010)
11. Baldan, P., Cocco, N., De Nes, F., Llabrés Segura, M., Simeoni, M.: MPath2PN - Translating metabolic pathways into Petri nets. In: Heiner, M., Matsuno, H. (eds.) BioPPN2011 Int. Workshop on Biological Processes and Petri Nets. CEUR Workshop Proceedings, vol. 724, pp. 102–116 (2011), http://ceur-ws.org/Vol-724

12. Baldan, P., Cocco, N., Simeoni, M.: Comparison of metabolic pathways by considering potential fluxes. In: Heiner, M., Hofestädt, R. (eds.) BioPPN2012 - 3rd International Workshop on Biological Processes and Petri Nets, Satellite Event of Petri Nets 2012, Hamburg, Germany, June 25. CEUR Workshop Proceedings, vol. 852, pp. 2–17. ceur-ws.org (2012), http://ceur-ws.org/Vol-852

13. Casasnovas, J., Clemente, J.C., Miró-Julià, J., Rosselló, F., Satou, K., Valiente, G.: Fuzzy clustering improves phylogenetic relationships reconstruction from metabolic pathways. In: Proc. of the 11th Int. Conf. on Information Processing and Management of Uncertainty in Knowledge-Based Systems (2006)

14. Chen, M., Hofestadt, R.: Web-based information retrieval system for the prediction of metabolic pathways. IEEE Trans. on NanoBioscience 3(3), 192–199 (2004)

15. Cheng, Q., Harrison, R., Zelikovsky, A.: MetNetAligner: a web service tool for metabolic network alignments. Bioinformatics 25(15), 1989–1990 (2009)

16. Clemente, J., Satou, K., Valiente, G.: Reconstruction of phylogenetic relationships from metabolic pathways based on the enzyme hierarchy and the gene ontology. Genome Informatics 16(2), 45–55 (2005)

17. Ebenhöh, O., Handorf, T., Heinrich, R.: A cross species comparison of metabolic network functions. Genome Informatics 16(1), 203–213 (2005)

18. Esparza, J., Nielsen, M.: Decidability issues for Petri Nets - a survey. Journal Inform. Process. Cybernet. EIK 30(3), 143–160 (1994)

19. Forst, C.V., Flamm, C., Hofacker, I.L., Stadler, P.F.: Algebraic comparison of metabolic networks, phylogenetic inference, and metabolic innovation. BMC Bioinformatics 7(1), 1–11 (2006)

20. Forst, C.V., Schulten, K.: Evolution of metabolism: a new method for the comparison of metabolic pathways using genomics information. Journal of Computational Biology 6(3/4), 343–360 (1999)

21. Forst, C.V., Schulten, K.: Phylogenetic analysis of metabolic pathways. Journal of Molecular Evolution 52(16), 471–489 (2001)

22. Grafahrend-Belau, E., Schreiber, F., Heiner, M., Sackmann, A., Junker, B.H., Grunwald, S., Speer, A., Winder, K., Koch, I.: Modularization of biochemical networks based on classification of Petri net t-invariants. BMC Bioinformatics 9(1), 1–17 (2008)

23. Hardy, S., Robillard, P.N.: Petri net-based method for the analysis of the dynamics of signal propagation in signaling pathways. Bioinformatics 24(2), 209–217 (2008)

24. Heiner, M., Koch, I.: Petri net based model validation in systems biology. In: Cortadella, J., Reisig, W. (eds.) ICATPN 2004. LNCS, vol. 3099, pp. 216–237. Springer, Heidelberg (2004)

25. Heymans, M., Singh, A.M.: Deriving phylogenetic trees from the similarity analysis of metabolic pathways. Bioinformatics 19(1), i138–i146 (2003)

26. Hofestädt, R.: A Petri net application of metabolic processes. Journal of System Analysis, Modelling and Simulation 16, 113–122 (1994)

27. Hong, S.H., Kim, T.Y., Lee, S.Y.: Phylogenetic analysis based on genome-scale metabolic pathway reaction content. Applied Microbiology and Biotechnology 65(2), 203–210 (2004)

28. Jaccard, P.: Distribution de la flore alpine dans le bassin des Dranses et dans quelques régions voisines. Bulletin del la Société Vaudoise des Sciences Naturelles 37, 241–272 (1901)

29. Kanehisa, M., Araki, M., Goto, S., Hattori, M., Hirakawa, M., Itoh, M., Katayama, T., Kawashima, S., Okuda, S., Tokimatsu, T., Yamanishi, Y.: KEGG for linking genomes to life and the environment. Nucleic Acids Research, 480–484 (2008)

30. Klau, G.W.: A new graph-based method for pairwise global network alignment. BMC Bioinformatics 10(suppl. 1), 1–9 (2009)
31. Koch, I., Heiner, M.: Petri nets. In: Junker, B.H., Schreiber, F. (eds.) Analysis of Biological Networks. Book Series in Bioinformatics, pp. 139–179. Wiley & Sons (2008)
32. Kuchaiev, O., Milenkovic, T., Memisevic, V., Hayes, W., Przulj, N.: Topological network alignment uncovers biological function and phylogeny. Journal of the Royal Society Interface 7(50), 1341–1354 (2010)
33. Li, Y., de Ridder, D., de Groot, M.J.L., Reinders, M.J.T.: Metabolic pathway alignment between species using a comprehensive and flexible similarity measure. BMC Systems Biology 2(1), 1–15 (2008)
34. Li, Z., Zhang, S., Wang, Y., Zhang, X.S., Chen, L.: Alignment of molecular networks by integer quadratic programming. Bioinformatics 23(13), 1631–1639 (2007)
35. Liao, L., Kim, S., Tomb, J.F.: Genome comparisons based on profiles of metabolic pathways. In: Proc. of the 6th Int. Conf. on Knowledge-Based Intelligent Information and Engineering Systems (KES 2002), pp. 469–476 (2002)
36. Lo, E., Yamada, T., Tanaka, M., Hattori, M., Goto, S., Chang, C., Kanehisa, M.: A method for customized cross-species metabolic pathway comparison. In: Proc. of Genome Informatics 2004. GIW 2004 Poster Abstract: P068 (2004)
37. Mithani, A., Preston, G.M., Hein, J.: Rahnuma: Hypergraph based tool for metabolic pathway prediction and network comparison. Bioinformatics 25(14), 1831–1832 (2009)
38. Murata, T.: Petri Nets: Properties, Analysis, and Applications. Proceedings of IEEE 77(4), 541–580 (1989)
39. Saitou, N., Nei, M.: The neighbor-joining method: a new method for reconstructing phylogenetic trees. Molecular Biology and Evolution 4(4), 406–425 (1987)
40. Oehm, S., Gilbert, D., Tauch, A., Stoye, J., Goessmann, A.: Comparative Pathway Analyzer - a web server for comparative analysis, clustering and visualization of metabolic networks in multiple organisms. Nucleic Acids Research 36, 433–437 (2008)
41. Pedersen, M.: Compositional definitions of minimal flows in petri nets. In: Heiner, M., Uhrmacher, A.M. (eds.) CMSB 2008. LNCS (LNBI), vol. 5307, pp. 288–307. Springer, Heidelberg (2008)
42. Pinter, R.Y., Rokhlenko, O., Yeger-Lotem, E., Ziv-Ukelson, M.: Alignment of metabolic pathways. Bioinformatics 21(16), 3401–3408 (2005)
43. Reddy, V.N.: Modeling Biological Pathways: A Discrete Event Systems Approach. Master's thesis, The Universisty of Maryland, M.S. 94-4 (1994)
44. Reddy, V.N., Liebman, M.N., Mavrovouniotis, M.L.: Qualitative Analysis of Biochemical Reaction Systems. Computers in Biology and Medicine 26(1), 9–24 (1996)
45. Reddy, V.N., Mavrovouniotis, M.L., Liebman, M.N.: Petri net representations in metabolic pathways. In: ISMB93: First Int. Conf. on Intelligent Systems for Molecular Biology, pp. 328–336. AAAI press (1993)
46. Schilling, C.H., Letscherer, D., Palsson, B.O.: Theory for the systemic definition of metabolic pathways and their use in interpreting metabolic function from a pathway-oriented perspective. Journal of Theoretical Biology 203, 229–248 (2000)
47. Schilling, C.H., Schuster, S., Palsson, B.O., Heinrich, R.: Metabolic pathway analysis: basic concepts and scientific applications in the post-genomic era. Biotechnology Progress 15(3), 296–303 (1999)
48. Schrijver, A.: Theory of linear and integer programming. Wiley-Interscience series in discrete mathematics and optimization. Wiley (1999)

49. Schuster, S., Dandekar, T., Fell, D.A.: Detection of elementary flux modes in bio-chemical networks: a promising tool for pathway analysis and metabolic engineering. Trends Biotechnology, 53–60 (March 1999)
50. Schuster, S., Fell, D.A., Dandekar, T.: A general definition of metabolic pathway useful for systematic organization and analysis of complex metabolic networks. Nature Biotechnology 18, 326–332 (2000)
51. Schuster, S., Hilgetag, C.: On elementary flux modes in biochemical reaction systems at steady state. Journal of Biological Systems 2, 165–182 (1994)
52. Schuster, S., Pfeiffer, T., Moldenhauer, F., Koch, I., Dandekar, T.: Exploring the pathway structure of metabolism: decomposition into subnetworks and application to Mycoplasma pneumoniae. Bioinformatics 18(2), 351–361 (2002)
53. Sestoft, P.: Programs for biosequence analysis, http://www.itu.dk/people/sestoft/bsa.html
54. Shasha, D., Wang, J.T.L., Zhang, S.: Unordered tree mining with applications to phylogeny. In: 20th Int. Conf. on Data Engineering, pp. 708–719. IEEE Computer Society (2004)
55. Sokal, R., Michener, C.: A statistical method for evaluating systematic relationships. University of Kansas Science Bulletin 38, 1409–1438 (1958)
56. Sørensen, T.: A method of establishing groups of equal amplitude in plant sociology based on similarity of species and its application to analyses of the vegetation on danish commons. Biologiske Skrifter / Kongelige Danske Videnskabernes Selskabg 5(4), 1–34 (1948)
57. Starke, P.H., Roch, S.: The Integrated Net Analyzer. Humbolt University Berlin (1999), http://www.informatik.hu-berlin.de/starke/ina.html
58. Tanimoto, T.T.: Technical report, IBM Internal Report, (November 17, 1957)
59. Tohsato, Y.: A method for species comparison of metabolic networks using reaction profile. IPSJ Digital Courier 2(0), 685–690 (2006)
60. Tohsato, Y., Matsuda, H., Hashimoto, A.: A multiple alignment algorithm for metabolic pathway analysis using enzyme hierarchy. In: Proc. Int. Conf. Intell. Syst. Mol. Biol., pp. 376–383 (2000)
61. Tohsato, Y., Nishimura, Y.: Metabolic pathway alignment based on similarity between chemical structures. IPSJ Digital Courier 3, 736–745 (2007)
62. Webb, E.C.: Enzyme nomenclature 1992: recommendations of the Nomenclature Committee of the International Union of Biochemistry and Molecular Biology on the nomenclature and classification of enzymes. Published for the International Union of Biochemistry and Molecular Biology by Academic Press, San Diego (1992)
63. Wernicke, S., Rasche, F.: Simple and fast alignment of metabolic pathways by exploiting local diversity. Bioinformatics 23(15), 1978–1985 (2007)
64. Zhang, K., Wang, J.T.L., Shasha, D.: On the editing distance between undirected acyclic graphs. International Journal of Foundations of Computer Science 3(1), 43–57 (1996)

Modeling and Analyzing
Wireless Sensor Networks with VeriSensor:
An Integrated Workflow

Yann Ben Maissa[1,2], Fabrice Kordon[2], Salma Mouline[1], and Yann Thierry-Mieg[2]

[1] LRIT – CNRST URAC29, Université Mohammed V-Agdal
4, Avenue Ibn Battouta, B.P. 1014 RP, Rabat, Maroc
mouline@fsr.ac.ma

[2] LIP6 – CNRS UMR7606, Université P. & M. Curie 4, Place Jussieu, 75005 Paris, France
{Yann.Ben-Maissa,Fabrice.Kordon,Yann.Thierry-Mieg}@lip6.fr

Abstract. A Wireless Sensor Network (WSN), made of distributed autonomous nodes, is designed to monitor physical or environmental conditions. WSNs have many application domains such as environment or health monitoring. Their design must consider energy constraints, concurrency issues, node heterogeneity, while still meeting the quality requirements of life-critical applications. Formal verification helps to obtain WSN reliability, but usually requires a high expertise, which limits its adoption in industry.

This paper presents VeriSensor, a domain specific modeling language (DSML) for WSNs offering support for formal verification. VeriSensor is designed to be used by WSN experts. It can be automatically translated into a formal specification for model checking. We present the language and its translation into a formal model (we use Instantiable Transition Systems – ITS).

A tool has been implemented. We used it to work on a case study, illustrating how several metrics and properties relevant to the domain can be evaluated.

Keywords: wireless sensor networks, domain specific modeling languages, model driven engineering, formal verification.

1 Introduction

Context. Wireless sensor networks (WSNs) are composed of distributed autonomous nodes, containing programs and sensors to monitor physical or environmental conditions. Each node is a small physical device embedding sensors, a small CPU, a battery, a wireless transceiver and an antenna for communication. WSN are useful in many contexts, such as environment or health monitoring, thus being a hot topic [4,20].

The design of WSNs is complex and error-prone due to their numerous constraints:

- *lifetime* is a crucial preoccupation (even more important than quality of service [3]). Overall lifetime of the WSN usually depends on sensor nodes lifetime because nodes have limited battery power.
- *concurrency and asynchrony* lead to important issues such as interleaving of actions and race conditions.

M. Koutny et al. (Eds.): ToPNoC VIII, LNCS 8100, pp. 24–47, 2013.

- *heterogeneity*, because WSNs may contain various types of nodes, each having different characteristics (embedded sensors, wireless range, battery capacity, etc.).
- *limited resources*, because nodes have limited CPU and memory capacities.

Problem. When WSNs are intended to handle critical functions, verification and validation must be performed to reach a significant confidence in such systems [37,18]. Several proposals in that direction have emerged in recent years (details are provided in section 2). We can classify them in the following way:

- case studies use formal verification techniques. While they show the practical and industrial relevance of performing formal analysis on WSNs, they use ad-hoc modeling of the system by experts in both WSNs and formal verification;
- domain specific modeling languages (DSMLs) providing concepts of the domain are also used within the context of model-driven engineering (MDE). These specifications can be simulated prior to code generation of the final system. However, simulation is not sufficient to ensure a high confidence in critical systems;
- Program model-checkers are intended to find bugs in implementations. However, these tools detect problems late in the development life-cycle, since an implementation must already be available.

So, at this stage, there is apparently no satisfactory solution for modeling a WSN and performing formal analysis on this model.

Contribution. This paper presents VeriSensor, a DSML for WSNs and its mapping to a formal language for verification and analysis. VeriSensor has the features of an architectural description language (ADL [32]) adapted to a modular description of WSNs. This is an extension of the work presented in [7].

VeriSensor offers "natural" modeling of a WSN to domain experts by providing high-level concepts that capture the main use cases of such systems – periodic data collection [31], event-detection [49], etc. VeriSensor can be transformed into a discrete formal model supporting analysis: Instantiable Transition Systems (ITS) [43]. At this stage, VeriSensor is not intended for code generation, but bridges to code generation tools such as MEDWSA [46] or Baobab [2] could be investigated.

To illustrate its capabilities, we modeled an example using VeriSensor. This example is translated into a formal model using our prototype tool. Then, analysis is performed using ITS-Tools [41].

Contents. Section 2 browses the main works in modeling and verification of WSNs we are aware of and positions our work. Section 3 gives an overview of VeriSensor. Section 4 presents the language concepts together with the case study [38] used as a running example (a body area network). Section 5 details the mapping of VeriSensor into ITS and section 6 shows the analysis results we compute on the case study.

2 Related Work

We classify the approaches dedicated to modeling and/or verification of wireless sensor networks in three categories:

- Ad-hoc modeling and verification, that usually focus on modeling one aspect of WSN and rely on formal methods,

– Program model-checkers, that consist in analyzing an implementation of WSNs,
– DSMLs, offering high-level concepts for the modeling of WSNs.

Ad-hoc Modeling and Verification. We investigate here some case studies of the literature, that use formal methods to improve the reliability of WSNs.

Olveczky et al. [36] model, simulate and verify the OGDC algorithm for maintaining optimal node coverage using Real-time Maude [35]. They first perform Monte-Carlo simulations then analyze time-bounded reachability and temporal logic properties but do not explore the full state space, hence possibly missing some rare behaviors.

Mounier et al. [33] model a WSN detecting a pollution cloud using the IF language [12]. They use the Kronos model-checker [11] to formally compute the worst-case lifetime of the network considering two alternate routing protocols: controlled flooding and directed-diffusion. The application layer is mostly abstracted away and, even then, analysis can only scale to a small number of nodes with a limited initial energy (40 units).

Tschirner et al. [45] specify a biomedical WSN using timed automata [5] and formally verify it with UPPAAL [8]. The case study focuses on a specific transceiver (Chipcon CC2420) and the verification of qualitative and quantitative network related properties in the context of periodic data collection.

Watteyne et al. [48] also use UPPAAL to compute the worst case execution and transmission times for the different phases of a real-time MAC protocol.

Coleri et al. [18] model with HyTech [23] a single node of a WSN. The model matches the TinyOS components of the implementation and is used to study its lifetime and verify some response properties.

Ghosh et al. [19] use AADL to model a WSN. Then, using Monte-Carlo simulations, they compute end-to-end average packet success rate, average latency and system lifetime.

While using formal methods to design a WSN can strongly increase confidence, modeling using a general purpose formal language requires an expert in both WSNs and formal modeling. Moreover, these case studies generally have a limited scope and must manually abstract many aspects of a WSN.

Program Model-Checkers. The works presented in this section deal with the analysis of WSN implementations. Since most WSNs are implemented using NesC on top of TinyOS, these tools mostly deal with these.

NesC@PAT [50] automatically generates PAT [40] models from NesC programs, and verifies the absence of deadlock, state reachability, and liveness properties.

Tos2CProver [13] is a prototype tool-chain that translates NesC programs of a single node into ANSI-C. The CBMC model checker [17] is then used to verify memory access related properties (*e.g.*, memory violations, state of registers).

T-check [30] is a tool for finding bugs in WSN implementations. It is built on top of TOSSIM [29], an event-driven simulator for sensor networks. It performs random walks and bounded depth model checking of safety and liveness propositional properties.

SLEDE [22] is a framework focused on automatic-verification of sensor network security protocols. It builds an intrusion model from NesC protocol descriptions and a set of verification goals. Analysis with SPIN [24] generates counterexamples in NesC.

Analysis of NesC programs clearly increases confidence in WSNs. However, program verification comes late in the development life-cycle, thus increasing risks, and may lead to costly redeployment of software.

DSMLs for WSNs. We focus here on model-driven approaches for WSNs design using Domain Specific Modeling Languages (DSMLs). Most of the time, these languages offer simulation as an analysis method and/or code generation to produce an implementation.

VisualSense [6] is a graphical editor and simulator built on top of Ptolemy II [28] allowing experts to build detailed specifications of radio communication and communication protocols. VisualSense is used to evaluate and plot protocol performance metrics (*e.g.*, latency, message loss) as well as energy consumption metrics.

Matilda/UML [47] defines a UML profile dedicated to Biologically inspired WSN (BisNet). A virtual machine (Matilda) then enables model execution and debugging.

Baobab [2] and MEDWSA [46] are code generators (to NesC/TinyOS) proposing visual notations to describe WSN nodes. No analysis facilities are provided.

Cavi [10] proposes a graphical DSML for WSNs. Translations are defined to support simulation with Castalia [9] and probabilistic model checking with PRISM [27]. It focuses on the modeling of network protocols and radio propagation. Cavi only supports two common routing protocols in WSNs: flooding and gossiping.

Discussion. None of the approaches listed above is fully satisfactory.

Ad-hoc formal modeling enables one to verify qualitative and/or quantitative properties on a WSN (such as worst-case analysis). However, to deal with scaling issues an expert in formal methods is needed. This expert must also interact with a WSN designer. Manual abstraction is needed to limit the complexity of verification, but this raises the problem of the relationship between the verified model and its implementation.

Program model-checking solves this relationship issue by building formal models from the code. This enables formal debugging of common memory errors for instance, but still faces scalability issues. For this reason, some tools focus on single node behavior. Also, program verification takes place late in the development process, increasing the cost of error correction.

High-level DSMLs dedicated to WSNs bridge the gap between domain experts on the one hand, analysis tools and implementation (via code generators) on the other hand. However, most of them (except [10]) only rely on simulation for analysis, which makes it difficult to catch rare behaviors. Except in [39], no tool provides both simulation and code generation. Also, none of the DSMLs supporting code generation defines information about the deployment topology of the WSN.

VeriSensor, the language we propose, is a DSML for WSNs supporting efficient formal verification of quantitative and qualitative properties by model checking. This DSML is translated into a formal model to be analyzed.

It is clear that WSNs are time-constrained and thus require appropriate formalisms to express time. We chose time Petri nets (TPN) that combine a good modeling of concurrency with an appropriate modeling of time.

Since our translation procedure is automated, it can embed dedicated abstractions for TPN and rely on efficient techniques that cope with combinatorial explosion. Automation reduces the expertise needed in formal methods to operate verification.

Our DSML reuses from other studies some useful notions about structuring brought by the component notion of ADL.

This work is complementary of other approaches presented above. While simulation provides averages or performance indices, we can offer a full worst case analysis. While program model checking focuses on debugging an implementation during the late phases of the development life-cycle, we propose to verify the system at early stages of the design.

We do not focus in this paper on code generation that will be investigated in further work. A way to do this is to define a translation procedure to existing code generation tools such as *MEDWSA* [46] or *Baobab* [2].

3   Overview of VeriSensor

A VeriSensor specification is composed of the definition of the nodes themselves, a description of the physical environment surrounding these nodes, the deployment of the system, and the specification of all queries to be processed by the WSN (see Fig. 1).

Description of the Nodes. There can be several classes of nodes in a WSN (*e.g.*, in a heterogeneous network), each one having its own characteristics such as:

- its sensors (which physical quantities to be measured and how they are captured), and their energy consumption,
- its application operating mode (periodic data collection, event detection, etc.) and the way it manipulates data as well as the related energy consumption,
- its interface with the network (wireless range, routing, etc.), and the corresponding energy consumption,
- the initial energy provided to the node (*e.g.*, battery capacity).

Several node classes can share common submodels and a node class can be instantiated several times when several nodes have the same characteristics.

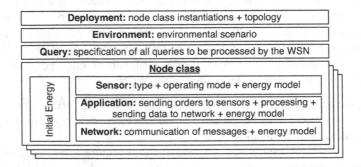

Fig. 1. Structure of a VeriSensor specification

Deployment Model. It defines how instances of node classes are spread in the physical environment and may change position over time[1]. Engineers use this model to define the topology of the system (number of instances per class and their coordinates) as well as the logical routing of messages among the nodes.

The topology is fundamental to provide an instantiation of the model elements. This type of model is found in simulation oriented DSMLs, but not in code-generation oriented DSMLs.

Environment Model. It defines physical quantities as a function of space (x, y, z) and time (t). Thus, the designer may describe a particular scenario in which the WSN runs. These scenarios are used to test qualitative properties of models on given problem instances. A given environment represents a particular situation in which a given behavior of the WSN is expected.

The Query Model. It describes the queries to broadcast and process in the WSN. Queries ask to periodically sample physical quantities for a certain duration. A *periodic* query requires the node to regularly send sampled data to the base station. A *conditional* query only signals the base station when the condition is met. This allows to model both periodic data collection [31] with a periodic query of an infinite duration, and event detection [49], using a conditional query that characterizes the event.

Architecture of VeriSensor. The various submodels are defined separately in VeriSensor to support *modularity* and *reusability* of WSN components. The deployment model of a system is the entry point of a VeriSensor specification. It references the Environment model and instantiates all nodes from the definition of their classes.

Inspiration from other DSMLs. The notion of node class in VeriSensor is inspired from the *sensor nodes* of Matilda. Similarly to Mounier et al. [33] we separate definitions of components from the routing, and further decompose nodes according to various aspects (energy, application...). The notions of environment and deployment models are inspired from VisualSense [6]. Also, as in Baobab [2] and MEDWSA [46], we describe the application layer, that is usually left unspecified in simulation oriented DSMLs.

4   Modeling with VeriSensor

This section presents VeriSensor through the specification of a case study.

4.1   The Body Area Network (BAN)

Our case study takes place in the context of home medical monitoring of patients who need constant care but can stay out of hospitals. Home medical monitoring allows to avoid hospitalization, which is as good for medical staff as for their patients.

The Body Area Network [38] is part of a wireless health monitoring system. It is composed of (see Fig. 2): *i)* a set of sensor nodes capable of sensing, processing and

---

[1] We do not yet support mobility in our approach but this is a natural extension that is semantically possible in VeriSensor.

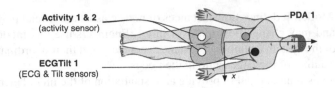

Fig. 2. The Body Area Network (BAN)

communicating vital signs to a personal server ; *ii)* a Portable Digital Assistant (PDA) that forwards patient data to a medical center through internet (3G or WIFI).

The BAN monitors the vital signs of the patient recovering from a heart attack. It checks whether he is exercising regularly as recommended by the doctors. WSNs, due to their small size and wireless nature, reduce system intrusiveness in patients lives.

As shown in Fig. 2, two redundant activity nodes detect periods of physical exercise (when the body activity level is above 8 $Watts.kg^{-1}$) while a third one periodically collects both heartbeat with an electrocardiogram (ECG) sensor and the tilt (*i.e.*, upper body orientation) in terms of the absolute angle relative to a vertical position.

The system designer (*i.e.*, the end-user of VeriSensor) wants to assess some critical aspects of his system. To do so, he needs to evaluate classes of properties such as:

p_1 evaluate which node limits the system lifetime according to a given scenario,
p_2 identify scenarios leading to undesirable situations that should be avoided,
p_3 check that the system behaves as expected by "replaying" existing situations identified by doctors,
p_4 compare alternative hardware solutions according to their characteristics (energy consumption of sensors, processing duration, etc.),

4.2 Modeling the BAN in VeriSensor

This section illustrates the VeriSensor syntax and structure through the modeling of the BAN. We follow a "path" going from the more general aspects of the system (its elements) to the implementation of some nodes and the description of its environment.

The Deployment Model. Figure 3 shows the deployment parameters of the BAN system. Each node instance is parameterized by its position (shown on Fig. 3) and next hop. For instance, the only node of class ECGTilt is located at position $\langle 0.1, 0.4, 0 \rangle$ (when a position parameter is unspecified, its value is 0) and routes messages to the pda1 instance. Distances are expressed in meters. We only consider here a static routing scheme based on the **nextHop** parameter defined in the deployment model.

The Query Model. Figure 4 shows the queries of the BAN. For example, AskHeart-Beat collects the heart beat every 13 time units and processes it for 2 time units, during

```
System BAN {environment => HumanBody;
            ECGTilt       => ecgtilt1  (x=0.1, y=0.4, nextHop = pda1 );
            Activity      => activity1 (x=0.1, y=-0.3, nextHop = pda1 ),
                             activity2 (x=-0.1 , y=-0.3, nextHop = pda1 );
            PDA           => pda1      (x=-0.1, y=0.3, nextHop = null );}
```

Fig. 3. Deployment of the BAN system

```
Queries medical {
  cond_query AskHeartBeat (condition = [HeartBeat < 40], duration = infinity,
  sensing_period = 13, processing_cost = 4 , processing_duration = 2);

  periodic_query AskTilt (quantities = [Tilt], duration = infinity,
  sensing_period = 8, processing_cost = 0, processing_duration = 0);

  cond_query AskActivity1 (condition = [Activity > 8], duration = infinity,
  sensing_period = 6, processing_cost = 4, processing_duration = 2);

  cond_query AskActivity2 (condition = [Activity > 8], duration = infinity,
  sensing_period = 9, processing_cost = 4, processing_duration = 2);}
```

Fig. 4. Query model for the BAN

the whole run (duration = infinity). It reports the heart beat value to the base station when it is below 40 (bradycardia). Processing costs 4 energy units per period.

The Node Class Model. A node class (Figure 5, left) specifies the physical characteristics of a node. It relates the information dispatched in the following aspects: sensing, application, network, and the initial energy.

The application defines the queries processed by a node. Here, ECGTilt is able to process both AskHeartBeat and AskTilt (Figure 5, left). Physical quantities are defined in a dedicated model (Figure 6, left).

Figure 5 (right) describes the sensors of the ECGTilt node class. In our study, it samples the upper body orientation (Tilt) and the heartbeat (Heartbeat). Sensors are described through their main technical characteristics: the measured physical quantity, the startup time (*i.e.*, the time for the sensor to be operational after being turned on), the sensing duration (*i.e.*, the time for the sensor to sense the value), and the energy cost of collecting a sample. For instance, ECGSensor measures the heartbeat, starts-up in 4 time units and consumes 2 energy units.

```
NodeClass ECGTilt {                     include types.def;
  sensing => ECGTsensing;               sensing ECGTsensing {
  application => ECGTApplication;         sensor ECGSensor (
  network => static_routing;                physical_quantity = Heartbeat,
  initial_energy = 1000;}                   startup_time = 4,
                                            sensing_duration = 1,
application ECGTApplication {               sensing_cost = 2);
  queries = AskHeartBeat,               sensor TiltSensor (
            AskTilt;}                       physical_quantity = Tilt,
                                            startup_time = 0,
                                            sensing_duration = 2,
                                            sensing_cost = 3);}
```

Fig. 5. ECGTilt, node and application description (left), sensing description (right)

The Physical Quantities Model. This model describes physical quantities as discrete ranges of values (see Fig. 6 left). The underlying semantics is the one of discrete event systems, so, continuous values must be mapped to an integer range. This mapping is user-defined; the designer must evaluate the trade-off between precision of quantities units and the analysis complexity.

```
type HeartBeat is 0..200;       include types.def;
type Tilt is 0..180;            environment cyclic HumanBody {context {}
type Activity is 0..15;           body {
                                    cycle 60; // cyclic behavior (in time units)
                                    HeartBeat function HeartBeatFunc (x,y,z,t) {
                                      if (0 <= t and t < 10) then return(95);
                                      elsif (10 <= t and t < 14) then return(40);
                                      else return (75);}
                                    Tilt function TiltFunc (x,y,z,t) {...}
                                    Activity function ActivityFunc (x,y,z,t) {...}}}
```

Fig. 6. Physical quantities definition (left) and an example of Environment Model (right)

The Environment Model. The evolution of each physical quantity q is defined by the environment which must provide a function returning its value for any point in time and space. There is one such function per physical quantity of the system. For instance, Fig. 6 (right) specifies the evolution of HeartBeatFunc that is sampled by the ECGTilt node. In this example, values of HeartBeat depend on time only.

For some properties of interest such as worst case scenarios, instead of using one of the user supplied environments we can use the provided unconstrained environment, which might return any value at any time.

The *clear separation* between the input conditions (environment) and the system specification is important in the analysis phase described below.

5   Formal Analysis of VeriSensor Specifications

Formal analysis by model checking of a system is a powerful technique that allows to capture subtle defects as well as to reason about worst case scenarios and occurrence of rare events by exhaustively analyzing all possible behaviors. However, it is limited in the scale of the systems it can analyze due to the combinatorial state space explosion, characteristic of concurrent asynchronous systems. To partly overcome this problem, techniques and tools have emerged such as SAT solvers [16] or shared decision diagrams [14].

Since WSNs are highly time driven and complex, we need a tool supporting a large amount of concurrency, the notion of time and able to tackle combinatorial explosion. VeriSensor emphasizes two typical aspects of WSNs: symmetries (thanks to the notion of node class) and locality in components (via the modular architecture of the language).

Instantiable Transition Systems (ITS): initially dedicated to distributed systems [43] and enriched to support time [41], they handle appropriately such characteristics. It is a model checking tool relying on a powerful decision diagrams library to cope with the complexity of large systems.

ITS also provide a way to define a structured and hierarchical specification of a system as well as a way to instantiate components. This is useful since VeriSensor is inherently hierarchical. ITS were previously experimented to analyze UML activity diagrams through a model transformation approach [44] similar to the one outlined here. ITS also showed excellent performance for this kind of specifications during the model checking contests @ Petri nets in 2011 [25] and 2012 [26].

Behavior of components is described using time Petri nets, a simple yet expressive formalism well adapted to modeling concurrent systems, process synchronizations, shared resources, as well as time constraints.

5.1 The Underlying Formal Model

Two formalisms are involved in the underlying formal description of VeriSensor: labeled time Petri nets to describe elementary behavior and ITS to structure the specification. We only provide here an intuitive definition (see [43,41] for a formal presentation, or the web page http://ddd.lip6.fr for more details on the supporting tools).

Instantiable Transition Systems. ITS allow hierarchical and compositional modeling, through a notion of type and instance and an application of the composite design pattern at a behavioral level. A type has an interface, defined as a set of action labels, and some definition of its internal behavior. Similarly to component oriented models, an ITS *composite* is a type that contains *instances* of ITS *types*. The composition mechanism is based only on transition synchronization. This mechanism is very well suited for compositional verification algorithms [15,21].

Figure 7 shows a simple example of a composite ITS type. States of the Client-Server model are the cartesian product between the Client and Server states. The system offers one interface, (begin, represented as a white square), that is synchronized with the start interfaces of the nested components (Client and Server). To fire begin, both client and server must fire a transition labeled by start. This system also contains a local synchronization (ε, represented as a black square) that is not exported. Similarly, to fire ε, the client must fire send and the server must fire get. Client and Server are elementary components that contain an automaton where local transitions are labeled by ε too. Client and Server can fire such local transitions without synchronizing together.

In practice, we use labeled time Petri nets to define elementary ITS types. We will use a high level graphical notation in the paper to describe the compositions, since the actual models which are generated are a bit complex.

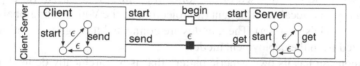

Fig. 7. Small example of composite-ITS

Labeled Time Petri Nets. Petri nets are well suited for concurrent asynchronous systems [34] such as WSNs and are well supported by tools.

In a Petri net, places (circles) contain tokens representing resources that are consumed by transitions (rectangles) when they fire, producing new tokens. A state of a Petri net assigns to each place of the net an integer representing the number of tokens it contains. In a given state, a transition is enabled if all its input places (connected by an arc from place to transition) contain enough tokens. Each arc may be labeled by an integer that indicates how many tokens are consumed or produced (the value 1 is assumed if there is no annotation). When firing, a transition produces tokens in the places connected by outgoing arcs.

Time Petri nets (TPNs) add a notion of clock to each transition, constrained by an earliest and latest firing time noted $[\alpha, \beta]$. As soon as a transition is enabled, the associated clock starts. This transition cannot fire before α time units have elapsed and must occur if the transition's clock reaches β. Hence a transition with $[0, \infty[$ can occur at any date if it is enabled, like Petri nets without time. This is assumed to be the default values and it is not explicitly shown in the figures.

The time model is discrete: a special transition *elapse* represents the evolution of time by one unit. All clocks progress simultaneously when *elapse* is fired.

Labels add a notion of interface to Petri nets, where some transitions (represented with thick borders) are called *public* and allow communication with the outside world. These transitions define the ITS interface. *Private* transitions can occur locally, independently from any situation outside the net, and typically represent an autonomous control flow.

5.2 Mapping VeriSensor to a Formal Specification

The mapping of VeriSensor into formal specifications relies on patterns, based on ITS and time Petri nets, associated to its syntactic elements. It is also based on a set of automatically computed abstractions that help containing the combinatorial explosion due to large data types.

The Transformation Process. To automatically transform the specification into a formal model we define a set of ITS patterns, modeling behaviors corresponding to the VeriSensor execution semantics. Instances of these ITS patterns are parameterized using values and types taken from the VeriSensor specification. Instances are then synchronized according to the deployment model, node class definitions, etc.

Thus, the transformation process uses parameters from the VeriSensor specification to customize patterns. The formal model is structured in *dimensions* describing orthogonal aspects of the WSN behavior extracted from the VeriSensor specification. The model of each node is composed of the following dimensions: network, application, sensors, energy, and local environment (a projection of the VeriSensor global environment over the node's position). Then, nodes are connected through the routing dimension computed from the deployment model.

Each dimension has its own generic pattern that is hierarchically defined, thus taking benefits from the ITS mechanisms. The final model is obtained by assembling and instantiating these patterns.

Each dimension respects a given fixed interface that does not depend on the internal behavior. This composition model allows an easy substitution of dimensions. This is of particular interest when studying several environmental scenarios or several energy consumption models.

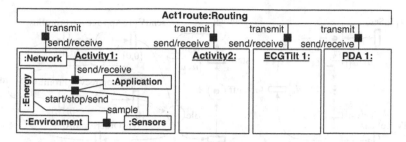

Fig. 8. Informal overview of the structure of the BAN specification according to the deployment given in Fig. 3. We only detail the node Activity1 and only show the routing instance of Activity1.

We define here a transformation from VeriSensor to ITS that have a formal semantics defined in [43]. There is no separate definition of the VeriSensor semantics. Hence, our transformation can be used to define the VeriSensor semantics.

Global Architecture of the Formal Model. Figure 8 informally illustrates the overall structure of the final formal specification for the BAN case study, based on the Veri-Sensor architecture. In this diagram, we distinguish instance names (followed by ":") from ITS pattern names (preceded by ":").

The assembling of a node class is illustrated for Activity1. We show how the dimensions interfaces are synchronized one to another. For example, the start label represents a synchronization between the application, energy and sensor dimensions. Similarly, sample synchronizes the sensor, energy and environment dimensions.

Routing and network transmission are handled by a dedicated ITS component (Routing). It exports one label per ⟨source, destination, message⟩ tuple. Its role is to transmit the message to the appropriate destination instance. Each node has its own routing instance ; its pattern will be detailed later in this section.

As each node class is instantiated according to the deployment model, Fig. 8 shows two activity nodes, one ECGTilt and one PDA.

Structure of a Node in the Formal Description. A node encompasses five dimensions:

- local environment: it represents the physical quantities functions projected at the physical position of the node. It is deduced from the VeriSensor environment model or corresponds to an "unconstrained" default environment for worst case analysis.
- sensors: it describes the behavior of sensors embedded in the node. It incorporates parameters (sensing duration, startup time, etc.) taken from the sensing model. The sensors sample values from the environment and forwards them to the application.
- application: it describes the behavior of the node in reaction to queries. It is deduced from the query model and the application description of a node. It controls the sensors (start/stop) and exchanges messages with the network.
- network: it models the network layer of a node. It transmits queries and results. In multi-hop scenarios it handles message forwarding.

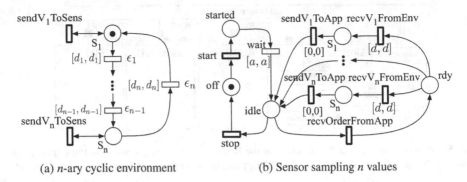

(a) *n*-ary cyclic environment   (b) Sensor sampling *n* values

Fig. 9. Two generic ITS, interface transitions are outlined in bold

- energy: it explicits the energy consumption model for the node. It synchronizes with any energy consuming operation. It is deduced from the energy costs declared in the input specification.

The Local Environment Pattern. Figure 9a represents the environment as seen by a given node. To obtain this behavior, the environment function $q(x, y, z, t)$ is projected over the coordinates of the node, yielding a function $q(t)$ of time only that is specific to the considered node sensor. This function is finally discretized, and encoded as a series of plateau values that have a certain duration d_i.

Each public transition is labeled by a possible value of the physical quantity. The time bound on local transitions (ε) represents the evolution of $q(t)$ as time progresses. The last transition ε_n can be added to represent a cyclic environment. This ITS is parameterized by n, the number of values sent in the cycle, and by d_i for $i \in [1..n]$, the duration for sending these values. Its ITS interface is the set of possible values sendV$_i$ToSens of the physical quantity.

The Sensor Pattern. Figure 9b represents the behavior of a sensor (as for the BAN system in Fig. 5 right) and is parameterized by: n (number of potential values in the physical quantity), a (startup time), and d (capture time). Its ITS interface is composed of the control commands (start, stop) connected to the application and sampling connected to the environment and application dimensions (recvV$_i$FromEnv, sendV$_i$ToApp).

The transmission of a value V$_k$ from the environment to the sensor is represented by a synchronization between sendV$_k$ToSens and recvV$_k$FromEnv. The transition sendV$_i$ToApp transmits sampled values to the application dimension. Because these definitions of the sensor and the environment are clearly separated we can easily associate the specification to any arbitrary environment instead of a fixed scenario. Such an association is described in the deployment model.

The Application Pattern. The application handles requests coming from the network. Since reaction to a query depends on its nature, each query defined in VeriSensor is transformed separately, and connected to the appropriate sensors. A dispatcher is defined for each node: as in a middleware, it filters and dispatches only the queries

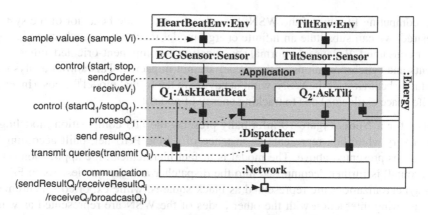

Fig. 10. Pattern for a node (the gray zone is the application pattern)

concerning the node. Figure 10 (gray zone) shows this pattern for ECGTilt. The two queries that this node can process are instantiated and connected to the dispatcher.

A conditional query (see an example in Fig. 4) is modeled as a time Petri net (not shown here). It has a cyclic behavior: when it receives start from the dispatcher, it starts the sensor, then collects a value at every period (defined as the sensing_period). For each sampled value, if the condition of the query is met, it sends a notification to the base station. A periodic query, once started, will sample values, process them and send them to the base station. In both cases, execution stops after duration time units, as defined in the query.

The TPN representing the query is controlled by a dispatcher and is synchronized with the sensor, network, and energy models (see Fig. 10).

The Network Pattern. The interface of the network allows to transmit queries and their results. So it defines, for each query, a set of services: broadcast/receive (a query), send/receive (a query result). It handles the forwarding of broadcasted queries and eliminates duplicates using a flood control algorithm. It receives values to be sent to the base station from the application as well as from peer nodes. Queries addressed to the node are transmitted to the dispatcher (see Fig. 10). Transmission to the network consumes energy, hence, the pattern is also connected to the Energy dimension.

The behavior of the network is specified using a Petri net that may consider transmission errors when necessary. To model loss of packets when energy is too low for reception, the pattern includes dummy reception transitions that discard the message (when energy is insufficient) and let the emitter fire the synchronization. This is important to preserve the modularity of the specification as well as to consider realistic behavior under degraded conditions (*e.g.*, some nodes are down).

The Energy Pattern. It encodes the energy of a node as a single place holding initial_energy tokens (see the definition of a node in Fig. 5). Public transitions consume energy ; there is one such transition for each possible energy consumption value.

Thus the lack of energy (*i.e.*, no token in the place) blocks energy consuming operations in the node (sampling, access to the network, etc.). When all nodes are out of energy, the system cannot execute anymore. This energy consumption model is used when computing lifetime of the WSN. If study of steady state behavior of the system is desired, we can substitute an infinite energy model for the nodes, where no energy is ever consumed. Because the formal specification is component-oriented, other components and synchronizations of the model are not impacted. This allows analysis of qualitative behaviors of the WSN, without paying in the formal model the cost (in terms of state space explosion) due to tracking energy of nodes.

Pattern for a Node. Figure 10 informally presents the ITS composition modeling a node. Every white box represents an instance of a time Petri net, built according to the patterns presented above. The model is in fact hierarchical: the application (gray background) is further decomposed into the dispatcher and the queries. As in Fig. 7, local synchronizations are represented as black squares, while exported synchronizations allowing interaction with the other nodes of the WSN are represented as white squares. To help readability, we only draw one synchronization to represent a set of similar synchronizations (the relevant synchronized labels are indicated on the left).

For example, ECGSensor can sample one of V_i $1 \leq i \leq n$ values from the environment. Each sample V_i synchronizes the corresponding sendV$_i$ToSens and recvV$_i$-FromEnv transitions from Fig. 9.

The two queries addressed by this node are synchronized to the dispatcher, the involved sensors, and the network. Finally, all energy-consuming operations are synchronized to the energy pattern.

Communication services are the resulting interface of this composite ITS. All nodes have the same interface.

Pattern for Routing. We first compute the routing table of each node, based on the deployment model (position, distance, range, etc.) and the specification of the next-hops. Each routing table is then encoded as a Petri net, with one place for each other node in the WSN. Only one of these places is initially marked (or more if routing between nodes can vary), reflecting the routing topology (*nextHop* for outgoing messages).

We then build a set of synchronizations to relate a source node, a destination node and the routing table for the source node. Structurally, this allows for arbitrary communications between nodes but only the synchronizations enabled by the routing table are actually activated (token in the corresponding place). This transformation pattern also allows to support updates to the routing table, without altering the nodes or the synchronizations between them.

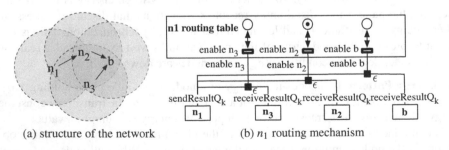

(a) structure of the network   (b) n_1 routing mechanism

Fig. 11. Routing in the BAN, its structure shows both communication range and routing

Broadcast is implemented similarly, but all neighboring nodes (*e.g.*, those within range) are synchronized. A broadcast is an atomic operation, thus avoiding any interleaving effect (source of combinatorial explosion in model checking). This construction also allows a realistic energy consumption: any node receiving a broadcast decreases energy, whether it will handle the query or not.

Figure 11a represents a network topology where n_i and b represent nodes, circles show communication range and arrows the routing graph. Figure 11b shows a Petri net modeling the routing table for n_1 (the only activated link is between n_1 and n_2 as the routing shows). Each *sendResultQ$_k$* transition (for query Q_k) is synchronized with both an *enable n$_i$* transition and a *receiveResultQ$_k$* transition from node n_j. When n_1 sends the result , only *enable n$_2$* transition will be enabled, which makes n_2 the only node to receive the result. Indeed, n_2 is n_1's next hop.

Abstractions. The resulting formal model has good modularity, allowing partial reuse in various scenarios. However, its size grows rapidly when data with a large number of potential values are used. Indeed, each possible value creates one or more synchronization labels throughout the model which is a source of complexity.

A first abstraction consists in using an id (*e.g.*, AskHeartBeat) per query of the VeriSensor specification and encode the associated behavior directly in the node (see the description of the application pattern above).

The underlying verification techniques require discrete sets of values; continuous physical quantities must be discretized, as described when presenting the local environment. For this purpose, it is only necessary to retain one symbolic value per range producing the same behavior of the system (*i.e.*, equivalence class). For instance, the behavior of a conditional query depends on sampled values that can be deduced from their thresholds. In the BAN system, for the conditional query AskHeartBeat (see Fig. 4), the domain of HeartBeat can be reduced to two values: strictly below 40, and over 40.

Thus, starting from the assumption that all domain values are symmetric, symbolic domains can be computed through structural analysis of the VeriSensor specification. All constraints are combined to produce a minimal set of values for each domain. Such techniques are derived from automatic symmetry detection [42] or symbolic trajectory evaluation [1]. The complexity of these techniques is low, since it relies on the size of the specification instead of the size of the state space.

This technique is very efficient for verifying properties such as worst case lifetime because the content of messages can mostly be abstracted away. When properties observe specific values of the physical quantities in the system, the symbolic domains must be further refined to consider the thresholds located in the property.

Deriving such abstractions automatically is important because: *i*) they are then correct by construction *ii*) using abstractions does not imply any end-user knowledge of the underlying techniques.

About the Formal Description of the BAN System. The resulting model for the BAN case study is composed of 19 ITS types of which 11 are elementary. All together, the enclosed Petri nets contain 84 places and 89 transitions of which 44 are time constrained. Thus, each state is a vector of 128 variables (places marking + transition clocks).

6   Analyzing the Case Study

This section discusses the analysis we performed on our case study. On the resulting ITS model, we evaluated the properties identified in section 4.1. All experiments were run on a high-end Xeon 64 bits at 2.6 GHz with 128 GB of RAM, on a single processor.

Prototype Implementation of a VeriSensor Formal Analyzer. Our publicly available prototype tool[2] is implemented in Java. It offers an Xtext[3]-based front-end in Eclipse (syntax highlighting, context-sensitive content assist, etc.). A transformation engine based on the VeriSensor EMF metamodel builds the ITS representation according to the rules defined in the previous section. Then, the produced model is analyzed using ITS-Tools [41]. Translation rules are written in Java (8260 LOC).

Scalability Analysis. The model of the BAN case study is associated with an "unconstrained" environment overapproximating all possible situations the BAN can face, thus allowing the analysis of worst and best cases scenarios in the system. Figure 12 shows the evolution, as initial energy increases, of the number of states in the system, the time to compute and the memory required to build it. As the charts show, the state space grows fast up to about 4×10^{13} states. Its representation in memory, as well as the computation time, behaves in a much more favorable way (charts 12b

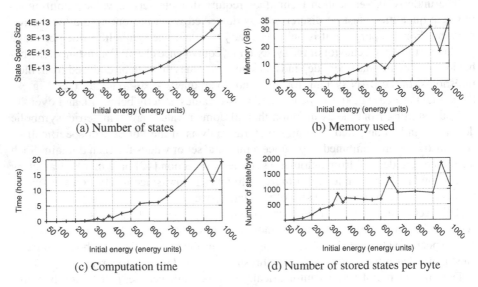

| (a) Number of states | (b) Memory used |
| (c) Computation time | (d) Number of stored states per byte |

Fig. 12. Evolution of the state space complexity when the initial energy allocated for each node increases (activity sensor period is 3 and 1 time units for activity1 and activity2 respectively. ECG sensor period is one time unit and Tilt sensor period is 2 time units. Message emission for every node takes 5 energy units, and message reception require 4 time units. Sensing cost 2 energy units for all sensors and processing data require 3 energy units for all nodes.

---

[2] http://lip6.fr/Yann.Ben-Maissa (subversion repository)

[3] http://www.eclipse.org/Xtext/: Xtext is a framework for development of programming languages and domain specific languages.

and 12c), thus validating the choice of ITS, based on decision diagrams, that already proved their efficiency for such systems [43].

Charts 12b and 12c show the evolution of memory and time required for state space construction according to the initial energy allocated to each node. We can scale this energy up to 1000 units (34.5 GBytes and 19 hours). From an industrial point of view, it becomes feasible to process larger values on current high-performance servers. Useful results from the designer point of view have been reported in [33] with smaller values. Our techniques provides more data on steady state behavior for the BAN study.

Figure 12d shows that we represent up to 1850 states per byte. As common with symbolic techniques, some variation in performances are observed, which are not directly related to the growth of the state space size.

This experiment shows a good scalability potential for the overall approach and, in particular, the feasibility of tracking "rare events" (which is difficult with simulation only) by means of reachability properties (*e.g.*, p_2 in section 4.1). However, if a Yes/No answer for reachability properties is reported within a reasonable time, we measured that computation of a counterexample needs significantly more time and memory.

Which Node Limits the System Lifetime (p_1). Exhibiting the energy consumption of the WSN in the worst case scenario allows the end-user to evaluate a lower bound of the system lifetime. Figure 13a shows the worst case lifetime evolution of the BAN nodes.

To compute this chart, we associate the BAN model with an *unconstrained environment* allowing any action. This environment consists in a set of transitions representing all the possible values of all physical quantities, where all transitions are always fireable. Therefore, when a sensor samples the environment, it can collect any possible value.

We then build a superset of all the possible behaviors from which we can obtain a worst case scenario before computing S_{end}, the set of states where at least one node cannot communicate anymore (its energy is below *Min*, the minimum energy to send a message). The lifetime is obtained by counting the minimum occurrences of the *elapse* transition located in the shortest transition sequence leading from the initial state to one state of S_{end}.

The objective is not to provide quantitative information since the initial number of energy units allocated to nodes is not sufficient (Figure 13a shows a system duration in hours range[4], while, at least, weeks would be needed). However, a designer can get an

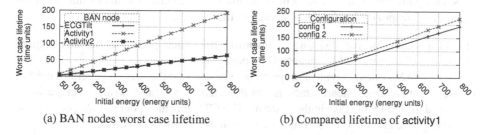

(a) BAN nodes worst case lifetime   (b) Compared lifetime of activity1

Fig. 13. Lifetime analysis on the BAN case study

---

[4] We did not set an exact duration for time units but, considering our abstractions, it should be minutes.

idea of the most critical component (*i.e.*, the one that fails first) according to various scenarios. This result is complementary of simulation that can tackle longer durations but not in an exhaustive way. Our exhaustive analysis exhibits the worst scenario the system can have. Computation of minimal traces is more costly than reachability, but still possible for large values: for Activity1 with 500 energy units, it takes less than 4 hours to compute the minimal trace (447 transitions) with a memory of 6.7 GB.

Figure 13a shows that ECGTilt and Activity2 are the limiting nodes in the system (*i.e.*, the ones that lack energy first). ECGTilt early death is problematic because it monitors a critical vital sign (heart beat). The designer may increase its lifetime by providing it a bigger battery (reducing the heart beat sensing period is not an option here because we can miss quick heart beat abnormalities). The lower lifetime of Activity2 is less problematic because it monitors a less critical parameter and is redundant with Activity1.

We show later how two alternative designs for Activity1 can be explored.

Detecting Undesirable Situations such as Deadlocks (p_2). Before evaluating lifetime properties on the WSN model, we used an infinite energy model and removed counters (*e.g.*, number of messages received by the base station) and checked that the state space is finite (4.03×10^7 states, computed in 2.8 seconds with 17.1 MB). This model allows to study steady state behavior (*i.e.*, the infinite traces of the system). Tracking energy consumption to compute lifetimes creates a more complex model, but is not suitable for all types of properties. A typical and interesting reachability property deals with unexpected deadlocks in the system (expected ones being those where all nodes exhausted their energy). This can reveal real deadlocks in the system, or allow the identification of crucial nodes whose activity is required to keep the system working. Such a situation can be detected using the following reachability formula, computed with no additional cost with respect to state space generation:

$$dead \ \wedge \ \bigwedge_{i \in Nodes} (energy(i) > Min_i) \qquad (1)$$

Where Min_i corresponds to the minimum energy required by node i to send a message and *dead* is the boolean meaning that the current state of the state space has no successor.

Formula 1 was evaluated on the BAN with an initial configuration of 300 energy units. Our prototype tool computed in 44 minutes and 1.3 GB of memory that all deadlocks are corresponding to a lack of energy in the system.

Checking Behavior for Existing Situations (p_3). Such properties usually require causal formulas expressed by means of temporal logic.

For the BAN system, a typical property is to ensure that the system generates neither a false negative (*i.e.*, a heart attack is not detected) nor a false positive (*i.e.*, a heart attack is detected by mistake in the system). The CTL formula 2 detects the presence of a false negative and the CTL formula 3 the existence of a false positive.

$$AG(occurs_{heart\,attack} \implies AF(detected_{heart\,attack})) \qquad (2)$$

Parameter	value in $config_1$	value in $config_2$
sensing frequency	3 TU	4 TU
acquisition time	0 TU	1 TU
acquisition energy	2 EU	3 EU
processing time	0 TU	1 TU
processing energy	3 EU	4 EU
emission time	1 TU	2 TU
emission energy	5 EU	6 EU
reception time	1 TU	2 TU
reception energy	4 EU	5 EU

Fig. 14. Data for the two studied variants in time units (TU) or energy units (EU)

$$AG(\neg occurs_{heart\,attack} \implies AF(\neg detected_{heart\,attack})) \tag{3}$$

In these formula the AG and AF operators respectively mean "in all cases" and "in all futures". $occurs_e$ is either true or false for a given environment e. In the BAN system, a given environment corresponds to a patient behavior which is annotated by the doctors as being sick or healthy. $detected_e$ is a state property. In our case ($e = heart\,attack$), it involves the PDA and corresponds to the detection of low activity (gathered from the activity sensors) and bradycardia detected by ECGTilt.

Properties 2 and 3 are verified for several environments representing different kinds of patients. Such a computation is less complex in time and memory than the worst case lifetime analysis, since the system is more constrained. With an initial amount of 300 initial energy units per node, formula 2 was computed in 38 minutes with 2.4 GB and formula 3 in 84 minutes with 2.6 GB.

Comparing Alternative Solutions (p_4). The choice of a given component may have an impact on WSN lifetime or on some important characteristics of the system. VeriSensor can be useful to compare two possible solutions. To do so, the designer may either change the characteristics of the nodes to be replaced (if only those change) or replace the node by an instance of another node class.

For the BAN case study, let us evaluate the impact of two configurations for Activity1 on the system lifetime (*e.g.*, when at least one node cannot communicate anymore). All previous measures where done using the $config_1$ presented in Fig. 14. We choose another hardware for Activity1, $config_2$, which characteristics are also provided in Fig. 14. Since these configurations are close one to another, it is difficult to predict which one will provide a better lifetime.

Comparison of the two configurations are displayed in the chart of Fig. 13b. It shows that the alternate solution increases the lifetime of the system.

7 Conclusion

This paper presented VeriSensor, a domain specific modeling language for wireless sensor networks (WSNs), designed to be used by WSN experts and offering support for modeling and formal verification. The objective is to evaluate both quantitative results (*e.g.*, estimation of the system's lifetime or average consumption per time unit) as well as qualitative results (*e.g.*, detection of unexpected situations such as deadlocks).

VeriSensor enables the modeling of a WSN by providing high-level concepts that support the main use cases of the domain. Thus, specifying WSNs consists in defining the node characteristics, how nodes are deployed and the physical environment in which the system runs. The notion of environment allows to evaluate the system in dedicated conditions and scenarios. A generic environment is provided: the "unconstrained environment" that allows any action in the system. It is useful to analyze the WSN in the worst possible conditions.

Instantiable Transition Systems (ITS) and time Petri nets are the underlying formal techniques used for verification. They show encouraging scalability capabilities, thus enabling the analysis of industrial systems with more significant parameters than in the state of the art.

The main advantage of the overall approach is to make formal specification and verification more accessible to the end-users (*i.e.*, the designers of WSNs). From a methodological point of view, model-driven techniques ease the use of formal models by designers. This eases the building of complex ITS models with low-level formal notations and potentially reduces the risks of modeling errors.

Even if we focus in this paper on the verification aspects, our approach does not exclude simulation which is a useful complementary approach. In fact, since VeriSensor has a formal semantic, it is executable and thus, can be simulated. The definition by the user of (several) environment and deployment models allows to specify specific scenarios under study.

Future Work. Experimentation shows that analysis can be performed on a VeriSensor specification. However, additional property-specific semantic preserving optimizations of the formal model could be performed to scale to larger system descriptions. Some ordering heuristics exploiting the structure of the generated formal models could also be proposed, since the underlying decision diagram based verification technology is very sensitive to this point. Finally, code generation of VeriSensor specifications could be supported by bridging it with existing tools dedicated to this purpose such as *MEDWSA* or *Baobab*.

References

1. Adams, S., Björk, M., Melham, T.F., Seger, C.-J.H.: Automatic abstraction in symbolic trajectory evaluation. In: Formal Methods in Computer-Aided Design, pp. 127–135. IEEE Computer Society (2007)
2. Akbal-Delibas, B., Boonma, P., Suzuki, J.: Extensible and precise modeling for wireless sensor networks. In: Yang, J., Ginige, A., Mayr, H.C., Kutsche, R.-D. (eds.) UNISCON. LNBIP, vol. 20, pp. 551–562. Springer, Heidelberg (2009)
3. Akyildiz, I.F., Su, W., Sankarasubramaniam, Y., Cayirci, E.: A survey on sensor networks. IEEE Communications Magazine 40(8), 102–114 (2002)
4. Akyildiz, I., Vuran, M.C.: Wireless Sensor Networks. John Wiley & Sons, Inc. (2010)
5. Alur, R., Dill, D.L.: Automata for modeling real-time systems. In: Paterson, M. (ed.) ICALP 1990. LNCS, vol. 443, pp. 322–335. Springer, Heidelberg (1990)

6. Baldwin, P., Kohli, S., Lee, E.A., Liu, X., Zhao, Y., Brooks, C.H., Krishnan, N.V., Neuendorffer, S., Zhong, C., Zhou, R.: Visualsense: Visual modeling for wireless and sensor network systems. Tech. rep., U.C. Berkeley (2005)
7. Ben Maïssa, Y., Kordon, F., Mouline, S., Thierry-Mieg, Y.: Modeling and Analyzing Wireless Sensor Networks with VeriSensor. In: Petri Net and Software Engineering (PNSE 2012), vol. 851, pp. 60–76. CEUR, Hamburg (2012)
8. Bengtsson, J., Larsen, K.G., Larsson, F., Pettersson, P., Yi, W.: UPPAAL — a Tool Suite for Automatic Verification of Real–Time Systems. In: Alur, R., Sontag, E.D., Henzinger, T.A. (eds.) HS 1995. LNCS, vol. 1066, pp. 232–243. Springer, Heidelberg (1996)
9. Boulis, A.: Castalia: revealing pitfalls in designing distributed algorithms in wsn. In: 5th International Conference on Embedded Networked Sensor Systems, pp. 407–408. ACM (2007)
10. Boulis, A., Fehnker, A., Fruth, M., McIver, A.: Cavi–simulation and model checking for wireless sensor networks. In: Fifth International Conference on Quantitative Evaluation of Systems, QEST 2008, pp. 37–38. IEEE (2008)
11. Bozga, M., Daws, C., Maler, O., Olivero, A., Tripakis, S., Yovine, S.: Kronos: A model-checking tool for real-time systems. In: Vardi, M.Y. (ed.) CAV 1998. LNCS, vol. 1427, pp. 546–550. Springer, Heidelberg (1998)
12. Bozga, M., Graf, S., Ober, I., Ober, I., Sifakis, J.: Tools and Applications: the IF toolset. In: 4th Int. School on Formal Methods for the Design of Computer, Communication and Software Systems: Real Time, SFM-04:RT (2004)
13. Bucur, D., Kwiatkowska, M.Z.: Software verification for tinyos. In: 9th ACM/IEEE International Conference on Information Processing in Sensor Networks, pp. 400–401. ACM (2010)
14. Burch, J.R., Clarke, E.M., McMillan, K.L., Dill, D.L., Hwang, L.J.: Symbolic model checking: 10^{20} states and beyond. In: 5th Annual Symposium on Logic in Computer Science, pp. 1–33. IEEE Press (1990)
15. Ciardo, G., Lüttgen, G., Miner, A.S.: Exploiting interleaving semantics in symbolic state-space generation. Formal Methods in System Design 31(1), 63–100 (2007)
16. Cimatti, A., Clarke, E., Giunchiglia, E., Giunchiglia, F., Pistore, M., Roveri, M., Sebastiani, R., Tacchella, A.: NuSMV 2: An openSource tool for symbolic model checking. In: Brinksma, E., Larsen, K.G. (eds.) CAV 2002. LNCS, vol. 2404, pp. 359–364. Springer, Heidelberg (2002)
17. Clarke, E., Kroening, D., Lerda, F.: A tool for checking ansi-c programs. Tools and Algorithms for the Construction and Analysis of Systems, 168–176 (2004)
18. Ergen, S.C., Ergen, M., Koo, T.J.: Lifetime analysis of a sensor network with hybrid automata modelling. In: WSNA, pp. 98–104 (2002)
19. Ghosh, A., Pereira, L., Yan, T.: Modeling wireless sensor network architectures using aadl. In: 4th European Congress on Embedded Real Time Software, ERTS (2008)
20. Gnawali, O., Welsh, M.: Sensor networks architectures and protocols. In: Emerging Wireless Technologies and the Future Mobile Internet, pp. 125–153. Cambridge University Press (2011)
21. Gupta, A., McMillan, K.L., Fu, Z.: Automated assumption generation for compositional verification. In: Damm, W., Hermanns, H. (eds.) CAV 2007. LNCS, vol. 4590, pp. 420–432. Springer, Heidelberg (2007)
22. Hanna, Y., Rajan, H.: Slede: Framework for automatic verification of sensor network security protocol implementations. In: 31st International Conference on Software Engineering – Companion, pp. 427–428. IEEE (2009)
23. Henzinger, T.A., Ho, P.H., Toi, H.W.: HYTECH: A Model Checker for Hybrid Systems. Int. Journal on Software Tools for Technology Transfer 1(1-2), 110–122 (1997)
24. Holzmann, G.: Spin model checker, the: primer and reference manual. Addison-Wesley Professional (2003)

25. Kordon, F., Linard, A., Buchs, D., Colange, M., Evangelista, S., Lampka, K., Lohmann, N., Paviot-Adet, E., Thierry-Mieg, Y., Wimmel, H.: Report on the Model Checking Contest at Petri Nets 2011. In: Jensen, K., van der Aalst, W.M., Ajmone Marsan, M., Franceschinis, G., Kleijn, J., Kristensen, L.M. (eds.) ToPNoC VI. LNCS, vol. 7400, pp. 169–196. Springer, Heidelberg (2012)

26. Kordon, F., Linard, A., Buchs, D., Colange, M., Evangelista, S., Fronc, L., Hillah, L.M., Lohmann, N., Paviot-Adet, E., Pommereau, F., Rohr, C., Thierry-Mieg, Y., Wimmel, H., Wolf, K.: Raw Report on the Model Checking Contest at Petri Nets, Tech. rep (2012)

27. Kwiatkowska, M., Norman, G., Parker, D.: Prism: Probabilistic symbolic model checker. Computer Performance Evaluation: Modelling Techniques and Tools, 113–140 (2002)

28. Lee, E.A., John, I.: Overview of the ptolemy project. Electronics Research Laboratory, College of Engineering, University of California (1999)

29. Levis, P., Lee, N., Welsh, M., Culler, D.: Tossim: Accurate and scalable simulation of entire tinyos applications. In: 1st International Conference on Embedded Networked Sensor Systems, pp. 126–137. ACM (2003)

30. Li, P., Regehr, J.: T-check: bug finding for sensor networks. In: 9th ACM/IEEE Int. Conf. on Information Processing in Sensor Networks, pp. 174–185. ACM (2010)

31. Mainwaring, A., Culler, D., Polastre, J., Szewczyk, R., Anderson, J.: Wireless sensor networks for habitat monitoring. In: 1st ACM Int. Workshop on Wireless Sensor Networks and Applications (WSNA), pp. 88–97. ACM (2002)

32. Medvidovic, N., Taylor, R.N.: A classification and comparison framework for software architecture description languages. IEEE Trans. Softw. Eng. 26, 70–93 (2000)

33. Mounier, L., Samper, L., Znaidi, W.: Worst-case lifetime computation of a wireless sensor network by model-checking. In: 4th ACM Workshop on Performance Evaluation of Wireless ad Hoc, Sensor, and Ubiquitous Networks (PE-WASUN), pp. 1–8. ACM (2007)

34. Murata, T.: Petri nets: Properties, analysis and applications. Proceedings of the IEEE 77(4), 541–580 (1989)

35. Ölveczky, P.C., Meseguer, J.: Semantics and pragmatics of Real-Time Maude. Higher-Order and Symbolic Computation 20(1-2), 161–196 (2007)

36. Ölveczky, P.C., Thorvaldsen, S.: Formal modeling and analysis of the OGDC wireless sensor network algorithm in real-time maude. In: Bonsangue, M.M., Johnsen, E.B. (eds.) FMOODS 2007. LNCS, vol. 4468, pp. 122–140. Springer, Heidelberg (2007)

37. Ölveczky, P.C., Thorvaldsen, S.: Formal modeling, performance estimation, and model checking of wireless sensor network algorithms in real-time maude. Theor. Comput. Sci. 410, 254–280 (2009)

38. Otto, C., Milenković, A., Sanders, C., Jovanov, E.: System architecture of a wireless body area sensor network for ubiquitous health monitoring. J. Mob. Multimed. 1, 307–326 (2005)

39. Sadilek, D.A.: Domain-specific languages for wireless sensor networks. In: Modellierung, pp. 237–241 (2008)

40. Sun, J., Liu, Y., Dong, J.S., Pang, J.: PAT: Towards flexible verification under fairness. In: Bouajjani, A., Maler, O. (eds.) CAV 2009. LNCS, vol. 5643, pp. 709–714. Springer, Heidelberg (2009)

41. Thierry-Mieg, Y., Bérard, B., Kordon, F., Lime, D., Roux, O.H.: Compositional Analysis of Discrete Time Petri nets. In: 1st Workshop on Petri Nets Compositions (CompoNet 2011), vol. 726, pp. 17–31. CEUR (2011)

42. Thierry-Mieg, Y., Dutheillet, C., Mounier, I.: Automatic symmetry detection in well-formed nets. In: van der Aalst, W.M.P., Best, E. (eds.) ICATPN 2003. LNCS, vol. 2679, pp. 82–101. Springer, Heidelberg (2003)

43. Thierry-Mieg, Y., Poitrenaud, D., Hamez, A., Kordon, F.: Hierarchical Set Decision Diagrams and Regular Models. In: Kowalewski, S., Philippou, A. (eds.) TACAS 2009. LNCS, vol. 5505, pp. 1–15. Springer, Heidelberg (2009)

44. Thierry-Mieg, Y., Hillah, L.-M.: UML behavioral consistency checking using Instantiable Petri nets. ISSE 4(3), 293–300 (2008)
45. Tschirner, S., Xuedong, L., Yi, W.: Model-based validation of QoS properties of biomedical sensor networks. In: 8th Int. Conf. on Embedded Software, pp. 69–78. ACM (2008)
46. Vicente-Chicote, C., Losilla, F., Álvarez, B., Iborra, A., Sánchez, P.: Applying mde to the development of flexible and reusable wireless sensor networks. Int. J. Cooperative Inf. Syst. 16(3/4), 393–412 (2007)
47. Wada, H., Boonma, P., Suzuki, J., Oba, K.: Modeling and executing adaptive sensor network applications with the Matilda UML virtual machine. In: 11th IASTED Int. Conf. on Software Engineering and Applications (SEA), pp. 216–225. ACTA Press (2007)
48. Watteyne, T., Augé-Blum, I., Ubéda, S.: Dual-mode real-time mac protocol for wireless sensor networks: a validation/simulation approach. In: 1st Int. Conf. on Integrated Internet ad hoc and Sensor Networks (InterSense), ACM (2006)
49. Werner-Allen, G., Lorincz, K., Welsh, M., Marcillo, O., Johnson, J., Ruiz, M., Lees, J.: Deploying a wireless sensor network on an active volcano. IEEE Internet Computing 10(2), 18–25 (2006)
50. Zheng, M., Sun, J., Liu, Y., Dong, J.S., Gu, Y.: Towards a model checker for NesC and wireless sensor networks. In: Qin, S., Qiu, Z. (eds.) ICFEM 2011. LNCS, vol. 6991, pp. 372–387. Springer, Heidelberg (2011)

Local State Refinement and Composition of Elementary Net Systems: An Approach Based on Morphisms

Luca Bernardinello[1], Elisabetta Mangioni[1,2], and Lucia Pomello[1]

[1] Dipartimento di Informatica, Sistemistica e Comunicazione,
Università degli studi di Milano - Bicocca,
Viale Sarca, 336 - Edificio U14 - I-20126 Milano, Italia
[2] Istituto per la Dinamica dei Processi Ambientali,
Consiglio Nazionale delle Ricerche (CNR-IDPA),
Piazza della Scienza, 1 - Edificio U1 - I-20126 Milano, Italia

Abstract. In the design of concurrent and distributed systems, modularity and refinement are basic conceptual tools. We propose a notion of refinement/abstraction of local states for a basic class of Petri Nets, associated with a class of morphisms. The morphisms, from a refined system to an abstract one, associate suitable subnets to abstract local states. We define an operation of composition ruled by morphisms of that class. The main results concern behavioural properties preserved and reflected by the morphisms. In particular, we focus on the conditions under which reachable markings are preserved or reflected, and the conditions under which a morphism induces a weak bisimulation between net systems.

Keywords: Petri Nets, morphisms, local state refinement, composition.

1 Introduction

Refinement and composition of modules are among the basic conceptual tools of a system designer. Several formal approaches are available. One of the main challenges consists in developing languages and methods allowing to derive properties of the refined system from properties of the abstract one, as well as properties of a composed system from properties of its components.

We propose an approach based on Petri nets, where the refinement of a model is supported by so-called α-morphisms on the class of Elementary Net Systems, in particular SMD-EN Systems. We focus on the refinement of local states. Given a net N_2, interpreted as an abstract description of a system, the local states of N_2 are replaced by subnets, giving a new net, say N_1, so that there is an α-morphism from N_1 to N_2.

Moreover, following the same approach proposed in [1], [16] and in [5], on the basis of α-morphisms, it is possible to compose two different refinements of an abstract net system, called interface, yielding a system which comprises the details of both operands, while respecting the same abstract view. Even if this

M. Koutny et al. (Eds.): ToPNoC VIII, LNCS 8100, pp. 48–70, 2013.

operation is not a limit in the category of nets here considered, the composed system results to be related to both the components and the interface by means of α-morphisms, and the resulting diagram is commutative.

Our approach is motivated by the attempt to define a refinement operation preserving behavioural properties on the basis of structural and only local behavioural constraints. The additional restrictions, with respect to general morphisms, aim, on one hand, to capture typical features of refinements, and on the other hand to ensure that some behavioural properties of the abstract model still hold in the refined model.

Using morphisms to formalize the relation between a refined net and a more abstract one is not new. Most approaches, in Petri net theory, are based on transition refinement and, less frequently, on place refinement; for a survey, see [6]. Another survey paper, [15], describes a set of techniques which allow to refine transitions in Place/transition nets, so that the relation between the abstract net and its refinement is given by a morphism. There, the emphasis is on refinement rules that preserve specific behavioural properties, within the wider context of general transformation rules on nets.

A very general class of morphisms, interpreted as abstraction of system requirements, with less focus on strict preservation of behavioural properties, is defined in [7]. An attempt to define abstractions based on morphisms which preserve both structural and behavioural properties is described in [9] for Coloured Petri Nets. These morphisms are consistent with an operation of composition of nets.

The approach we present in this paper is similar in spirit to the refinement operation proposed in [14]. In that approach, refinement is defined on transition systems, but is strictly related to refinement of local states in nets, through the notion of region.

α-morphisms can be seen as a special case of the morphisms introduced in [20] and in [13], as it is formally shown in [4] and in [10]. Other morphisms introduced in the literature on the same line of [20] are the ones given in [19] and [2].

The use of products in a suitable category of nets as a way to model composition by synchronization has been studied by several authors, starting from [20] and in [11]. A variation on this theme, more similar to ours, proposed in [8], applies to safe nets and is built on the notion of pullback.

In the rest of this section, the main ideas of refinement and related morphisms are explained by means of a simple example. In Section 2 we collect preliminary definitions related to Petri nets which are used in the rest of the paper. Section 3 contains the definition of α-morphism; Section 4 contains the main results of the paper: in particular, we show that reachable markings are preserved, we characterize the local conditions under which reachable markings are reflected, i.e.: under which the inverse image of reachable markings are reachable markings, and such that morphisms induce a weak bisimulation between the related net systems. In Section 5 we present the composition of SMD-EN Systems guided by α-morphisms and show under which structural and local behavioural properties the composed net is weakly bisimilar to its components. Finally, in Section 6 we discuss some critical issues in our approach and suggest possible developments.

1.1   An Example

The example presented in this section aims at explaining, informally, how α-morphisms support refinement of local states in Elementary Net Systems. The morphism maps nodes of a refined system, N_1, on a more abstract one, N_2.

The Elementary Net System shown in Fig. 1 represents an abstract view of the interaction between a student and an University secretariat office. A student may ask the office either to emit an English proficiency certificate or to admit her to the final exam. Note that, at this level of abstraction, the model does not

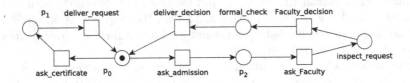

Fig. 1. Abstract view (N_2)

distinguish a positive answer from a negative one. Suppose that the local state inspect_request corresponds to the actual inspection of the request by a Faculty board, which delivers the decision to the secretariat.

We might want to refine formal_check, in order to distinguish two cases: positive answer and negative answer.

The actual decision has been taken in state inspect_request, so the refinement of formal_check requires splitting the event Faculty_decision, thus reflecting the choice between the two answers. The result of the refinement is shown in Fig. 2, where the subnet refining formal_check is enclosed in a shaded oval. Note that the operation has required also splitting the outgoing transitions, in order to reflect the alternative outcomes. As suggested by the labels, the morphism $\varphi : N_1 \to N_2$ maps the elements enclosed in the shaded oval to the condition formal_check, the events Faculty_decision_ok and Faculty_decision_ko to the event Faculty_decision, and the events deliver_decision_receipt, deliver_decision_ documents_ko and deliver_decision_career_ko to the event deliver_decision, respectively.

2   Preliminary Definitions

In this section, we recall the basic definitions of net theory, in particular Elementary Net Systems [18], and bisimulation [12].

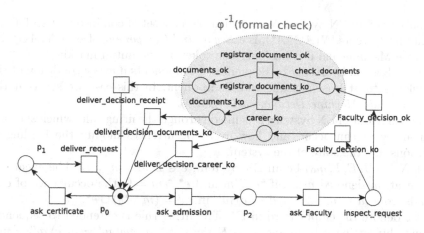

Fig. 2. Refined model (N_1)

2.1 Petri Nets

In net theory, models of distributed systems are based on objects called nets which specify local states, local transitions and the relations among them. A *net* is a triple $N = (B, E, F)$, where B is a set of *conditions* or local states, E is a set of *events* or transitions such that $B \cap E = \emptyset$ and $F \subseteq (B \times E) \cup (E \times B)$ is the *flow relation*.

We adopt the usual graphical notation: conditions are represented by circles, events by boxes and the flow relation by arcs. The set of elements of a net will be denoted by $X = B \cup E$; we allow nets with isolated elements.

The *preset* of an element $x \in X$ is ${}^\bullet x = \{y \in X | (y, x) \in F\}$; the *postset* of x is $x^\bullet = \{y \in X | (x, y) \in F\}$; the *neighbourhood* of x is given by ${}^\bullet x^\bullet = {}^\bullet x \cup x^\bullet$. These notations are extended to subsets of elements in the usual way.

For any net N we denote the *in-elements* of N by ${}^\circ N = \{x \in X : {}^\bullet x = \emptyset\}$ and the *out-elements* of N by $N^\circ = \{x \in X : x^\bullet = \emptyset\}$.

A net is *simple* if for all $x, y \in X$, if ${}^\bullet x = {}^\bullet y$ and $x^\bullet = y^\bullet$, then $x = y$.

A net $N' = (B', E', F')$ is a *subnet* of $N = (B, E, F)$ if $B' \subseteq B, E' \subseteq E$, and $F' = F \cap ((B' \times E') \cup (E' \times B'))$. Given a subset of elements $A \subseteq X$, we say that $N(A)$ is the *subnet of N identified* by A if $N(A) = (B \cap A, E \cap A, F \cap (A \times A))$. Given a subset of conditions $A \subseteq B$, we say that $N(A)$ is the *subnet of N generated* by A if $N(A) = (A, {}^\bullet A^\bullet, F \cap (\{A \cup \{{}^\bullet A^\bullet\}\} \times \{A \cup \{{}^\bullet A^\bullet\}\}))$.

A *State Machine* is a connected net such that each event e has exactly one input condition and exactly one output condition: $\forall e \in E, |{}^\bullet e| = |e^\bullet| = 1$.

Elementary Net (EN) Systems are a basic system model in net theory. An *Elementary Net System* is a quadruple $N = (B, E, F, m_0)$, where (B, E, F) is a net such that B and E are finite sets, self-loops are not allowed, isolated elements are not allowed, and the *initial marking* is $m_0 \subseteq B$.

The elements in the initial marking are interpreted as the conditions which are true in the initial state.

A subnet of an EN System N identified by a subset of conditions A and all its pre and post events, $N(A \cup {}^\bullet A^\bullet)$, is a *Sequential Component* of N if $N(A \cup {}^\bullet A^\bullet)$ is a State Machine and if it has only one token in the initial marking.

An EN System is *covered* by Sequential Components if every condition of the net belongs to at least a Sequential Component. In this case we say that the system is *State Machine Decomposable (SMD)*.

The behaviour of EN Systems is defined through the firing rule, which specifies when an event can occur, and how event occurrences modify the holding of conditions, i.e. the state of the system.

Let $N = (B, E, F, m_0)$ be an EN System, $e \in E$ and $m \subseteq B$. The event e is *enabled* at m, denoted $m\,[e\rangle$, if ${}^\bullet e \subseteq m$ and $e^\bullet \cap m = \emptyset$; the occurrence of e at m leads from m to m', denoted $m\,[e\rangle\,m'$, iff $m' = (m \setminus {}^\bullet e) \cup e^\bullet$.

Let ϵ denote the empty word in E^*. The firing rule is extended to sequences of events by setting $m\,[\epsilon\rangle\,m$ and $\forall e \in E, \forall w \in E^*, m\,[ew\rangle\,m' = m\,[e\rangle\,m''[w\rangle m''$; w is called a *firing sequence*.

A subset $m \subseteq B$ is a *reachable marking* of N if there exists a $w \in E^*$ such that $m_0\,[w\rangle\,m$. The *set of all reachable markings* of N is denoted by $[m_0\rangle$.

An EN System is *contact-free* if $\forall e \in E, \forall m \in [m_0\rangle$: ${}^\bullet e \subseteq m$ implies $e^\bullet \cap m = \emptyset$. An EN System covered by Sequential Components is contact-free [18]. An event is called *dead* at a marking m if it is not enabled at any marking reachable from m. A reachable marking m is called *dead* if no event is enabled at m. An EN System is *deadlock-free* if no reachable marking is dead.

2.2   Unfoldings

The semantics of an EN System can be given as its *unfolding*. The unfolding is an acyclic net, possibly infinite, which records the occurrences of its elements in all possible executions.

Definition 1. *Let $N = (B, E, F)$ be a net, and let $x, y \in X$. We say that x and y are in* conflict, *denoted by $x \,\#_N\, y$, if there exist two distinct events $e_x, e_y \in E$ such that $e_x F^* x$, $e_y F^* y$, and ${}^\bullet e_x \cap {}^\bullet e_y \neq \emptyset$.*

Definition 2. *An occurrence net is a net $N = (B, E, F)$ satisfying:*

1. *if $e_1, e_2 \in E, e_1{}^\bullet \cap e_2{}^\bullet \neq \emptyset$ then $e_1 = e_2$;*
2. *F^* is a partial order,*
3. *for any $x \in X, \{y : y F^* x\}$ is finite;*
4. *$\#_N$ is irreflexive,*
5. *the minimal elements with respect to F^* are conditions.*

A branching process of N is an occurrence net whose elements can be mapped to the elements of N.

Definition 3. *Let $N = (B, E, F, m_0)$ be an EN System, and $\Sigma = (P, T, G)$ be an occurrence net. Let $\pi : P \cup T \to B \cup E$ be a map.*
   The pair (Σ, π) is a branching process of N if:

- $\pi(P) \subseteq B$, $\pi(T) \subseteq E$;
- π restricted to the minimal elements of Σ is a bijection on m_0;
- for each $t \in T$, π restricted to ${}^\bullet t$ is injective and π restricted to $t^\bullet$ is injective;
- for each $t \in T$, $\pi({}^\bullet t) = {}^\bullet(\pi(t))$ and $\pi(t^\bullet) = ({}^\bullet\pi(t))$.

The unfolding of an EN System N, denoted by $Unf(N)$, is the maximal branching process of N, namely the unique, up to isomorphism, branching process such that any other branching process of N is isomorphic to a subnet of $Unf(N)$. The map associated to the unfolding will be denoted u and called *folding*.

2.3   Bisimulation

Bisimulation relations have been introduced as equivalence notions with respect to event observation [12]. We define the observability of events of a system by using a labelling function which associates the same label to different events, when viewed as equal by an observer, and the label τ to unobservable events.

Definition 4. *Let* $N = (B, E, F, m_0)$ *be an EN System,* $l : E \to L \cup \{\tau\}$ *be a labelling function where* L *is the alphabet of observable actions and* $\tau \notin L$ *the unobservable action. Let* ϵ *denote the empty word both of* E^* *and* L^*. *The function* l *is extended to a homomorphism* $l : E^* \to L^*$ *in the following way:*

$$l(\epsilon) = \epsilon$$

$$\forall e \in E, \forall w \in E^*, l(ew) = \begin{cases} l(e)l(w) & \text{if } l(e) \neq \tau \\ l(w) & \text{if } l(e) = \tau \end{cases}$$

The pair (N, l) *is called Labelled EN System.*
   Let $m, m' \in [m_0\rangle$ *and* $a \in L \cup \{\epsilon\}$; *then:*

- *a is enabled at* m, *denoted* $m \langle a \rangle$, *iff* $\exists w \in E^* : l(w) = a$ *and* $m [w\rangle$;
- *if a is enabled at* m, *then the occurrence of a can lead from* m *to* m', *denoted* $m \langle a \rangle m'$, *iff* $\exists w \in E^* : l(w) = a$ *and* $m [w\rangle m'$.

We define weak bisimulation as a relation between reachable markings of Labelled EN Systems [17].

Definition 5. *Let* $N_i = (B_i, E_i, F_i, m_0^i)$ *be an EN System for* $i = 1, 2$, *with the labelling function* $l_i : E_i \to L \cup \{\tau\}$. *Then* (N_1, l_1) *and* (N_2, l_2) *are weakly bisimilar, denoted* $(N_1, l_1) \approx (N_2, l_2)$, *iff* $\exists r \subseteq [m_0^1\rangle \times [m_0^2\rangle$ *such that:*

- $(m_0^1, m_0^2) \in r$;
- $\forall(m_1, m_2) \in r, \forall a \in L \cup \{\epsilon\}$ *it holds*

$$\forall m_1' : m_1 \langle a \rangle m_1' \Rightarrow \exists m_2' : m_2 \langle a \rangle m_2' \wedge (m_1', m_2') \in r$$

and (vice versa)

$$\forall m_2' : m_2 \langle a \rangle m_2' \Rightarrow \exists m_1' : m_1 \langle a \rangle m_1' \wedge (m_1', m_2') \in r$$

Such a relation r *is called* weak bisimulation.

3   A Class of Morphisms

In this section we recall the formal definition of α-morphisms for State Machine Decomposable Elementary Net Systems (SMD-EN Systems), and show that SMD-EN Systems together with α-morphisms form a category [4].

α-morphisms are defined as the restriction of a more general class of morphisms for EN Systems, called ω-morphisms. We will discuss the preservation of both structural and behavioural properties of α-morphisms in the next section.

Definition 6. *Let $N_i = (B_i, E_i, F_i, m_0^i)$ be an EN System, for $i = 1, 2$. An ω-morphism from N_1 to N_2 is a total surjective map $\varphi : X_1 \to X_2$ such that:*

1. $\varphi(B_1) = B_2$;
2. $\varphi(m_0^1) = m_0^2$;
3. $\forall e_1 \in E_1$, if $\varphi(e_1) \in E_2$, then $\varphi(^\bullet e_1) = {}^\bullet\varphi(e_1)$ and $\varphi(e_1{}^\bullet) = \varphi(e_1)^\bullet$;
4. $\forall e_1 \in E_1$, if $\varphi(e_1) \in B_2$, then $\varphi(^\bullet e_1{}^\bullet) = \{\varphi(e_1)\}$;

We require that the map is total and surjective because N_1 refines the abstract model N_2, and any abstract element must be related to its refinement.

In particular, a subset of nodes can be mapped on a single condition $b_2 \in B_2$; in this case, we will call *bubble* the subnet identified by this subset, and denote it by $N_1(\varphi^{-1}(b_2))$; if more than one element is mapped on b_2, we will say that b_2 is *refined* by φ.

Definition 7. *Let $N_i = (B_i, E_i, F_i, m_0^i)$ be a SMD-EN System, for $i = 1, 2$. An α-morphism from N_1 to N_2 is an ω-morphism satisfying*

5. $\forall b_2 \in B_2$
   (a) $N_1(\varphi^{-1}(b_2))$ *is an acyclic net;*
   (b) $\forall b_1 \in {}^\circ N_1(\varphi^{-1}(b_2))$, $\varphi(^\bullet b_1) \subseteq {}^\bullet b_2$ and $(^\bullet b_2 \neq \emptyset \Rightarrow {}^\bullet b_1 \neq \emptyset)$;
   (c) $\forall b_1 \in N_1(\varphi^{-1}(b_2))^\circ$, $\varphi(b_1{}^\bullet) = b_2{}^\bullet$;
   (d) $\forall b_1 \in \varphi^{-1}(b_2) \cap B_1$,
       $(b_1 \notin {}^\circ N_1(\varphi^{-1}(b_2)) \Rightarrow \varphi(^\bullet b_1) = \{b_2\})$ and $(b_1 \notin N_1(\varphi^{-1}(b_2))^\circ \Rightarrow \varphi(b_1{}^\bullet) = \{b_2\})$;
   (e) $\forall b_1 \in \varphi^{-1}(b_2) \cap B_1$, *there is a sequential component N_{SC} of N_1 such that $b_1 \in B_{SC}$ and $\varphi^{-1}(^\bullet b_2{}^\bullet) \subseteq E_{SC}$.*

As we can see in Fig. 3a and 3b, in-conditions and out-conditions have different constraints, 5b and 5c respectively. As required by 5c, we do not allow that choices, which are internal to a bubble, constrain a final marking of that bubble: i.e., each out-condition of the bubble must have the same choices of the condition it refines. Instead, pre-events do not need this strict constraint (5b): hence it is sufficient that pre-events of any in-condition are mapped on a subset of the pre-events of the condition it refines. For example, in this particular case, we know that the choice between e_1 and f_1 of Figure 3a is made before the bubble, and this is implied also by the requirement 5e) on sequential components. Moreover, the conditions that are internal to a bubble must have pre-events and post-events which are all mapped to the refined condition b_2, as required by 5d.

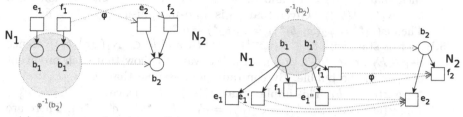

(a) Pre events of an in-condition   (b) Post events of an out-condition

Fig. 3. Pre and post event of a bubble

By requirement 5e, events in the neighbourhood of a bubble are not concurrent, and the same holds for their images. Within a bubble, there can be concurrent events; however, post events are in conflict, and firing one of them will empty the bubble, as it will be shown in Lemma 1 of the next section.

As shown in the following Proposition, α-morphisms are closed by composition; moreover, the identity function on X is an α-morphism, and the composition is associative. Hence, the family of SMD-EN Systems together with α-morphisms forms a category.

Proposition 1. *Let $N_i = (B_i, E_i, F_i, m_0^i)$ be a SMD-EN System for $i = 1 \ldots 3$. Let φ_i, with $i = 1, 2$, be an α-morphism from N_i to N_{i+1}.*
The map $\varphi : N_1 \rightarrow N_3$, $\varphi = \varphi_2 \circ \varphi_1$ is an α-morphism.

Proof. The first part of the proof is a simple verification. We have to prove only the last item of the α-morphism (Def. 7):

5: let $b_3 \in B_3$; by definition $N_1(\varphi^{-1}(b_3)) = N_1(\varphi_1^{-1}(\varphi_2^{-1}(b_3)))$.
If $b_1 \in N_1(\varphi^{-1}(b_3))$, then $\exists b_2 \in B_2 : \varphi_1(b_1) = b_2 \wedge \varphi_2(b_2) = b_3$.
5a: it is immediate to see that the bubble is acyclic;
5b: let $b_1 \in {}^\circ N_1(\varphi^{-1}(b_3))$, hence $b_1 \in {}^\circ N_1(\varphi_1^{-1}(b_2))$.
We want to prove that $b_2 \in {}^\circ N_2(\varphi_2^{-1}(b_3))$. By contradiction, let $e_2 \in {}^\bullet b_2$ and $\varphi_2(e_2) = b_3$. From Def. 7, point 5b ${}^\bullet b_1 \neq \emptyset$, then $\exists e_1 \in E_1$ such that $e_1 \in {}^\bullet b_1$. Given that $b_2 \notin {}^\circ N_2(\varphi_2^{-1}(b_3))$, then from Def. 7, point 5d $\varphi_2({}^\bullet b_2) = \{b_3\}$. From Def. 6, point 3 we know that $\varphi_1(e_1) \in {}^\bullet b_2$, then $\varphi(e_1) = b_3$ but this is a contradiction.
From Def. 7, point 5b:
 - $\varphi_2({}^\bullet b_2) \subseteq {}^\bullet b_3$ and if ${}^\bullet b_3 \neq \emptyset$ then ${}^\bullet b_2 \neq \emptyset$ and
 - $\varphi_1({}^\bullet b_1) \subseteq {}^\bullet b_2$ and if ${}^\bullet b_2 \neq \emptyset$ then ${}^\bullet b_1 \neq \emptyset$.
Then we have $\varphi({}^\bullet b_1) = \varphi_2(\varphi_1({}^\bullet b_1)) \subseteq \varphi_2({}^\bullet b_2) \subseteq {}^\bullet b_3$, and if ${}^\bullet b_3 \neq \emptyset$ then ${}^\bullet b_2 \neq \emptyset$ then ${}^\bullet b_1 \neq \emptyset$;
5c: let $b_1 \in N_1(\varphi^{-1}(b_3))^\circ$, hence $b_1 \in N_1(\varphi_1^{-1}(b_2))^\circ$. Given that φ_1 is an α-morphism, $\varphi_1(b_1{}^\bullet) = b_2{}^\bullet$.
Now, we want to prove that $b_2 \in N_2(\varphi_2^{-1}(b_3))^\circ$. By contradiction, let $e_2 \in b_2{}^\bullet$ and $\varphi_2(e_2) = b_3$. Given that φ_1 is an α-morphism, $\exists e_1 \in E_1$,

such that $\varphi_1(e_1) = e_2$ and $e_1 \in b_1{}^\bullet$ but this is a contradiction since $b_1 \in N_1(\varphi^{-1}(b_3))^\circ$. Given that φ_2 is an α-morphism, $\varphi_2(b_2{}^\bullet) = b_3{}^\bullet$. Then $\varphi(b_1{}^\bullet) = \varphi_2(\varphi_1(b_1{}^\bullet)) = \varphi_2(b_2{}^\bullet) = b_3{}^\bullet$;

5d: let us start with $b_1 \in N_1(\varphi^{-1}(b_3)) \cap B_1$ and $b_1 \notin {}^\circ N_1(\varphi^{-1}(b_3))$; Hence $\exists e_1 \in E_1 : e_1 \in {}^\bullet b_1 \wedge \varphi(e_1) = b_3$. We want to show that each pre-event of b_1 is in the bubble. By contradiction, assume that $\exists e_1' \in E_1 : e_1' \in {}^\bullet b_1 \wedge \varphi(e_1') \neq b_3$. This implies that $\varphi_1(e_1') \neq b_2$, hence $\exists e_2' \in E_2 \wedge \exists e_3' \in E_3 : \varphi(e_1') = \varphi_2(\varphi_1(e_1')) = \varphi_2(e_2') = e_3' \wedge e_2' \in {}^\bullet b_2 \wedge e_3' \in {}^\bullet b_3$. There are two cases:

- $b_2 \notin {}^\circ N_2(\varphi^{-1}(b_3))$, then from Def. 7, point 5d $\varphi_2({}^\bullet b_2) = \{b_3\}$ and this is a contradiction;
- $b_2 \in {}^\circ N_2(\varphi^{-1}(b_3))$ then there are two cases:
  - $\varphi_1(e_1) \in B_2$, then from Def. 6, point 4 $\varphi_1(e_1{}^\bullet) = \varphi_1(e_1)$, hence $\varphi_1(e_1) = b_2$ and then $b_1 \notin {}^\circ N_1(\varphi^{-1}(b_2))$. Then from Def. 7, point 5d $\varphi_1({}^\bullet b_1) = \{b_2\}$, hence $\varphi_1(e_1') = b_2$ and this is a contradiction;
  - $\varphi_1(e_1) = e_2$, then from Def. 6, point 3 $\varphi_1(e_1{}^\bullet) = e_2{}^\bullet \wedge b_2 \in e_2{}^\bullet \wedge \varphi_2(e_2) \neq b_3$ because b_2 is an in-condition in the bubble of b_3. But then $\varphi(e_1) = \varphi_2(\varphi_1(e_1)) = \varphi_2(e_2) \neq b_3$ and this is a contradiction.

For conditions of the bubble that are not out-conditions the proof is symmetrical;

5e: we want to prove that exists a sequential component N_{SC} of N_1 such that $b_1 \in B_{SC}$ and $\varphi^{-1}({}^\bullet b_3{}^\bullet) \subseteq E_{SC}$.

We use here Prop. 3 that will be proved in Section 4 with the other properties. That proposition says that the inverse image of a sequential component is covered by sequential components.

Take a sequential component of N_3 that contains b_3. Using Prop. 3 construct one sequential component of N_2 containing b_2. Using the same Lemma construct one sequential component of N_1 containing b_1.   □

Any ω-morphism, being a total map defined on the set of elements of a net N_1, naturally induces a partition of those elements. We now show how to define an elementary net on the set of equivalence classes generated by that partition.

Definition 8. *Let $N_i = (B_i, E_i, F_i, m_0^i)$ be an EN System, for $i = 1, 2$. An ω-morphism, φ, from N_1 to N_2 defines an equivalence relation on X_1, where the equivalence class of $x \in X_1$ is $[x] = \{y \in X_1 |\; \varphi(y) = \varphi(x)\}$. The quotient of N_1 with respect to φ is $N_1/\varphi = (B_1/\varphi, E_1/\varphi, F_1/\varphi, m_0^1/\varphi)$, where*

- $B_1/\varphi = \{[x] : x \in X_1, \varphi(x) \in B_2\}$;
- $E_1/\varphi = \{[x] : x \in X_1, \varphi(x) \in E_2\}$;
- $F_1/\varphi = \{([x], [y]) : x, y \in X_1, [x] \neq [y], (x, y) \in F_1\}$;
- $m_0^1/\varphi = \{[x] : x \in m_0^1\}$.

The quotient so defined is isomorphic to N_2, as shown below.

Proposition 2. *Let $\varphi : N_1 \to N_2$ be an ω-morphism. Then N_1/φ is an EN System isomorphic to N_2.*

Proof. Define a map $\lambda : B_1/\varphi \cup E_1/\varphi \rightarrow X_2$, by $\lambda([x]) = \varphi(x)$. Since ω-morphisms are surjective, λ is a bijection. We will now show that $([x], [y]) \in F_1\varphi \Leftrightarrow (\lambda([x]), \lambda([y])) \in F_2$.

Let $([x], [y]) \in F_1/\varphi$. Then, by definition, there are $x_1, y_1 \in X_1$ such that $x_1 \in [x]$, $y_1 \in [y]$, $[x] \neq [y]$, and $(x_1, y_1) \in F_1$. By definition of ω-morphism, it then follows that $(\varphi(x_1), \varphi(y_1)) \in F_2$.

Let $(x, y) \in F_2$. Suppose $x \in B_2$ and $y \in E_2$ (the case where $x \in E_2$ and $y \in B_2$ is analogous). Since φ is surjective, $\varphi^{-1}(x)$ and $\varphi^{-1}(y)$ are both non-empty; moreover, the elements in $\varphi^{-1}(y)$ are all events. Take e such that $\varphi(e) = y$; by Def. 6, point 3, we know that $\varphi(^\bullet e) = {}^\bullet y$. Then, from $x \in {}^\bullet y$, follows the existence of some $b \in {}^\bullet e$ such that $\varphi(b) = x$, and $([x], [y]) \in F_1/\varphi$.   □

4   Properties Preserved and Reflected by α-morphisms

Since we consider SMD-EN Systems, it is natural to ask whether α-morphisms preserve and reflect sequential components. Let φ be an α-morphism from N_1 to N_2. If a condition b_2 belongs to a sequential component, then also its pre- and post-events belong to the same sequential component. Hence, if b_2 is refined by a bubble $N_1(\varphi^{-1}(b_2))$, by requirement 5e of α-morphisms any condition of the bubble belongs to a sequential component containing any event in $\varphi^{-1}(^\bullet b_2{}^\bullet)$. Then, the sequential components of N_2 are reflected by φ, in the sense that the inverse image of a sequential component is covered by sequential components.

Proposition 3. *Let $\varphi : N_1 \rightarrow N_2$ be an α-morphism. Let N_{SC2} be a sequential component of N_2. Then $\varphi^{-1}(N_{SC2})$ is covered by sequential components, each one containing the whole inverse image of the neighbourhood of each condition of N_{SC2}.*

Proof. Let us assume that there is a unique condition of N_{SC2}, b_2, that is refined by the morphism. It is easy to see that $\varphi^{-1}(N_{SC2})$ is a subnet of N_1, and that it is isomorphic to N_{SC2} except for b_2 and its neighbourhood. Take $b_1 \in \varphi^{-1}(b_2) \cap B_1$. For Def. 7, point 5e we know that there is a sequential component N_{SC1} of N_1 such that $b_1 \in B_{SC1}$ and $\varphi^{-1}(^\bullet b_2{}^\bullet) \subseteq E_{SC1}$. Now build up a sequential component generated by $(B_{SC1} \cap \varphi^{-1}(b_2)) \cup \varphi^{-1}(B_{SC2} \setminus \{b_2\})$. This procedure can be easily extended to the refinement of multiple conditions by applying it to a single condition at a time.   □

Sequential components are not preserved, as we can see in Fig. 4. The sequential component of N_1 generated by $\{\varphi^{-1}(b_1), b_{5-1}, b_{6-1}\}$ is such that its image, the net generated by $\{b_1, b_5, b_6\}$, is not a sequential component of N_2 since e_3, which belongs to $^\bullet b_5$, is such that $^\bullet e_3 \cap \{b_1, b_5, b_6\} = \emptyset$.

The idea driving our interpretation of bubble is that the subnet corresponding to a condition "behaves" in the same way as the condition it refines. In a SMD-EN System, each condition at any time can be true or false. It is not possible that this condition is partially true or partially false; hence, also the bubble should behave like this. The next lemma states that firing an output event of a bubble

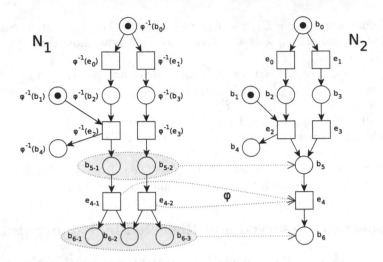

Fig. 4. Two SMD-EN Systems related by an α-morphism

empties the bubble, and that no input event of a bubble is enabled whenever a token is inside the bubble.

Lemma 1. *Let $\varphi : N_1 \to N_2$ be an α-morphism. Then:*

1. *Let $e_1 \in E_1, b_2 \in B_2$: $e_1 \in \varphi^{-1}(b_2^{\bullet})$; $m_1, m_1' \in [m_0^1\rangle$: $m_1 [e_1\rangle m_1'$, then $m_1' \cap \varphi^{-1}(b_2) = \emptyset$.*
2. *Let $e_1 \in E_1, b_2 \in B_2$: $e_1 \in \varphi^{-1}({}^{\bullet}b_2)$; $m_1, m_1' \in [m_0^1\rangle$: $m_1 [e_1\rangle m_1'$ then $m_1 \cap \varphi^{-1}(b_2) = \emptyset$.*

Proof. Take a marking m_1 in which a condition $b_1 \in \varphi^{-1}(b_2)$ is marked.

We know by Def. 7, point 5e) that there exists a sequential component SC of N_1 such that $b_1 \in B_{SC}$ and $\varphi^{-1}({}^{\bullet}b_2^{\bullet}) \subseteq E_{SC}$.

1. By contradiction, take $e_1 \in \varphi^{-1}(b_2^{\bullet})$ such that $b_1 \notin {}^{\bullet}e_1$ and $m_1 [e_1\rangle$; hence all its preconditions are marked. Since SC contains e_1, one of its preconditions belongs to SC as well as b_1, this is a contradiction because the sequential component has only one token.
2. By contradiction, take $e_1 \in \varphi^{-1}({}^{\bullet}b_2)$ such that $m_1 [e_1\rangle$; hence all its preconditions are marked. Since SC contains e_1, one of its preconditions belongs to SC as well as b_1, and this is a contradiction because the sequential component has only one token. $\qquad\square$

In the next proposition, we show that α-morphisms preserve reachable markings.

Proposition 4. *Let $\varphi : N_1 \to N_2$ be an α-morphism, and $m_1 \in [m_0^1\rangle$. Then $\varphi(m_1) \in [m_0^2\rangle$. If $m_1 [e\rangle m_1'$ then:*

- *if $\varphi(e) \in E_2$ then $\varphi(m_1) [\varphi(e)\rangle \varphi(m_1')$*
- *if $\varphi(e) \in B_2$ then $\varphi(m_1) = \varphi(m_1')$.*

Proof. The proof is by induction on the length of a firing sequence σ from m_0^1 to m_1.

Suppose $|\sigma| = 0$. Then $m_1 = m_0^1$. By definition, $\varphi(m_0^1) = m_0^2$. Now, take an event e enabled in m_0^1: $m_0^1 [e\rangle m_1'$, hence $m_1' = (m_0^1 \setminus {}^\bullet e) \cup e^\bullet$. Either $\varphi(e) \in E_2$ or $\varphi(e) \in B_2$. If $\varphi(e) \in E_2$, then for Def. 6 point 3 we have $\varphi({}^\bullet e) = {}^\bullet\varphi(e)$ and $\varphi(e^\bullet) = \varphi(e)^\bullet$. Moreover, by Lemma 1 point 1 we know that when a post event of a bubble fires, it empties the bubble, hence $m_0^2 [\varphi(e)\rangle m_0^2 \setminus {}^\bullet\varphi(e) \cup \varphi(e)^\bullet$. If $\varphi(e) \in B_2$, then for Def. 6 point 4 we have $\varphi({}^\bullet e^\bullet) = \{\varphi(e)\}$, hence $\varphi(m_0^1) = \varphi(m_1')$.

Suppose now $|\sigma| = n + 1$. Then we can write $\sigma = \sigma_1 e$, with $m_0^1 [\sigma_1\rangle m_1 [e\rangle m_1'$. By the induction hypothesis, there is $m_2 \in [m_0^2\rangle$ such that $\varphi(m_1) = m_2$. Either $\varphi(e) \in E_2$ or $\varphi(e) \in B_2$. If $\varphi(e) \in E_2$, then for Def. 6 point 3 we have $\varphi({}^\bullet e) = {}^\bullet\varphi(e)$ and $\varphi(e^\bullet) = \varphi(e)^\bullet$. Moreover, by Lemma 1 point 1 we know that when a post event of a bubble fires, it empties the bubble, hence $m_2 [\varphi(e)\rangle m_2 \setminus {}^\bullet\varphi(e) \cup \varphi(e)^\bullet$. If $\varphi(e) \in B_2$, then for Def. 6 point 4 we have $\varphi({}^\bullet e^\bullet) = \{\varphi(e)\}$, hence $\varphi(m_1) = \varphi(m_1')$.   □

As for other morphisms in the literature, α-morphisms do not reflect reachable markings. This can happen, in particular, when a condition is refined by a subnet leading to a block before reaching a marking enabling out-events, or whenever the refinements of conditions "interfere" with each other so that, even if in each bubble a "final" local marking is reached, the global marking doesn't enable any event, as for example in the case of the α-morphism given in Fig. 6. The two above cases suggest to require both that any condition is refined by a subnet such that, when a final marking is reached, this one enables events which correspond to the post-events of the refined condition; and also that different refinements do not "interfere" with each other. The non interference is guaranteed when any event of N_2 has at most a unique condition in its neighbourhood that is properly refined in N_1.

In order to reflect the reachable markings we have to introduce behavioural constraints. We now show that this can be done through local constraints, by considering the unfolding of subnets related to the bubbles.

The following auxiliary construction is needed. Given an α-morphism φ : $N_1 \to N_2$, and a condition $b_2 \in B_2$ with its refinement $N_1(\varphi^{-1}(b_2))$, we define two new SMD-EN Systems. The first one, denoted $S_1(b_2)$, contains (a copy of) the subnet $N_1(\varphi^{-1}(b_2))$, its pre and post-events in E_1 and two new conditions: b_1^{in}, which is pre of all the pre-events, and b_1^{out}, which is post of all the post-events. The initial marking of $S_1(b_2)$ will be $\{b_1^{in}\}$. The second system, denoted $S_2(b_2)$ contains b_2, its pre- and post-events and two new conditions: b_2^{in}, which is pre of all the pre-events, and b_2^{out}, which is post of all the post-events. The initial marking of $S_2(b_2)$ will be $\{b_2^{in}\}$.

In Fig. 5 we show the two systems $S_1(b_2)$ and $S_2(b_2)$ for the nets showed in the initial example (Fig. 1 and 2), in Section 1, with b_2 = formal_check.

Definition 9. *Let $\varphi : N_1 \to N_2$ be an α-morphism and $b_2 \in B_2$.*

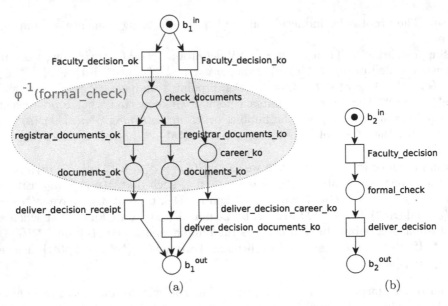

(a)   (b)

Fig. 5. (a): S_1(formal_check) of Fig. 2 and (b): S_2(formal_check) of Fig. 1

*Construct the SMD-EN Systems, $S_1(b_2) = (B_{S1}, E_{S1}, F_{S1}, m_0^{S1})$ and $S_2(b_2) =$
$(B_{S2}, E_{S2}, F_{S2}, m_0^{S2})$ in this way:*

$$B_{S1} = \begin{cases} (\varphi^{-1}(b_2) \cap B_1) \cup \{b_1^{out}\} & \text{if } {}^\bullet b_2 = \emptyset \\ (\varphi^{-1}(b_2) \cap B_1) \cup \{b_1^{in}\} & \text{if } b_2^\bullet = \emptyset \\ (\varphi^{-1}(b_2) \cap B_1) \cup \{b_1^{in}, b_1^{out}\} & \text{otherwise} \end{cases}$$

$E_{S1} = (\varphi^{-1}(b_2) \cap E_1) \cup \varphi^{-1}({}^\bullet b_2) \cup \varphi^{-1}(b_2^\bullet);$

$F_{S1} = (F_1 \cap ((B_{S1} \cup E_{S1}) \times (E_{S1} \cup B_{S1}))) \cup F_{S1}^{in} \cup F_{S1}^{out}$, *where*
$F_{S1}^{in} = \{(b_1^{in}, e) : e \in \varphi^{-1}({}^\bullet b_2)\}$ *and* $F_{S1}^{out} = \{(e, b_1^{out}) : e \in \varphi^{-1}(b_2^\bullet)\};$

$$m_0^{S1} = \begin{cases} m_0^1 \cap \varphi^{-1}(b_2) & \text{if } {}^\bullet b_2 = \emptyset \\ \{b_1^{in}\} & \text{otherwise} \end{cases}$$

$$B_{S2} = \begin{cases} \{b_2, b_2^{out}\} & \text{if } {}^\bullet b_2 = \emptyset \\ \{b_2, b_2^{in}\} & \text{if } b_2^\bullet = \emptyset \\ \{b_2, b_2^{in}, b_2^{out}\} & \text{otherwise} \end{cases}$$

$E_{S2} = {}^\bullet b_2^\bullet;$

$F_{S2} = (F_2 \cap ((B_{S2} \cup E_{S2}) \times (E_{S2} \cup B_{S2}))) \cup F_{S2}^{in} \cup F_{S2}^{out}$, *where*
$F_{S2}^{in} = \{(b_2^{in}, e) : e \in {}^\bullet b_2\}$ *and* $F_{S2}^{out} = \{(e, b_2^{out}) : e \in b_2^\bullet\};$

$$m_0^{S2} = \begin{cases} m_0^2 \cap \{b_2\} & \text{if } {}^\bullet b_2 = \emptyset \\ \{b_2^{in}\} & \text{otherwise} \end{cases}$$

Define φ^S as a map from $S_1(b_2)$ to $S_2(b_2)$, which restricts φ to the elements of
$S_1(b_2)$, and extends it with $\varphi^S(b_1^{in}) = b_2^{in}$ and $\varphi^S(b_1^{out}) = b_2^{out}$. Note that $S_1(b_2)$
and $S_2(b_2)$ are SMD-EN Systems and that φ^S is an α-morphism.

Let $\varphi : N_1 \to N_2$ be an α-morphism and $\varphi^S : S_1(b_2) \to S_2(b_2)$ as in Def. 9. By using φ^S, consider two labelling functions l_1 and l_2 such that the events in E_{S2} are all observable, i.e.: l_2 is the identity function, and the invisible events of $S_1(b_2)$ are the ones mapped to conditions, i.e.:

$$\forall e \in E_{S1} : l_1(e) = \begin{cases} \varphi^S(e) & \text{if } \varphi^S(e) \in E_{S2} \\ \tau & \text{otherwise} \end{cases}$$

Let $Unf(S_1(b_2))$ be the unfolding of $S_1(b_2)$ with $u : Unf(S_1(b_2)) \to S_1(b_2)$ folding function. The following lemma shows that if $\varphi^S \circ u$ is an α-morphism, then $S_1(b_2)$ and $S_2(b_2)$ are weakly bisimilar.

Lemma 2. *Let $\varphi : N_1 \to N_2$ be an α-morphism, and φ^S as in Def. 9. Let $Unf(S_1(b_2))$ be the unfolding of $S_1(b_2)$ with u folding function. If $\varphi^S \circ u$ is an α-morphism from $Unf(S_1(b_2))$ to $S_2(b_2)$, then $r = \{(m_1, \varphi^S(m_1)) : m_1 \in [m_0^{S1}\rangle\}$ is a weak bisimulation, and $(S_1(b_2), l_1)$ and $(S_1(b_2), l_2)$ are weakly bisimilar.*

Proof. Since φ^S is an α-morphism, Prop. 4 assures that $S_2(b_2)$ simulates $S_1(b_2)$, by $(\varphi^S)^{-1}$.

Then, we need only to prove that $S_1(b_2)$ simulates $S_2(b_2)$, by φ^S.

We prove that r is a weak bisimulation between $(S_1(b_2), l_1)$ and $(S_2(b_2), l_2)$. The reachable markings of $S_2(b_2)$ are $\{\{b_2^{in}\}, \{b_2\}, \{b_2^{out}\}\}$, let us discuss the three corresponding set of markings of $S_1(b_2)$ separately:

- the initial marking of $S_2(b_2)$ is $m_0^{S2} = \{b_2^{in}\}$ and it is related to the initial marking of $S_1(b_2)$, $m_0^{S1} = \{b_1^{in}\}$.
  We have two possible cases:
  - $\{b_2^{in}\} [\epsilon\rangle \{b_2^{in}\}$: in $S_1(b_2)$ it is not possible to fire one of the pre-events of the bubble, that are the ones enabled in the initial marking, because they are all labelled, so it is only possible to fire the empty word and remain in the initial marking,
  - $\{b_2^{in}\} [a\rangle \{b_2\}$: for the surjectivity of the α-morphism, in $S_1(b_2)$ there is, at least, one event mapped on a, let us call it a_1. For the Def. 6, point 3, a_1 has an environment corresponding to the one of a, hence $\{b_1^{in}\} [a_1\rangle \{m_1\}$ with $\varphi^S(m_1) = \{b_2\}$. After this firing, all the events internal to the bubble can freely fire because each one is mapped on b_2, hence for Def. 6, point 4 the new marking is again related to $\{b_2\}$. It is not possible that a post-event of the bubble fires, because in that case the visible action will not be a;
- let $(m_1, \{b_2\}) \in r$ such that $m_1 \subseteq \varphi^{-1}(b_2)$.
  We have two possible cases:
  - $\{b_2\} [\epsilon\rangle \{b_2\}$: this part of the proof is equivalent to the last part of the previous item,
  - $\{b_2\} [a\rangle \{b_2^{out}\}$: we prove $m_1 (a) \{b_1^{out}\}$ by induction on the distance between one of the initial markings of the bubble and m_1.
    base $\exists e_1 \in S_1(b_2) : {}^\bullet e_1 = b_1^{in} \wedge e_1{}^\bullet = m_1$.

Note that m_1 is generated, in the unfolding, by an event in conflict with all the other pre-events of the bubble, hence all its future is completely disjoint from the rest of the unfolding of the bubble. Def. 7, point 5c assure that in its future there will be, at least, one event for each post-events of b_2, hence it is possible to fire one event mapped on a,

induction   let m_1 be a marking internal to the bubble such that $m_1(a)$, let $m_1', m_1[e_1]m_1'$, be such that $\neg(m_1'(a))$. Hence e_1 is in conflict with all the events with label a. Thus all the future of e_1 is in conflict with all the events with label a. This is a contradiction because the morphism from the unfolding to $S_2(b_2)$ assures that each run will end in b_1^{out} and Def. 7, point 5c assures that each out-condition of the bubble should have a post-event with label a.

– the final marking of $S_2(b_2)$ is $\{b_2^{out}\}$ and it is related to the final marking of $S_1(b_2)$, $\{b_1^{out}\}$. Both are deadlock markings.   □

When the morphism corresponds to the refinement of a marked condition, we require that all the tokens of the corresponding bubble are placed into in-conditions which are post-conditions of a pre-event, if it exists. System N_1 is then called *well marked* with respect to φ.

Definition 10. *Let* $\varphi : N_1 \to N_2$ *be an* α*-morphism. System* N_1 *is* well marked *with respect to* φ *if for each* $b_2 \in B_2$ *one of the following conditions hold:*

– $\varphi^{-1}(b_2) \cap m_0^1 = \emptyset$ *or*
– *if* ${}^\bullet b_2 \neq \emptyset$ *then there is* $e_1 \in \varphi^{-1}({}^\bullet b_2)$ *such that* $\varphi^{-1}(b_2) \cap m_0^1 = e_1^\bullet$ *or*
– *if* ${}^\bullet b_2 = \emptyset$ *then* $\varphi^{-1}(b_2) \cap m_0^1 = {}^\circ\varphi^{-1}(b_2)$

The following proposition states a set of conditions under which reachable markings are reflected by α-morphisms.

Proposition 5. *Let* $\varphi : N_1 \to N_2$ *be an* α*-morphism such that* N_1 *is well marked w.r.t.* φ, φ^S *be as in Def. 9, and* $Unf(S_1(b_2))$ *be the unfolding of* $S_1(b_2)$ *with* u *folding function. If* $\varphi^S \circ u$ *is an* α*-morphism from* $Unf(S_1(b_2))$ *to* $S_2(b_2)$, *then, for all* $m_2 \in [m_0^2\rangle$, *there is* $m_1 \in [m_0^1\rangle$ *such that* $\varphi(m_1) = m_2$.

Proof. We will actually show a slightly stronger property, namely that m_1 can be chosen so that its intersection with the set of conditions in the bubble refining b_2 only contains elements in $(N_1(\varphi^{-1}(b_2)))^\circ$. The proof is by induction on the length of a firing sequence σ from m_0^2 to m_2.

Suppose $|\sigma| = 0$. Then $m_2 = m_0^2$. By definition, $\varphi(m_0^1) = m_0^2$. If $b_2 \notin m_0^2$, then $m_0^1 \cap \varphi^{-1}(b_2) = \emptyset$. If $b_2 \in m_0^2$, then we use Lemma 2 to reach in N_1 a marking in the bubble of b_2 that contains only out-conditions, and we are done.

Suppose now $|\sigma| = n+1$. Then we can write $\sigma = \sigma_1 e_2$, with $m_0^2[\sigma_1\rangle m_1^2[e_2\rangle m_2$. By the induction hypothesis, there is $m_1^1 \in [m_0^1\rangle$ such that $\varphi(m_1^1) = m_1^2$ and $m_1^1 \cap \varphi^{-1}(b_2) \subseteq (N_1(\varphi^{-1}(b_2)))^\circ$.

Since φ is surjective, there is at least one event in E_1 that φ maps on e_2. If $b_2 \notin {}^\bullet e_2$, then there exists $e_1 \in \varphi^{-1}(e_2)$ such that $m_1^1[e_1\rangle$. If $b_2 \in {}^\bullet e_2$, by Lemma 2 there exists $e_1 \in \varphi^{-1}(e_2)$ such that $m_1^1[e_1\rangle$.   □

Let $N_i = (B_i, E_i, F_i, m_0^i)$ be a SMD-EN System for $i = 1, 2$ and let $\varphi : N_1 \to N_2$ be an α-morphism. By using φ, we define two labelling functions such that all events in E_2 are observable, i.e.: l_2 is the identity function, and the invisible events of N_1 are the ones mapped to conditions, i.e.:

$$\forall e \in E_1 : l_1(e) = \begin{cases} \varphi(e) & \text{if } \varphi(e) \in E_2 \\ \tau & \text{otherwise} \end{cases}$$

The next proposition, which states the conditions under which N_1 and N_2 are weakly bisimilar, is a consequence of Prop. 4 and of the proof of Prop. 5.

Proposition 6. *Let $\varphi : N_1 \to N_2$ be an α-morphism such that N_1 is well marked and $\varphi^S \circ u$ is an α-morphism from $Unf(S_1(b_2))$ to $S_2(b_2)$, then (N_1, l_1) and (N_2, l_2) are weakly bisimilar: $(N_1, l_1) \approx (N_2, l_2)$.*

Prop. 5 and Prop. 6 are stated in the case in which only one condition is refined, but they can be generalized to multiple refinements, provided that in the neighbourhood of each event of N_2 there is, at most, one refined condition. The examples in Fig. 6 show why this constraint is required. In order to refine two conditions which are both neighbourhood of the same event, it would also be possible to consider the composition of the two systems, each one refining one of the two conditions. Such a composition is presented in the following section.

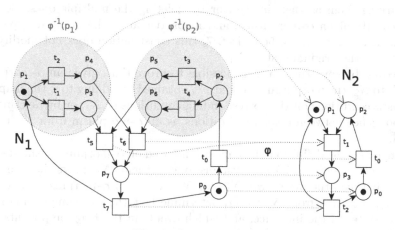

Fig. 6. An α-morphism

5 Composition Based on α-morphisms

In this section, we define a way of composing SMD-EN Systems, based on α-morphisms, in a similar way as in [5] and in [16].

The two systems to be composed must be mapped onto a common *interface*, which is another SMD-EN System. The two morphisms, from the components to the interface, determine which elements are to be identified, as shown later by means of an example. The interface can be seen, intuitively, as a protocol of interaction, with which the components must comply, or as a common abstraction; in this second view, each component can refine some parts of the common abstraction.

We will first give some following preliminary definitions, then the formal definition of the operation, and finally an example. Given an α-morphism φ from N_1 to N_2, we say that N_1 is *canonical* with respect to φ if, for any abstract condition b_2 in N_2, N_1 contains a condition b_1 as *representation* of b_2.

Definition 11. *Let $\varphi : X_1 \to X_2$ be an α-morphism from N_1 to N_2. N_1 is canonical with respect to φ if every bubble, $\varphi^{-1}(b_2)$ with $b_2 \in B_2$, contains one, and only one, condition, $b_1 \in \varphi^{-1}(b_2) \cap B_1$, that satisfies the following constraints:*

- *$b_1 \in m_0^1 \Leftrightarrow b_2 \in m_0^2$;*
- *${}^\bullet b_1 = \varphi^{-1}({}^\bullet b_2)$;*
- *$b_1{}^\bullet = \varphi^{-1}(b_2{}^\bullet)$.*

We will say that condition b_1 is a representation *of b_2, denoted $r_{N_1}(b_2)$. The subnet of a bubble, obtained by removing the representation, is denoted: $N_1^{-rep}(b_2) = N_1(\varphi^{-1}(b_2) \setminus \{r_{N_1}(b_2)\})$.*

If N_1 is not canonical, it is always possible to construct its unique (up to isomorphisms) *canonical version*, denoted $N_1^{\mathcal{C}}$, by adding the missing representations, and marking them as their images, or by deleting the multiple ones. Because of the constraint on α-morphisms, and in particular of the ones on sequential components, i.e.: condition 5e of Def. 7, this construction does not modify the behaviour of the original system N_1.

Moreover, by construction, it is possible to prove that, given an α-morphism from N_1 to N_2, the morphism, denoted $\varphi^{\mathcal{C}}$, obtained by adding to φ the mapping of the new conditions on the corresponding conditions of N_2, or by deleting the correspondence between deleted conditions, is an α-morphism from $N_1^{\mathcal{C}}$ to N_2, see [10].

We give now the definition of composition based on α-morphisms, the starting point is a set of three SMD-EN Systems; one of them, N_I, plays the role of an interface between the other two, N_1 and N_2. A pair of α-morphisms, one from N_1 to N_I, the other from N_2 to N_I, determine how the two components refine the local states of the interface, and which events in the two components have to synchronize.

The crucial point in the definition concerns the choice of synchronizing events. Suppose that the morphisms onto the interface map bubbles A_1 and A_2 to the same local state b (where A_i is taken in N_i). Then, the representations of A_1 and A_2 are local states which are identified in composing the two nets. This implies that any event in N_1 which puts a token in the representation of A_1 must be synchronized with any event doing the same in the representation of A_2. This explains the definition of the sets E_{sync}, below.

It is assumed that N_1, N_2 and N_I are disjoint and that N_1 and N_2 are canonical with respect to the corresponding morphisms.

Definition 12. *Let $N_i = (B_i, E_i, F_i, m_0^i)$ be an SMD-EN System for $i = 1, 2, I$. Let φ_i, with $i = 1, 2$, be an α-morphism from N_i to N_I. Let N_i be canonical with respect to φ_i. Define $N = N_1\langle N_I \rangle N_2 = (B, E, F, m_0)$ by*

$$B = \bigcup_{b_I \in B_I} B_{Bubble(b_I)} \qquad E = \left(\bigcup_{e_I \in E_I} E_{sync}(e_I) \right) \cup \left(\bigcup_{b_I \in B_I} E_{Bubble(b_I)} \right)$$

$$F = \bigcup_{b_I \in B_I} \left(F(b_I) \cup F_{Bubble(b_I)} \right)$$

$$b \in m_0 \iff b \in m_0^I \text{ or } b \in m_0^1 \text{ or } b \in m_0^2$$

where: $E_{sync}(e_I) = \{ e = \langle e_1, e_2 \rangle : e_1 \in E_1, e_2 \in E_2, \varphi_1(e_1) = e_I = \varphi_2(e_2) \}$
For $b_I \in B_I$, define:

$$Bubble(b_I) = ((B_{N_1^{-rep}(b_I)} \cup \{b_I\} \cup B_{N_2^{-rep}(b_I)}),$$
$$(E_{N_1^{-rep}(b_I)} \cup E_{N_2^{-rep}(b_I)}),$$
$$(F_{N_1^{-rep}(b_I)} \cup F_{N_2^{-rep}(b_I)}))$$

$$F(b_I) = {}^\bullet F(b_I) \cup F^\bullet(b_I)$$

Let $e = \langle e_1, e_2 \rangle \in \bigcup_{e_I \in {}^\bullet b_I} E_{sync}(e_I)$,

$${}^\bullet F(b_I) = \{(e, b) : b \in {}^\circ Bubble(b_I), (e_1, b) \in F_1\} \cup$$
$$\{(e, b_I)\} \cup \{(e, b) : b \in {}^\circ Bubble(b_I), (e_2, b) \in F_2\}$$

Let $e = \langle e_1, e_2 \rangle \in \bigcup_{e_I \in b_I{}^\bullet} E_{sync}(e_I)$,

$$F^\bullet(b_I) = \{(b, e) : b \in Bubble(b_I)^\circ, (b, e_1) \in F_1\} \cup$$
$$\{(b_I, e)\} \cup \{(b, e) : b \in Bubble(b_I)^\circ, (b, e_2) \in F_2\}$$

Note that in order to simplify the notation, $N_1\langle N_I \rangle N_2$ does not refer to the morphisms φ_i. By construction, $N = N_1\langle N_I \rangle N_2$, as defined above, is an EN System. Moreover, it is covered by sequential components. To see this, take $b \in B$. If $b \in B_I$, then b belongs to a sequential component in N_I, and all the conditions in this component are also in N, and these, together with their neighbourhood, identify a sequential component in N. If $b \in B_i$, then b belongs to a sequential component in N_i, and all the conditions in this component have a corresponding condition in N. It is easy to check that these, together with their neighbourhood, identify a sequential component in N.

We now define a map φ_i' from $N = N_1\langle N_I \rangle N_2$ onto N_i, and we will show in Prop. 7 that it is an α-morphism.

Definition 13. *Define φ_i' as follows, for each $x \in X$:*

$$\varphi_i'(x) = \begin{cases} x, & \text{if } x \in X_i \\ r_{N_i}(x), & \text{if } x \in B_I \\ r_{N_i}(\varphi_{3-i}(x)), & \text{if } x \in B_{3-i} \\ e_i, & \text{if } x = \langle e_1, e_2 \rangle \\ r_{N_i}(\varphi_{3-i}(x)), & \text{if } x \in E_{3-i} \end{cases}$$

Proposition 7. *The map φ_i' is an α-morphism from $N = N_1\langle N_I\rangle N_2$ to N_i, $i = 1, 2$.*

Proof. $\varphi_i' : X \to X_i$ is a total surjective function by construction.

Let $x, y \in X, e \in E$,

1: $\varphi_i'(B) = B_i$: take $b \in B$, we have three cases:
- $b \in B_i$, hence $\varphi_i'(b) = b$,
- $b \in B_I$, hence $\varphi_i'(b) = r_{N_i}(b)$,
- $b \in B_{3-i}$, hence $\varphi_i'(b) = r_{N_i}(b)$;

2: $\varphi_i'(m_0) = m_0^i$: given by construction;

3: let $\varphi_i'(e) \in E_i$ we have two cases:
- $e \in E_i$: this means that e is an event in a bubble of N_i and the construction respects its pre and post conditions and all the arcs;
- $e = \langle e_1, e_2 \rangle$, hence $\varphi_i(e_i) = e_I$. Let us start with preconditions. Take $b \in {}^\bullet e$, then for Def. 6, point 1 $\exists b_i \in B_i : \varphi_i'(b) = b_i \wedge \exists b_I \in B_I : \varphi_i(b_i) = b_I$; if $(b, e) \in F$ there are two cases:
  - $b_i \in \text{Bubble}(b_I)^\circ$ and $(b_i, e_i) \in F_i$,
  - $b \in B_I$ or $b_i \in \text{Bubble}(b_I)^\circ$ and $(b_i, e_{3-i}) \in F_{3-i}$, hence $\varphi_i'(b) = r_{N_i}(b_I)$, hence $(r_{N_i}(b_I), e_i)$.

  Take $b_i \in {}^\bullet e_i$, then for Def. 6 there is a condition of N mapped on it. For construction, we have that $b_i \in \text{Bubble}(b_I)^\circ$, and it can be a representation or not. If it is not a representation, $b_i \in B$, $\varphi_i'(b_i) = b_i$ and $(b_i, e) \in F$. If it is a representation, $b_I \in B$, $\varphi_i'(b_I) = b_i$ and $(b_I, e) \in F$. The proof for post-conditions is analogous;

4: $\varphi_i'(e) = r_{N_i}(b_I) \in B_i$, hence it was in a bubble of b_I in N_2: $e \in E_{3-i}$ and $\varphi_{3-i}(e) = b_I \in B_I$, hence for construction also b is in that bubble: $\varphi_i'(b) = r_{N_i}(b_I)$;

5: take $b_i \in B_i$, $N(\varphi_i'^{-1}(b_i))$ and $b_I = \varphi_i(b_i) \in B_I$.
If b_i is not a representation in N_i, by construction its bubble in N consists in the condition itself alone: in that case all the constraints are easily verified. If b_i is a representation in N_i ($b_i = r_{N_i}(b_I)$), by construction, its bubble in N is made by b_I plus the bubble of b_I in the other component. For b_I is exactly as we stated before. That bubble is clearly acyclic. The composition rebuilds the same relations between elements in the bubble of the other component, respecting constraint 5d. It creates the Cartesian product of events of N_1 and N_2 mapped on the same event of N_I and, consequently, it creates an arc

between all this copies and the neighbour conditions, respecting constraints 5b and 5c.

We will prove for representation b_i the constraint 5e on the conditions in the bubble of the other component, $b \in B_{3-i}$. Let $b \in \varphi_i'^{-1}(b_i) \cap B$, such that $b \notin B_I$.

Let N_{SC_i} be a sequential component of N_i containing b_i. Clearly, this sequential component contains also its pre and post events. Given that b_i is a representation, these are exactly all the events in the inverse image of pre and post events of b_I.

Let $N_{SC_{3-i}}$ be a sequential component of N_{3-i} containing b and all the events in the inverse image of pre and post events of b_I.

Take a sequential component generated by all the conditions of N_{SC_i} but for b_i plus the conditions of $N_{SC_{3-i}}$ that are in the bubble of b_I. That sequential component contains all the events in the neighbourhood of these condition, hence also all the events in the inverse image of pre and post events of b_i. $\square$

By construction, it is possible to prove that the system $N = N_1\langle N_I\rangle N_2$ is *canonical* with respect to φ_1' and to φ_2' and that the following diagram commutes.

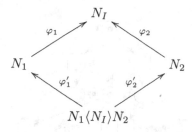

These results say that the composed system refines both the components, as well as the interface. For each abstract condition there is a corresponding condition in the composed system. An example of composition of net systems is given in Fig. 7. The interface, N_I, is a simple sequence of two events. The two components, N_1 and N_2, refine two different local state, b_1 and b_0, each one by a subnet, shown on a gray background. The composed net $N_1\langle N_I\rangle N_2$ contains both refinements of b_1 and b_0, while the rest of the net, not refined by the components, is taken as it is, but for the synchronizations of the events in the neighbourhood of the refinements/bubbles. By a construction similar to the one used in [5] (in Theorem 4.5), it is possible to prove the following Proposition.

Proposition 8. *Let $N_i = (B_i, E_i, F_i, m_0^i)$ be an SMD-EN System for $i = 1, 2, I$. Let φ_i, with $i = 1, 2$, be an α-morphism from N_i to N_I, and let $N = N_1\langle N_I\rangle N_2$ be be the composition of N_1 and N_2 using φ_1 and φ_2. If N_1 is weakly bisimilar to N_I then $N = N_1\langle N_I\rangle N_2$ is weakly bisimilar to N_2.*

Where, the labelling functions are derived from φ_1 and φ_2', respectively, in such a way that E_I and E_2 are all observable and the invisible events of E_1 and E are the ones which are mapped to conditions by φ_1 and φ_2', respectively.

For an indirect proof of the previous Proposition see [3]. This result tells us, in particular, that the composition of refinements N_1 and N_2, which are weakly bisimilar to a common interface N_I, yields a system N which is weakly bisimilar to N_I; and then, since bisimulation preserves deadlock-freeness, it is possible to deduce that N is also deadlock-free by verifying that N_I is deadlock-free. Remember that by Prop. 6 it is possible to check weak bisimilarity between two systems related by an α-morphism by considering their behaviour only locally.

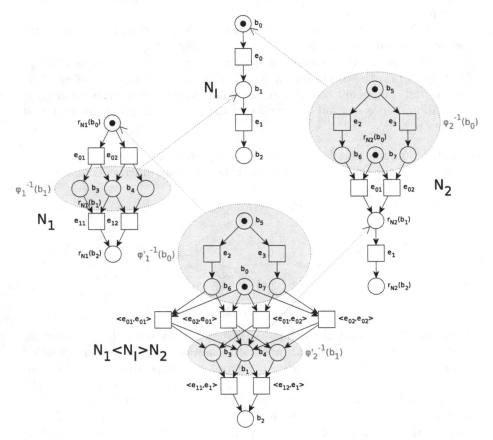

Fig. 7. An example of composition based on α-morphisms

6   Conclusions

We have presented a notion of morphism for a basic class of Petri nets with the aim of supporting refinement/abstraction of local states. The morphism, in fact, formalizes the relation between a refined net system and an abstract one, by replacing local states of the target net system with subnets. The main idea is that if one starts with an abstract model with some required behavioural properties, then, by refining local states with subnets respecting some constraints, the refined net system will maintain the required behavioural properties. Indeed, the main results concern behavioural properties preserved and reflected by the morphisms. In particular, reachable markings are preserved, and we have characterized some conditions under which reachable markings are reflected, and under which the morphisms induce a bisimulation between net systems. Since bisimulation preserves deadlock freeness, this implies for example that, starting from a deadlock-free abstract system it is possible to refine it obtaining a system which is still deadlock-free. The constraints in order to preserve/reflect behavioural properties are structural and behavioural, where the behavioural ones are only local. On this morphism we have defined a notion of composition based on interface in the line of [5]. We have shown that bisimilarity between a component and the interface can be lifted to bisimilarity between the other component and the composed system.

For what concerns future work, we plan to study the constraints under which this morphism can be defined for P/T nets and Coloured nets.

With respect to the application to system design, we plan to define a set of refinement operations which guarantee the existence of an α-morphism from the refined net to the original one.

Acknowledgments. Work partially supported by MIUR PRIN 2010-2011 grant H41J12000190001, "Automi e Linguaggi Formali: Aspetti Matematici e Applicativi". We thank the anonymous referees for their helpful comments.

References

1. Bednarczyk, M.A., Bernardinello, L., Caillaud, B., Pawłowski, W., Pomello, L.: Modular system development with pullbacks. In: van der Aalst, W.M.P., Best, E. (eds.) ICATPN 2003. LNCS, vol. 2679, pp. 140–160. Springer, Heidelberg (2003)
2. Bednarczyk, M.A., Borzyszkowski, A.M.: On concurrent realization of reactive systems and their morphisms. In: Ehrig, H., Juhás, G., Padberg, J., Rozenberg, G. (eds.) APN 2001. LNCS, vol. 2128, pp. 346–379. Springer, Heidelberg (2001)
3. Bernardinello, L., Mangioni, E., Pomello, L.: Composition of Elementary Net Systems based on α-morphisms. In: Köhler-Bußmeier, M. (ed.) Joint Proc. of LAM 2012, WooPS 2012, and CompoNet 2012, Hamburg, Germany, June 25-26. CEUR Workshop Proceedings, vol. 853, pp. 87–102. CEUR-WS.org (2012)
4. Bernardinello, L., Mangioni, E., Pomello, L.: Local State Refinement on Elementary Net Systems: an Approach Based on Morphisms. In: Cabac, L., Duvigneau, M., Moldt, D. (eds.) Proceedings of he Petri Nets and Software Engineering. International Workshop, PNSE 2012, Hamburg, Germany, June 25-26. CEUR Workshop Proceedings, vol. 851, pp. 138–152. CEUR-WS.org (2012)
5. Bernardinello, L., Monticelli, E., Pomello, L.: On preserving structural and behavioural properties by composing net systems on interfaces. Fundam. Inform. 80(1-3), 31–47 (2007)
6. Brauer, W., Gold, R., Vogler, W.: A survey of behaviour and equivalence preserving refinements of Petri nets. Advances in Petri Nets 1990, 1–46 (1991)
7. Desel, J., Merceron, A.: Vicinity respecting homomorphisms for abstracting system requirements. Transactions on Petri Nets and Other Models of Concurrency 4, 1–20 (2010)

8. Fabre, E.: On the construction of pullbacks for safe petri nets. In: Donatelli, S., Thiagarajan, P.S. (eds.) ICATPN 2006. LNCS, vol. 4024, pp. 166–180. Springer, Heidelberg (2006)
9. Lakos, C.A.: Composing abstractions of coloured petri nets. In: Nielsen, M., Simpson, D. (eds.) ICATPN 2000. LNCS, vol. 1825, pp. 323–342. Springer, Heidelberg (2000)
10. Mangioni, E.: Modularity for system modelling and analysis. PhD thesis, Università degli Studi di Milano-Bicocca, Dottorato di ricerca in Informatica, ciclo 24 (2013)
11. Meseguer, J., Montanari, U.: Petri nets are monoids. Information and Computation 88(2), 105–155 (1990)
12. Milner, R.: Communication and concurrency. Prentice-Hall, Inc., Upper Saddle River (1989)
13. Nielsen, M., Rozenberg, G., Thiagarajan, P.S.: Elementary transition systems. Theor. Comput. Sci. 96(1), 3–33 (1992)
14. Nielsen, M., Rozenberg, G., Thiagarajan, P.S.: Elementary transition systems and refinement. Acta Inf. 29(6/7), 555–578 (1992)
15. Padberg, J., Urbásek, M.: Rule-based refinement of Petri nets: A survey. In: Ehrig, H., Reisig, W., Rozenberg, G., Weber, H. (eds.) Petri Net Technology for Communication-Based Systems. LNCS, vol. 2472, pp. 161–196. Springer, Heidelberg (2003)
16. Pomello, L., Bernardinello, L.: Formal tools for modular system development. In: Cortadella, J., Reisig, W. (eds.) ICATPN 2004. LNCS, vol. 3099, pp. 77–96. Springer, Heidelberg (2004)
17. Pomello, L., Rozenberg, G., Simone, C.: A survey of equivalence notions for net based systems. In: Rozenberg, G. (ed.) APN 1992. LNCS, vol. 609, pp. 410–472. Springer, Heidelberg (1992)
18. Rozenberg, G., Engelfriet, J.: Elementary net systems. In: Reisig, W., Rozenberg, G. (eds.) APN 1998. LNCS, vol. 1491, pp. 12–121. Springer, Heidelberg (1998)
19. Vogler, W.: Executions: A new partial-order semantics of Petri nets. Theor. Comput. Sci. 91(2), 205–238 (1991)
20. Winskel, G.: Petri nets, algebras, morphisms, and compositionality. Inf. Comput. 72(3), 197–238 (1987)

From Code to Coloured Petri Nets: Modelling Guidelines

Anna Dedova and Laure Petrucci

LIPN, CNRS UMR 7030, Université Paris XIII
99, Avenue Jean-Baptiste Clément, F-93430 Villetaneuse, France
avd.nsu@gmail.com, Laure.Petrucci@lipn.univ-paris13.fr

Abstract. This paper presents a method for designing a coloured Petri net model of a system starting from its high-level object oriented source code. The entire process is divided into two parts: grounding and code analysis. For each part detailed step-by-step guidelines are given. The approach is illustrated with an industrial application case study, the NEO protocol.

1 Introduction

The modelling problem has been under investigation for many years. It features a lot of particular cases depending on 1) the nature of the description of the system to be modelled and 2) which formalism is chosen for the final model. According to the first criteria there are three basic groups of modelling approaches:

1. Starting from an informal description of a problem;
2. Starting from a detailed specification of a system;
3. Starting from the source code.

Some recent works tackle the first group of approaches. For example, in [6] the authors propose a modular design method and illustrate it on a model railway case study. One of the main points of [6] is using properties of the system at the modelling stage. In [8] an approach aggregating different views of the system is given. This method assumes that the system can be observed from several points of view: pre/post, process and lifeline views expressing respectively pre- and post-conditions of events, sequences of events, and sequences of states. Thus, steps in a process view correspond to system events and can be modelled by transitions in a Petri nets formalism. Similarly, steps of a lifeline view correspond to the states of the system and can be modelled by places of a Petri net. Then, by identifying the elements of these different representations of systems, places and transitions are glued together in order to get a complete Petri net.

The second group of modelling approaches includes various attempts to deliver a formal model from UML diagrams [14,12,11]. The advantage of these methods is that most developers are familiar with the UML and an automatic transformation of their diagrams into formal models and model-check them, would greatly simplify the software quality control. The difficulty is that UML diagrams allow

M. Koutny et al. (Eds.): ToPNoC VIII, LNCS 8100, pp. 71–88, 2013.

for much more freedom for the designer than formal models and the automatic translation is not trivial.

This paper addresses the third group of modelling approaches, which is not covered by a wide range of methods in the literature [16]. Such approaches are dedicated to systems for which the source code already exists, in order to guarantee it satisfies some requirements. They often do not support a complete language, but are restricted to some subset of it. Moreover, to the best of our knowledge, no work addressed a high level object oriented language, such as Python. Some works dedicated to ADA programs focus on the control flow and are limited to boolean variables [9] whereas we consider complex data structures.

Hence, what are the particular difficulties encountered by reverse-engineering from the source code? If a program is rather small (tens of lines) one can simply suppose that the operators are the system events and correspond to transitions, places between them model the intermediate states of the system, and some additional places model the states of variables used. But this approach is no more applicable when the system under consideration is as large as 3 MBytes of object oriented code. Of course it is possible to model all operators as in the previous case, but then the model becomes so huge that there is no means to analyse it and it becomes useless. Thus, it is necessary to choose an appropriate *level of abstraction* for the system. If it is too low and the model contains too many details, the same problem as above arises. If the level of abstraction is too high, there are too many hypotheses and assumptions and it may happen that nothing is left worth checking. The model is then trivial and its behaviour is completely correct while the system contains drawbacks that are hidden due to the modelling assumptions.

This paper reports the process adopted when modelling the NEO protocol using a reverse-engineering approach within the Neoppod project [4,5]. The project aimed a formally proving that some essential properties of a new distributed database management system were satisfied, thus giving sufficient confidence in its correct behaviour. This allowed us to gain experience on the methodology we used, derive finer and general guidelines for modelling which constitute the core of the paper, and check that the models obtained using these guidelines were as expected. Moreover, this work confirmed our opinion that Petri nets and more specifically high-level nets were an appropriate choice as modelling language for such purposes since they make the model fit quite closely the initial source code. These benefits of using Petri nets for software engineering purposes are exposed in [7]. Thus, even without prior knowledge of Petri nets, the protocol programmers/engineers could easily come to understand the model, which additionally gave them a synthetic overall view of their large program.

The paper is organised as follows. Section 2 gives detailed guidelines on how to derive step-by-step a coloured Petri net from the source code. Then Section 3 shows how this method was applied in practice to the NEO protocol. Finally, Section 4 draws some conclusions.

We assume the reader is familiar with coloured Petri nets [13].

2   Modelling Guidelines

This section discusses the guidelines to follow in order to deliver a coloured Petri net from high level object oriented source code. These guidelines are illustrated with the NEO protocol in Section 3, and the reader is invited to read both in parallel.

2.1   Grounding

Before the start of the modelling process some preparation work is required. It mainly concerns the deep understanding of the project structure and expected properties of the system. This helps a lot during the modelling by saving the time devoted to the consideration of unnecessary elements or restructuring model hierarchy. It is always possible to skip this stage and proceed directly to modelling the most interesting piece of code, but then the risk of choosing an inadequate abstraction level is very high. The main steps of grounding are listed below. They are depicted in Figure 1 together with the elements that are to be considered or are impacted.

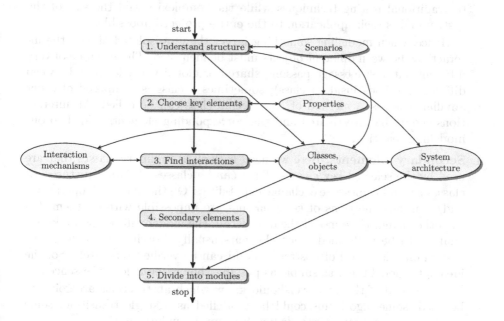

Fig. 1. Schema of the grounding process

1. **Understand the Structure.** First of all, we should pay attention to the architecture of the project. The key elements (classes) should be found as well as their roles in the whole system. It can be very useful to find the most common scenarios of the system use (or maybe scenarios that should

be verified later). We can look for the parts (classes or objects) of the system that are impacted by these scenarios. We also need to understand the class structure of the project (paying a particular attention to inheritance and polymorphism). During this step the most important result is global comprehension of how the system works from the inside.

2. **Choose Key Elements.** The second step focuses on the system properties to be checked. Properties can be proposed by developers, clients or anyone else. Then, they must be considered one by one in order to choose those that are the most crucial for the system. Selecting them before starting the modelling process is very important since this choice can influence a lot the model structure that will not be so easy to change later on.

    Once the properties are selected, we look for the scenarios they concern. Moreover, the classes and methods used within these scenarios are selected, according to the project structure from the previous step. Thus, the main pieces of code that are going to be modelled are defined.

3. **Find Interactions.** We should keep in mind that objects of chosen classes can be verified separately from one another. But the ultimate goal is usually to model-check the whole system altogether. Separate parts can be subjected to traditional testing techniques while the complexity and the size of the system makes their application to the entire project impossible.

    Hence, when modelling something larger than an isolated object, the interactions between different objects must be identified. These can be of very different natures: message passing; shared or global variables (e.g. between different methods inside a class); sometimes a class is composed of other auxiliary classes; a method of an external class can be called. All interactions should be investigated and the corresponding elements added to our modelling selection.

4. **Secondary Elements.** Here we need to look at auxiliary classes that are used by the selected key classes. They can be classes of data structures, or classes providing message exchange capabilities. On the one hand, operations and/or interconnections of key elements are impossible without them. On the other hand, if we model them in detail, the model will be too bulky for analysis to be performed. Such elements usually describe the work of the system on a low level of abstraction and can be verified separately. So, the idea is to model them as simple as possible, but without loss of essence.

    At the end of this step we should know which abstractions are going to be used: some algorithms could be modelled as a single transition, some complex data structures encoded with natural numbers, etc.

5. **Divide into Modules.** All the scenarios and methods that have been chosen for modelling are used to design a modular structure for the future model. Of course, it can be changed later during the modelling process.

    It is rather natural to associate a submodule with a class or a method. It is also important to pay attention to secondary elements and decide whether they are worth a separate module or not.

2.2   Code Analysis

During this stage, two processes are carried out in parallel: the analysis of the source code and the construction of the model. In order to streamline these processes we propose to divide them into five main activities, according to the scheme on Figure 2. Each activity requires to look for some elements in the source code as well as interpreting them in terms of the modelling formalism (in our case coloured Petri nets). At each step, the source code is observed from different points of view in order to extract the different components of the model. In practice, it is usually necessary to perform the cycle several times but at the

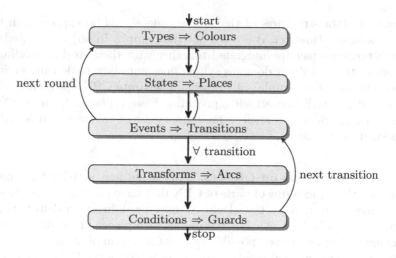

Fig. 2. Schema of the modelling process

start it is hard to tell how many times it should be done. It is also possible that some activities are skipped on later rounds, since a new element cannot be extracted from the source code. From one round to another the understanding of the chosen abstraction level is more and more accurate and the model is more and more complete.

Since the module hierarchy of the CPN can be different from the initial structure of classes and methods, the work within the five activities can be organised in different ways.

- Consider the modules of the future model (found at the fifth step of grounding) one by one. For each module examine scenarios, classes and methods it concerns and analyse them via all activities.
- Consider scenarios or methods (found at the second step of grounding) one by one. For each scenario/method perform each activity that will give refinement for different modules of the model.
- Consider activities one by one and look at the system as a whole, analysing different parts of code and changing different models, but from the chosen point of view.

In practice, the third approach is difficult to apply unless the model is almost ready and can be grasped at a glance. The first approach is the most effective one, but sometimes the second one may also prove useful by focusing on a particular behaviour. In this case, the behaviour is either described by an execution scenario, or the details of a method are tracked step-by-step.

Data Structures. It is important to start from this activity because it forms the basis of the future model. It is natural to start with colour domains in order to use them (and may be enhanced later with new details) during further activities.

In general, data structures of the source code *should* be expressed in terms of colour domains. However, it is often not that simple. In object oriented code, data structures are usually integrated together with their storing, loading and treatment methods. Colour domains syntax does not allow to do this, so, it may be needed to model a "simple" object with a separate CPN. Such cases can be left to further activities nevertheless providing basic types for future CPNs.

This phase provides as a result a preliminary list of colour domains and variables needed in the model.

States and Conditions on Objects. This is the first activity that assumes the modeller thinks in terms of parts of CPN that have no strict correspondence in the source code, namely the places. It may be difficult to deliver them in the situation of "blank sheet", but the model with places make other activities become much simpler or even possible (e.g. construction of arcs).

Hence, this phase aims at creating the set of places of the CPN which usually represent the states of the system or its parts (objects, variables, etc.). To begin with, the system flow of operations can be represented as a finite state automaton. The set of states of this automaton can be a first approximation of the set of places of the CPN. Then conditions required to proceed from one state to another are considered. These conditions often concern the states of some objects or variables. They should also be added to the set of places. Finally, a colour domain (defined during the previous activity) is associated with each place. If some variable or object is directly mentioned in the properties of the system, it can be directly represented as a place on the first round and may be transformed into a group of places or a subnet on later founds.

Events and Actions. This activity is in general simpler than the previous one. Each operator or method call in the source code can be considered as an action and thus be modelled as a transition. The main hindrance here is a tendency to model every operator with a transition. To avoid this we can apply information obtained during grounding (2nd and 4th steps).

The purpose is to select actions, essential for the processes to be verified. To start with, consider the changes of variables and data structures that are implicitly mentioned in the properties. If the properties are not formalised yet, main constructions of the system can serve as a basis. As for previous phases, on the first round only a preliminary view of transitions in the model can be given. After going through other activities it will be completed and refined.

Transformation of Data. During this phase, the modeller considers for each transition the three following questions, and performs the corresponding net construction:

1. What is taken as input? (Connect corresponding places with input arcs);
2. What is produced as output? (Connect corresponding places with output arcs);
3. How are the tokens transformed? (Provide input and output arc expressions).

If there is a special input format, it can be reflected in the input arc inscription. If the output is somehow calculated from input variables, the corresponding output arc must be assigned with a formula, representing these calculations in terms of CPN. Often, the formulae from the source code cannot be applied directly and need to be adapted w.r.t. the chosen level of abstraction.

Conditions on Events. Here, as in the previous phase, we consider the set of transitions. The focus this time is on the special conditions under which a transition can be fired. In practice the conditions for most transitions are modelled by the matching of tokens in input places with arc expressions. In this case the transition has a guard **true** that can be omitted in the model. But sometimes for better readability of the model, and also to prevent having too large sets of places and transitions, it can prove better to formulate such a condition as a guard of the transition.

The goal of this activity is to find such cases and to figure out the guards. It can happen that some condition is not possible to express on the selected level of data abstraction. If so, the colour domains created in the first activity must be revised, as well as their occurrences in parts of the CPN that have already been built. Thus, an additional round of activities is started.

So, in this section we gave the detailed guidelines to follow in order to model a system starting from high level object oriented source code. In the next section these guidelines will be applied step-by-step to the industrial case.

3   Application of the Guidelines to the NEO Protocol

This section illustrates modelling guidelines with examples from modelling process of the NEO protocol. The protocol, designed to handle a large distributed database over a cluster of machines, was described in [4,5]. Its main characteristics are shortly summarised in Section 3.1. This specification was part of an industrial project which aimed at validating the protocol and its prototype implementation both designed and developed by the NEXEDI company. It was implemented in Python, but our approach is not specific to this language.

3.1   Brief Description of the NEO Protocol

A more extensive description and analysis of the NEO protocol can be found in [4] and [5].

Different kinds of nodes play dedicated roles in the protocol, as depicted by the architecture in Figure 3:

storage nodes handle the database itself. Since the database is distributed, each storage node cares for a part of the database, according to a *partition table*. To avoid data loss in case of a node failure, data is duplicated, and is thus handled by at least two storage nodes.

master nodes handle the transactions requested by the client nodes and forward them to the appropriate storage nodes. A distinguished master node, called *primary master*, handles the operations. *Secondary masters* (i.e. the other master nodes) are ready to become primary master in case of a failure of this node. They also inform other nodes of the identity of the primary master.

the administration node is used for manual setup if needed.

client nodes correspond to the machines running applications concerned with the database objects. Thus, they request either read or write operations. They first ask the primary master which storage nodes are concerned with their data, and can then contact them directly.

The life cycle of the NEO protocol is depicted in Figure 4.

At the system start, the primary master is *elected* among all master nodes. The primary master maintains the key information for the protocol to operate.

After the election of a primary master, the system goes through various stages with the purpose of checking that all transactions were completely processed, and thus that the database is consistent across the different storage nodes (*bootstrap protocol*).

Finally, the system enters its *operational state*. Clients can then access the database through the elected primary master.

As for storage nodes, once they are connected to the primary master, they check the consistency of the information they detain, and initialise their service before being ready to serve requests.

3.2   Grounding

Each step described in Section 2.1 is now applied.

Understand Structure. This step is difficult to illustrate on a real example since it implies working on extensive code. The conclusions cannot be confirmed by a small piece of code. Nevertheless, for the NEO protocol, at this stage we can state the following, and confirm the brief description from Section 3.1.

The main entities are nodes of the cluster, of four types: master, storage, client and admin nodes. For each of these types there is a corresponding class in the source code.

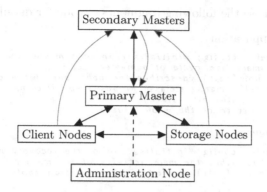

Fig. 3. Protocol architecture

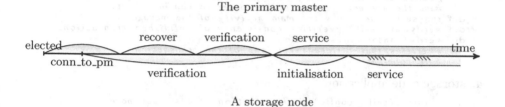

Fig. 4. Phases of bootstrap process

The life cycle of nodes leads them through different phases implemented by an auxiliary class (RecoveryManager, VerificationManager) or a method of the corresponding node class (ElectPrimary, VerifyData, Initialize, DoOperation). Also, depending on the phase of the protocol, a node changes its message handlers.

Choose Key Elements. Based on the conclusions of the previous step and on the verification issues, we decided to focus on master and storage nodes. This paper does not get into the details of the numerous properties to check, a large part of which can be found in [4] and [5]. Many properties were provided as an informal statement by the code developers. For example, only a single node is elected as a primary master; all shared information (partition tables, identifiers) has been made consistent for the service phase to take place.

Most attention is payed to the election of the primary master and to the bootstrap process (everything between election and operational state). Later on in this paper we focus on bootstrap phase. For this phase a successful scenario implies that the primary master (supposed to be correctly chosen during election phase) checks that its critical information is up-to-date (recovery phase), verifies the coherence of the unfinished transactions (verification phase) and allows storage nodes to start operation (service phase).

Therefore, we chose the following fragments of code for detailed analysis:

1. master node application

```
1  def __init__(self, config) #initialisation of a master node
2  def run(self) #main life cycle of a master node
3  def playPrimaryRole(self) #describes the behaviour of the primary master
4  def runManager(self, manager_class) #loads a specific manager
5  def changeClusterState(self, state)
6      #changes the state of the whole cluster
```

2. recovery manager class

```
1  def __init__(self, config)#initialisation of the recovery manager
2  def run(self) #describes the main activity of the manager
3  def buildFromScratch(self) #called if the partition table is injured
```

3. verification manager class

```
1  def __init__(self, app) #initialisation of the verification manager
2  def _askStorageNodesAndWait(self, packet, node_list)
3      #called each time when the same message is sent to all SN
4      #and the answers are required in order to continue boot.
5  def run(self) #describes the main activity of the manager
6  def verifyData(self) #verifies consistency of unfinished transactions
7  def verifyTransaction(self, tid)
8      #verifies that different replicas of the transaction
9      #are coherent
```

4. storage node application

```
1  def __init__(self, config) #initialisation of a storage node
2  def run(self) #main life cycle of a storage node
3  def connectToPrimary(self) #connects to the primary master
4  def verifyData(self) #launches verification phase
5  def initialize(self) #launches initialisation phase
```

Find Interactions. The nodes in the cluster need to communicate with one another. For this purpose they use a class EventManager. It describes the mechanism for sending and receiving messages. To treat them, each node has its own handlers, different for the different phases of the protocol. Thus, they should be added to our list of pieces of code.

Another means for nodes collaboration in the cluster is a partition table. It is implemented as a class that stores the distribution of data among storage nodes. This class is another key element and should also be added to the analysis list.

The master and storage applications also use some global variables to allow their methods to know the state of the application (primary, operational, has_pt — partition table). This information should be kept aside to be used during modelling.

Secondary Elements. When this stage occurs, all significant parts of the project and their communications are identified. It is then time to make rather crude abstractions on objects that could not be eliminated from the model, but must be simplified because of the abstraction level.

For example, for the NEO protocol we made following abstractions:

1. The complex message structure, defined in a class package is modelled as an integer number;

2. Connection, described as a group of classes, is modelled as a pair of nodes, that are considered to be connected;
3. Transaction and object of the database, that have a lot of fields, such as serial number, history, data, etc., are modelled by their identification numbers.

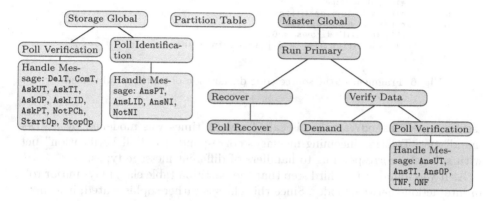

Fig. 5. Hierarchy of models

Divide into Modules. Figure 5 presents the subnets structure of the bootstrap model. Let us discuss how it was created step-by-step.

The methods chosen for detailed analysis in the second step can be divided into two groups: those concerning a master and a storage node. Thus, nets "Master Global" and "Storage Global" will be constructed starting from source code of methods __init__ and run of the corresponding cluster nodes. The master node net will also include the analysis of playPrimaryRole method and the storage node connectToPrimary method.

A storage node calls two methods corresponding to verification and initialisation phases. They can become sub-modules of "Storage Global". During each of these phases, a number of message types is treated. The nets, modelling the handlers of these messages, will be sub-nets of the "Verification" and "Initialisation" nets.

The primary master calls recovery and verification manager during the bootstrap. So, it is natural to model this with sub-modules corresponding to each manager. Thus, the "Recovery" net is the result of the code analysis of methods runManager and changeClusterState of the primary master and methods __init__, run and buildFromScratch of the recovery manager class. It has one sub-net that corresponds to method poll used for treating incoming messages. Similarly, "VerifyData" is built on the basis of methods runManager and changeClusterState of the primary master and all methods from verification manager class chosen for detailed analysis. During modelling, this sub-module has become too complicated, so it was decided to replace some parts of it by sub-nets. Thus, method

```
1  class Cell(object):
2    def __init__(self, node, state = CellStates.UP_TO_DATE):
3      self.node = node
4      self.state = state
5  ...
6
7  class PartitionTable(object):
8    def __init__(self, num_partitions, num_replicas):
9      self._id = None
10     self.np = num_partitions
11     self.nr = num_replicas
12     self.num_filled_rows = 0
13     self.partition_list = [[] for _ in xrange(num_partitions)]
14 ...
```

Fig. 6. Fragment of the source code declaration of partition table class

_askStorageNodesAndWait that is called several times was modelled by a "Demand" net. Treating incoming messages corresponds to "Poll Verification" net with sub-nets, corresponding to handlers of different message types.

As it was found at the third step that the partition table class plays major role in interactions between nodes. Since this class is rather sophisticated, it forms a separate net "Partition Table".

3.3 Code Analysis

In this subsection we will give some detailed examples of application the guidelines from Section 2.2 to the source code of the NEO protocol.

Data Structures. In order to show how the colour domains can be constructed from data structures, let us consider the piece of code in Figure 6. It is a fragment of the partition table class definition where the internal fields are declared. First, the class for a cell of the partition table is declared. It has two attributes: a storage node and a state. Knowing that a partition cell has two possible states (up-to-date or not), we can declare a colour domain PSTATE as a set of these two values and a colour domain PT_CELL as a product of storage node type and cell state.

```
colset PSTATE = with UTD | OOD; (* the set of states of partition*)
colset SN = index sn with 0..N; (* the set of storage nodes *)
colset PT_CELL = product SN*PSTATE; (* a cell of partition table *)
```

Now let us consider the beginning of the partition table class constructor. It starts with assigning the values of variables for the number of replicas and the number of partitions. Then it creates a two-dimension list. In one dimension its size is equal to the number of partitions, in the other dimension the size is not specified. So, we declare three auxiliary colour domains: a set of partitions, a list of partition cells and a partition row, that is a product of a partition and a list of cells. Finally, a partition table colour domain consists of a list of partition rows.

```
1  def run(self):
2      self.app.changeClusterState(ClusterStates.VERIFYING)
3      self.verifyData()
4      ...
5
6  def verifyData(self):
7      em, nm = self.app.em, self.app.nm
8      neo.lib.logging.debug('waiting_for_the_cluster_to_be_operational')
9      while not self.app.pt.operational(): em.poll(1)
10     neo.lib.logging.info('start_to_verify_data')
11     self._askStorageNodesAndWait(Packets.AskUnfinishedTransactions(),
12         [x for x in self.app.nm.getIdentifiedList() if x.isStorage()])
13     ...
14
15 def _askStorageNodesAndWait(self, packet, node_list):
16     poll = self.app.em.poll
17     operational = self.app.pt.operational
18     uuid_set = self._uuid_set
19     uuid_set.clear()
20     for node in node_list:
21         uuid_set.add(node.getUUID())
22         node.ask(packet)
23     while True:
24         poll(1)
25         if not uuid_set:
26             break
```

Fig. 7. Fragment of the source code of the verification phase

```
colset PART = index np with 0..NP (* the set of partitions *)
colset PT_CELLlist = list PT_CELL with 0..(NR+1); (* a cell list *)
colset PT_ROW = product PART*PT_CELLlist; (* a partition table row *)
colset PT = list PT_ROW with 0..NP; (* the partition table type *)
```

The following colour domain definitions will be used later on:

```
colset MN = index mn with 0..M; (* the set of master nodes *)
colset NODE =   union s1:SN + m1:MN; (* the set of all nodes *)
colset CSTATE = with VER | REC | RUN | STP; (* the set of cluster states *)
colset MTYPE = with StopOp | StartOp | AskUT | AskPT | AskNI | AskLID |
                    AskTI | AskOP | AnsUT | AnsNI | AnsPT | AnsLID |
                    AnsTI | AnsOP | NotNI | NotPCh| DelT | ComT;
                    (* the set of message types *)
colset MESS = product MTYPE*NODE*NODE*INT; (* the set of messages *)
colset SNlist list SN with 0..N; (* a list of storage nodes *)
colset MESSlist = list MESS 0..1000; (* a list of messages *)
```

States and Conditions on Objects. As an illustration of the next four steps, let us consider the beginning of the verification phase from the primary master point of view. The corresponding source code is listed in Figure 7.

The first three lines come from the run method of the verification manager class. We can see that the primary master changes cluster state to VERIFYING and calls the verifyData method. So, we can start by defining two places:

- ○ *start_verif* with colour domain MN (the state of the primary master at the start of the verification manager);
- ● *c_state* with colour domain CSTATE (the current state of the cluster).

Then, the primary master waits until the partition table becomes operational (line 9). We define a new place, corresponding to this state of the primary master:

- ○ *wait_pt* with colour domain MN.

After that, it calls a method _askStorageNodesAndWait, where it sends requests about unfinished transactions to storage nodes, and waits until the list uuid_set becomes empty. This waiting period can be modelled as a new place. In order to send messages to other nodes we need a channel place. According to the protocol, it must be a FIFO list. Hence, two places are added:

- ● *network* with colour domain MESSlist;
- ○ *wait_ut* with colour domain MN.

Finally, the primary master starts the verification of transactions one by one. This code is out of scope of our example, but we can at least give the next state of the primary master by adding a new place:

- ○ *verifying_trans* with colour domain MN.

Events and actions Now, we need to extract the important actions from the same piece of code. The first method call changeClusterState can be considered as one of them. So, we add the first transition:

- ▭ *change_c_state.*

When getting to the next lines, we see that line 7 contains nothing but shortcuts and line 8 writes the current state to the log. The next important action is em.poll(1) that is executed while the primary master waits for the partition table to be operational. Here, it is supposed to treat different messages. For the sake of readability of the model, we decide to organise message handlers in separate sub-nets. A new transition is added, coloured in black to symbolise there is a net behind.

- ▬ *poll_pm_verif.*

Line 10 is not important since it writes a log. Then the _askStorageNodesAndWait method is called with a list of all identified storage nodes as an argument. Inside this method some shortcuts occur (lines 16–18) and the list is cleared uuid_set. Then, considering the storage nodes from the input list one by one, they are added to uuid_set and send a request for unfinished transactions (which is also given as input parameter, defined in line 11). An additional place is needed to store the identified storage nodes. So, we go to the previous step, add this place, and return to add a new transition:

- ○ *s_iden* with colour domain SN.
- ▭ *ask_ut.*

Then the primary master is waiting once again, executing poll (line 24). So, we duplicate the corresponding transition. Finally, we add a transition that models the exit of this process.

- ▭ *got_ut.*

Transformations of Data. Let us consider the transitions we have up to now one by one in order to build arcs and provide their expressions. To do so, some variables should first be declared. Let pm: MN; cst: CSTATE. The whole net can be seen in Figure 8. Transition *change_c_state* moves the primary master token

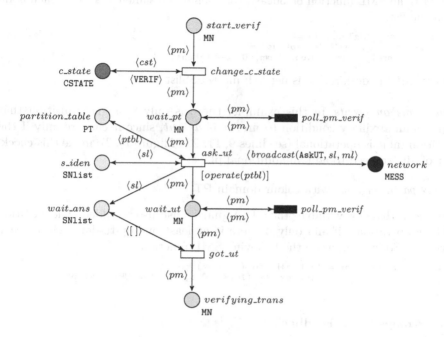

Fig. 8. Model of verification manager — part 1

from place *start_verif* to *wait_pt* and replaces the current cluster state token with a VERIF one.

Transition *got_ut* moves the primary master from place *wait_ut* to place *verifying_trans*. But it can fire only when all answers are received from the storage nodes. Here an additional place, similar to the variable uuid_set (line 25), is created, that will contain all storage nodes, answers from which the primary master is waiting. Transition *got_ut* must fire if and only if this place is empty. However, it is not possible to check if the multiset is empty without inhibitor arc. One of the solutions is to change the colour domain to SNlist, since a list can be checked for emptiness.

– ⃝ *wait_ans* with colour domain SNlist.

A new variable sl: SNlist is also declared.

Transition *poll_pm_verif* is replaced by a sub-net. Here it simply takes the primary master token and puts it back. Handlers of messages, that are hidden behind them, can change the state of some variables, e.g. uuid_set, and, respectively, the content of place *wait_ans*.

Transition *ask_ut* moves the primary master token from place *wait_pt* to *wait_ut*. It also sends messages to all storage nodes from place *s_iden*. Here we see that it could be convenient to change the colour domain of *s_iden* to SNlist. In this case we can directly put this list into place *wait_ans*. Also we can write an SML function broadcast, that sends the same message to each node from the list.

```
fun broadcast (msgType, l) =
    List.foldr (fn (sNode, tokens) =>
        1'(msgType, s1 (sNode), pm, 0) ++ tokens) [] l
```

A new variable declaration is needed: ml: MESSlist.

Conditions on events In this example, there is only a single transition that requires an auxiliary condition to fire. It is *ask_ut*, since it can fire only if the partition table is operational (see lines 9, 11, 22 of figure 7). To make this check, first of all, we need to add an additional place:

– ◯ *partition_table* with colour domain PT,

together with a new variable ptbl: PT. A guard must also be added. The partition table is operational if and only if there is at least one up-to-date cell for each partition. So, we can write the following SML function.

```
1  fun operational pt = List.all (fn (_, row) =>
2                       List.exists (fn (_, st) => st = UP) row) pt
```

3.4   Analysis and Feedback

The properties the protocol should satisfy were model-checked. The outcome of this analysis was suspicious scenarios. The design approach allowed for tracing back the execution sequence in the source code, and thus the engineers could check their validity. Properties for the election of a primary master node are detailed in [4] as well as their analysis. Some 70 properties were given by the engineers (in natural language). We first grouped these properties, and figured out which ones were relevant for our purposes. Examples of such properties are "At all times, there is at most one primary master node", which concerns only the master nodes election phase, "When the primary master is in the verification state, a partition table is selected", which deals with the overall system. Then those properties of interest for the primary master election were analysed using several tools:

– a graphical user interface, Coloane [2];
– the CPN-AMI verification platform [3];
– CPNTools for coloured nets interface and state space analysis [1];
– the HELENA high-level nets analyser [10].

Some scenarios were due to a too coarse abstraction level, but the assumptions made during modelling did hold and guarantee the appropriate behaviour of the code. An interesting erroneous scenario pointed out the possibility of a livelock in the primary master election process. However, this never happened in practice, as the developers found out it was prevented by a side-effect of a Python function. Nevertheless, they could fix it, such a side effect being undesirable, in case it doesn't happen in a future version of Python.

The lessons learned in the Neo protocol analysis project confirmed that the modelling approach from source code made it relatively easy to trace back potentially undesirable scenarios. Of course, the level of abstraction has some influence on the results, in that some of the scenarios examined do not actually lead to an error. However, it gave the engineers a better understanding of the details of their code, of the overall process flow, and served as a basis for discussions on the details of the protocol functioning. This was particularly useful since the programmers that wrote the initial code were not available anymore.

4 Conclusion

In this paper we gave detailed directions on how to construct a coloured Petri net model from a high level object oriented source code and illustrated it with a real case example. The modelling process is divided into 2 main parts: grounding and code analysis.

Now the following questions could be raised. Can this process be automated? The most complicated part of the modelling process is to choose objects and actions that are important for the goals of verification and separate them from those that are not as useful. If a programming language could provide some kind of priorities to data structures and methods, it may simplify the automation process. During the industrial project in which the NEO protocol was analysed, a code-tagging approach to facilitate both the modelling and the interpretation of the verification results was envisioned for future work. Moreover, part of our group works on a tool-supported Petri net model design method from a natural language description. That tool provides the user with specific guidelines for model construction, mainly based on a refinement approach. Its integration within a larger software platform, namely CoSyVerif [15] will also provide analysis capabilities. Further work could include the integration of both approaches so as to have a better feedback on the original source code.

Another interesting question is could these modelling guidelines be applied elsewhere? Even if not directly, but with some refinements, they could be applied to any reverse-engineering process providing a coloured Petri net or a similar model of concurrency.

References

1. CPN Tools Homepage: http://cpntools.org/
2. The Coloane tool Homepage, https://coloane.lip6.fr/
3. The CPN-AMI Homepage, http://move.lip6.fr/software/CPNAMI/
4. Choppy, C., Dedova, A., Evangelista, S., Hong, S., Klai, K., Petrucci, L.: The NEO protocol for large-scale distributed database systems: Modelling and initial verification. In: Lilius, J., Penczek, W. (eds.) PETRI NETS 2010. LNCS, vol. 6128, pp. 145–164. Springer, Heidelberg (2010)

5. Choppy, C., Dedova, A., Evangelista, S., Klaï, K., Petrucci, L., Youcef, S.: Modelling and formal verification of the NEO protocol. In: Jensen, K., van der Aalst, W.M., Ajmone Marsan, M., Franceschinis, G., Kleijn, J., Kristensen, L.M. (eds.) Transactions on Petri Nets and Other Models of Concurrency VI. LNCS, vol. 7400, pp. 197–225. Springer, Heidelberg (2012)

6. Choppy, C., Petrucci, L., Reggio, G.: A modelling approach with coloured Petri nets. In: Kordon, F., Vardanega, T. (eds.) Ada-Europe 2008. LNCS, vol. 5026, pp. 73–86. Springer, Heidelberg (2008)

7. Denaro, G., Pezzé, M.: Petri nets and software engineering. In: Desel, J., Reisig, W., Rozenberg, G. (eds.) Lectures on Concurrency and Petri Nets. LNCS, vol. 3098, pp. 439–466. Springer, Heidelberg (2004)

8. Desel, J., Petrucci, L.: Aggregating views for Petri net model construction. In: Proc. Workshop on Petri Nets and Distributed Systems, PNDS 2008, Associated with Petri Nets 2008, pp. 17–31. Xi'an, China (2008)

9. Duri, S., Buy, U., Devarapalli, R., Shatz, S.M.: Application and experimental evaluation of state space reduction methods for deadlock analysis in ada. ACM Trans. Softw. Eng. Methodol. 3(4), 340–380 (1994)

10. Evangelista, S.: High Level Petri Nets Analysis with Helena. In: Ciardo, G., Darondeau, P. (eds.) ICATPN 2005. LNCS, vol. 3536, pp. 455–464. Springer, Heidelberg (2005)

11. Farooq, U., Lam, C.P., Li, H.: Transformation methodology for UML 2.0 activity diagram into colored Petri nets. In: Proceedings of the Third Conference on IASTED International Conference: Advances in Computer Science and Technology, ACST 2007, Anaheim, CA, USA, pp. 128–133. ACTA Press (2007)

12. Kerkouche, E., Chaoui, A., Bourennane, E.-B., Labbani, O.: A uml and colored petri nets integrated modeling and analysis approach using graph transformation. Journal of Object Technology 9(4), 25–43 (2010)

13. Jensen, K.: Coloured Petri Nets. Basic Concepts, Analysis Methods and Practical Use. Basic Concepts. Springer (1992)

14. Saldhana, J.A., Shatz, S.M.: Uml diagrams to object petri net models: An approach for modeling and analysis. In: International Conference on Software Engineering and Knowledge Engineering, pp. 103–110 (2000)

15. The CosyVerif group. CosyVerif Web page, http://www.cosyverif.org

16. Voron, J., Kordon, F.: Transforming Sources to Petri Nets: A Way to Analyze Execution of Parallel Programs. In: International Workshop on Petri Nets Tools and APplications (PNTAP), pp. 1–10. ACM (2008)

Using Integer Time Steps for Checking Branching Time Properties of Time Petri Nets

Agata Janowska[1], Wojciech Penczek[2], Agata Półrola[3], and Andrzej Zbrzezny[4]

[1] Institute of Informatics, University of Warsaw, Poland
janowska@mimuw.edu.pl
[2] Institute of Computer Science PAS and UPH Siedlce, Poland
penczek@ipipan.waw.pl
[3] University of Łódź, FMCS, Poland
polrola@math.uni.lodz.pl
[4] Jan Długosz University, IMCS, Poland
a.zbrzezny@ajd.czest.pl

Abstract. Verification of timed systems is an important subject of research, and one of its crucial aspects is the efficiency of the methods developed. Extending the result of Popova which states that integer time steps are sufficient to test reachability properties of time Petri nets [8,11], in our work we prove that the discrete-time semantics is also sufficient to verify properties of the existential and the universal version of CTL* of TPNs with the dense semantics. To show that considering this semantics instead of the dense one is profitable, we compare the results for SAT-based bounded model checking of the universal version of CTL$_{-X}$ properties and the class of distributed time Petri nets.

1 Introduction

Verification of time-dependent systems is an important subject of research. The crucial problem to deal with is the state explosion: the state spaces of these systems are usually very large due to infinity of the dense time domain, and are likely to grow exponentially in the number of concurrent components of the system. This influences strongly the efficiency of the model checking methods.

The papers of Popova [8,11] show that in the case of checking reachability for systems modelled by time Petri nets (i.e., while testing whether a marking of a net is reachable) one can use discrete (integer) time steps instead of real-valued ones. This reduces the state space to be searched. The aim of our work is to investigate whether the result of Popova can be extended, i.e., whether the discrete-time semantics can replace the dense-time one also while verifying a wider class of properties of dense-time Petri net systems. In this paper we present our preliminary result, i.e., prove that the discrete-time model can be used instead of the dense-time one for verifying properties of the existential and the universal version of CTL*. To show that such an approach can be profitable we perform some experiments, using an implementation for SAT-based bounded model checking of the universal version of CTL$_{-X}$ and the class of distributed

M. Koutny et al. (Eds.): ToPNoC VIII, LNCS 8100, pp. 89–105, 2013.
© Springer-Verlag Berlin Heidelberg 2013

time Petri nets with the discrete-time semantics [6], as well as its modification for the dense-time case.

The rest of the paper is organised as follows: Sec. 2 discusses the related work. Sec. 3 introduces time Petri nets and their dense and discrete models. Sec. 4 presents the logics ECTL* and ACTL*. Sec. 5 deals with the theoretical considerations, while Sec. 6 presents the experimental results. Sec. 7 contains final remarks and sketches directions of our further work.

2   Related Works

In our work we are interested in branching time properties. To our best knowledge the fact that the discrete-time semantics is sufficient to verify ECTL* or ACTL* properties of time Petri nets (TPNs) with the dense-time semantics has never been proven before.

The topic of verification of dense-time Petri nets using integer time steps has been studied in several publications. In the paper [8] it is shown how to construct a reachability graph whose vertices are reachable integer states for a time Petri net in which all the latest firing times are finite. The main theorem of [8] states that for each run of a TPN, starting at its initial state, it is possible to find a corresponding run which starts at the initial state as well, and visits integer states only. Due to this theorem a discrete analysis of boundedness and liveness of a TPN is possible. The work [9] extends the results of [8] to arbitrary TPNs. It uses the idea of "freezing" the clock values of the transitions with infinite Lft once their Eft is reached. This way a reduced (finite) reachability graph of "essential" (integer) states is obtained.

In [10] and [11] the state space of a TPN is characterised parametrically. The main theorems of [11] state that for an arbitrary feasible execution path where the clocks have real values it is possible to replace these real values by integer ones to obtain another feasible path. The differences between the clock values of each enabled transition at a given marking in both paths are always smaller than 1, and so are the differences between the total times of both the executions. In the paper [10] an enumerative procedure for reducing the state space is introduced. The idea is to divide a problem into a finite number of smaller problems, which can be solved recursively with a methodology inspired from dynamic programming. Moreover, it extends the method of [11] to the nets with real-valued time steps (in [11] rational time steps are allowed only) and with infinite latest firing times.

The authors of the above-mentioned papers claim that the knowledge of the reachable integer states is sufficient to determine the entire behaviour of the net at any point in time. However, all these papers show the trace equivalence between a continuous model and a (restricted) discrete one. It is very well known that the trace equivalence preserves linear time properties, but it does not preserve branching time properties (see Fig. 1 and [3]), so the word "behaviour" should probably be understood in a way following from a fragment of [10]: *"The properties of a Petri net, both the classical one as well as the TPN, can be divided*

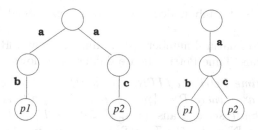

Fig. 1. Two trace equivalent models which are not (bi)similar. A formula distinguishing them is e.g. $\varphi = \mathrm{EF}(\mathrm{EX}p1 \wedge \mathrm{EX}p2)$ which holds for the model on the right only.

into two parts: There are static properties, like being pure, ordinary, free choice, extended simple, conservative, etc., and there are dynamic properties like being bounded, live, reachable, and having place- or transitions invariants, deadlocks, etc. While it is easy to prove the static behavior of a net using only the static definition, the dynamic behavior depends on both the static and dynamic definitions and is quite complicated to prove.", so as the dynamic properties listed. Moreover, the result of the papers [8,9] does not imply bisimulation between both the models, as the construction given in these papers cannot be used to prove it. We discuss this on p. 101, showing that the relation $\mathcal{R}$ used in our proof and derived from the result of [8,9] cannot be used to prove bisimulation. This follows from the fact that the integer run π' "justifying" $\sigma'\mathcal{R}\sigma$ (generated according to the construction of [8]) and the dense run π occurring in the relation do not need to "branch" in the same way. Similarly, the result of [10,11] does not imply (bi)simulation as well. Although it is not stated directly, the construction given in these papers is based on a parametric description of the classes of the *forward-reachability graph* for a net considered (i.e., a structure in which the initial state class contains the initial state of the net and all the time successors of this state, and the further classes are built according to the following scheme: given a state class C_x corresponding to firing a sequence of transitions x, its successor class on a transition t contains all the concrete states which can be obtained by firing t at a concrete state $\sigma \in C_x$ and then passing some time not disabling any enabled transition). It is well known that such a structure preserves reachability and linear time properties, but it does not preserve branching time properties. The discrete runs constructed in both the papers are retrieved from the dense ones to preserve nothing but visiting the same state classes as the runs they correspond to.

This paper is a modified and improved version of our work [5], which was published in the proceedings of a local workshop and contained a completely different proof without an explicit definition of simulation.

3   Time Petri Nets

We start with introducing some basic definitions related to time Petri nets. For simplicity of the presentation we focus on 1-safe time Petri nets only. However, our result applies also to unbounded nets, which is explained in more detail in the final section.

Let $\mathbb{N}$ be the set of natural numbers (including zero), and $\mathbb{R}$ ($\mathbb{R}_+$) be the set of (nonnegative) reals. Time Petri nets are defined as follows:

Definition 1. *A time Petri net (TPN, for short) is a six-element tuple* $\mathcal{N} = (P, T, F, Eft, Lft, m^0)$, *where* $P = \{p_1, \ldots, p_{n_P}\}$ *is a finite set of places,* $T = \{t_1, \ldots, t_{n_T}\}$ *is a finite set of transitions,* $F \subseteq (P \times T) \cup (T \times P)$ *is the flow relation,* $Eft : T \to \mathbb{N}$ *and* $Lft : T \to \mathbb{N} \cup \{\infty\}$ *are functions describing the earliest and the latest firing time of the transition, where for each* $t \in T$ *we have* $Eft(t) \leq Lft(t)$, *and* $m^0 \subseteq P$ *is the initial marking of* $\mathcal{N}$.

For a transition $t \in T$ we define its *preset* $\bullet t = \{p \in P \mid (p, t) \in F\}$ and *postset* $t \bullet = \{p \in P \mid (t, p) \in F\}$, and consider only the nets having the preset and the postset nonempty for each transition. We need also the following notations and definitions:

- a *marking* of $\mathcal{N}$ is any subset $m \subseteq P$,
- a transition $t \in T$ is *enabled* at m ($m[t\rangle$ for short) if $\bullet t \subseteq m$ and $t \bullet \cap (m \setminus \bullet t) = \emptyset$; and *leads from* m *to* m' if it is enabled at m, and $m' = (m \setminus \bullet t) \cup t \bullet$. The marking m' is denoted by $m[t\rangle$ as well, if this does not lead to misunderstanding.
- $en(m) = \{t \in T \mid m[t\rangle\}$;
- for $t \in en(m)$, $newly\_en(m, t) = \{u \in T \mid u \in en(m[t\rangle) \wedge (t \bullet \cap \bullet u \neq \emptyset \vee u \bullet \cap \bullet t \neq \emptyset)\}$.

Concerning the behaviour of time Petri nets, it is possible to consider the dense-time semantics, i.e., the one in which the time steps can be of an arbitrary (nonnegative) real-valued length, and the discrete one which considers integer time passings only. Below we define both of them.

3.1   Dense-Time Semantics

In the dense-time semantics (the *dense semantics* in short) a *concrete state* σ of a net $\mathcal{N}$ is defined as a pair $(m, clock)$, where m is a marking, and $clock : T \to \mathbb{R}_+$ is a function which for each transition $t \in en(m)$ gives the time elapsed since t became enabled most recently, and assigns zero to other transitions. Given a state $(m, clock)$ and $\delta \in \mathbb{R}_+$, denote by $clock + \delta$ the function defined by $(clock + \delta)(t) = clock(t) + \delta$ for each $t \in en(m)$, and $(clock + \delta)(t) = 0$ otherwise. By $(m, clock) + \delta$ we denote $(m, clock + \delta)$. The *dense concrete state space* of $\mathcal{N}$ is a structure $(T \cup \mathbb{R}_+, \Sigma, \sigma^0, \to_r)$, where Σ is the set of all the concrete states of $\mathcal{N}$, $\sigma^0 = (m^0, clock^0)$ with $clock^0(t) = 0$ for each $t \in T$ is the initial state of $\mathcal{N}$, and $\to_r \subseteq \Sigma \times (T \cup \mathbb{R}_+) \times \Sigma$ is a timed consecution relation defined by:

- for $\delta \in \mathbb{R}_+$, $(m, clock) \xrightarrow{\delta}_r (m, clock + \delta)$ iff $(clock + \delta)(t) \leq Lft(t)$ for all $t \in en(m)$ (*time successor*),
- for $t \in T$, $(m, clock) \xrightarrow{t}_r (m', clock')$ iff $t \in en(m)$, $Eft(t) \leq clock(t) \leq Lft(t)$, $m' = m[t\rangle$, and for all $u \in T$ we have $clock'(u) = 0$ for $u \in newly\_en(m, t)$ and $clock'(u) = clock(u)$ otherwise (*action successor*).

Notice that firing of a transition takes no time.

Given a set of propositional variables PV, we introduce a valuation function $V : \Sigma \to 2^{PV}$ which assigns the same propositions to the states with the same markings. We assume the set PV to be such that each $q \in PV$ corresponds to exactly one $p \in P$, and use the same names for the propositions and the places. The function V is then defined by $p \in V(\sigma)$ iff $p \in m$ for each $\sigma = (m, \cdot)$. The structure $M_r(\mathcal{N}) = (T \cup \mathbb{R}_+, \Sigma, \sigma^0, \to_r, V)$ is a *dense concrete model* of $\mathcal{N}$.

A *dense σ-run* of TPN $\mathcal{N}$ is a maximal (i.e., non-extendable) sequence of states: $\sigma_0 \xrightarrow{a_0}_r \sigma_1 \xrightarrow{a_1}_r \sigma_2 \xrightarrow{a_2}_r \ldots$, where $\sigma_0 = \sigma \in \Sigma$ and $a_i \in T \cup \mathbb{R}_+$ for each $i \geq 0$. A state σ is reachable in $M_r(\mathcal{N})$ if there is a dense σ^0-run $\sigma_0 \xrightarrow{a_0}_r \sigma_1 \xrightarrow{a_1}_r \sigma_2 \xrightarrow{a_2}_r \ldots$ such that $\sigma = \sigma_i$ for some $i \in \mathbb{N}$.

3.2   Discrete-Time Semantics

Alternatively, one can consider integer time passings only. In such a *discrete-time semantics* (*discrete semantics* in short) a (*discrete*) *concrete state* σ_n of a net $\mathcal{N}$ is a pair $(m, clock_n)$, where m is a marking, and $clock_n : T \to \mathbb{N}$ is a function which for each transition $t \in en(m)$ gives the time elapsed since t became enabled most recently, and assigns zero to the other transitions. Given a state $(m, clock_n)$ and $\delta \in \mathbb{N}$, we define $clock_n + \delta$ and $(m, clock_n) + \delta$ analogously as in the dense-time case. The *discrete concrete state space* of $\mathcal{N}$ is a structure $(T \cup \mathbb{N}, \Sigma_n, \sigma_n^0, \to_n)$, where Σ_n is the set of all the discrete concrete states of $\mathcal{N}$, $\sigma_n^0 = (m^0, clock_n^0)$ with $clock_n^0(t) = 0$ for each $t \in T$ is the initial state of $\mathcal{N}$, and $\to_n \subseteq \Sigma_n \times (T \cup \mathbb{N}) \times \Sigma_n$ is a timed consecution relation defined by:

- for $\delta \in \mathbb{N}$, $(m, clock_n) \xrightarrow{\delta}_n (m, clock_n + \delta)$ iff $(clock_n + \delta)(t) \leq Lft(t)$ for all $t \in en(m)$ (*time successor*),
- for $t \in T$, $(m, clock_n) \xrightarrow{t}_n (m', clock_n')$ iff $t \in en(m)$, $Eft(t) \leq clock_n(t) \leq Lft(t)$, $m' = m[t\rangle$, and for all $u \in T$ we have $clock_n'(u) = 0$ for $u \in newly\_en(m, t)$ and $clock_n'(u) = clock_n(u)$ otherwise (*action successor*).

Again, firing of a transition takes no time.

Given a set of propositional variables PV, we introduce valuation function $V_n : \Sigma_n \to 2^{PV}$ which assigns the same propositions to the states with the same markings. Similarly to the dense case, we assume the set PV to be such that each $q \in PV$ corresponds to exactly one $p \in P$, and use the same names for the propositions and the places. The function V_n is then defined by $p \in V_n(\sigma_n)$ iff $p \in m$ for each $\sigma_n = (m, \cdot)$. The structure $M_n(\mathcal{N}) = (T \cup \mathbb{N}, \Sigma_n, \sigma_n^0, \to_n, V_n)$ is a *discrete concrete model* of $\mathcal{N}$.

A *discrete σ_n-run* of TPN $\mathcal{N}$ is a maximal sequence of states: $\sigma_{n0} \xrightarrow{a_0}_n \sigma_{n1} \xrightarrow{a_1}_n \sigma_{n2} \xrightarrow{a_2}_n \ldots$, where $\sigma_{n0} = \sigma_n \in \Sigma_n$ and $a_i \in T \cup \mathbb{N}$ for each $i \geq 0$. A state σ_n is *reachable* in $M_n(\mathcal{N})$ iff there is a σ_n^0-run of $\mathcal{N}$ $\sigma_{n0} \xrightarrow{a_0}_n \sigma_{n1} \xrightarrow{a_1}_n \sigma_{n2} \xrightarrow{a_2}_n \ldots$ such that $\sigma_n = \sigma_{ni}$ for some $i \in \mathbb{N}$.

4   Temporal Logics ACTL* and ECTL*

In our work we deal with the verification of properties of time Petri nets expressed in certain sublogics of the standard branching time logic CTL*. Below, we define the logics of our interest.

4.1   Syntax and Sublogics of CTL*

Let $PV = \{\wp_1, \wp_2 \ldots\}$ be a set of propositional variables. The language of CTL* is given as the set of all the state formulas φ_s (interpreted at states of a model), defined using path formulas φ_p (interpreted along paths of a model), by the following grammar:

$$\varphi_s := \wp \mid \neg\varphi_s \mid \varphi_s \wedge \varphi_s \mid \varphi_s \vee \varphi_s \mid A\varphi_p \mid E\varphi_p$$
$$\varphi_p := \varphi_s \mid \varphi_p \wedge \varphi_p \mid \varphi_p \vee \varphi_p \mid X\varphi_p \mid U(\varphi_p, \varphi_p) \mid R(\varphi_p, \varphi_p).$$

In the above $\wp \in PV$, A ('for All paths') and E ('there Exists a path') are path quantifiers, whereas X ('neXt'), U ('Until') and R ('Release') are state operators. Intuitively, the formula $X\varphi_p$ specifies that φ_p holds in the next state of the path, whereas $U(\varphi_p, \psi_p)$ expresses that ψ_p eventually occurs and that φ_p holds continuously until then. The operator R is dual to U: the formula $R(\varphi_p, \psi_p)$ says that either ψ_p holds always or it is released when φ_p eventually occurs. Derived operators are defined as $G\varphi_p \stackrel{def}{=} R(false, \varphi_p)$ and $F\varphi_p \stackrel{def}{=} U(true, \varphi_p)$, where $true \stackrel{def}{=} \wp \vee \neg\wp$, and $false \stackrel{def}{=} \wp \wedge \neg\wp$ for an arbitrary $\wp \in PV$. Intuitively, the formula $F\varphi_p$ specifies that φ_p occurs in some state of the path ('Finally'), whereas $G\varphi_p$ expresses that φ_p holds in all the states of the path ('Globally').

Next, we define some sublogics of CTL*:

ACTL* : the fragment of CTL* in which the state formulas are restricted such that negation can be applied to propositions only, and the existential quantifier E is not allowed,

ECTL* : the fragment of CTL* in which the state formulas are restricted such that negation can be applied to propositions only, and the universal quantifier A is not allowed,

ACTL : the fragment of ACTL* in which the temporal formulas are restricted to positive boolean combinations of $AU(\varphi, \psi)$, $AR(\varphi, \psi)$, and $AX\varphi$ only.

ECTL : the fragment of ECTL* in which the temporal formulas are restricted to positive boolean combinations of $EU(\varphi, \psi)$, $ER(\varphi, \psi)$ and $EX\varphi$ only.

L_{-X} denotes the logic L without the next-step operator X.

4.2   Semantics of CTL*

Let PV be a set of propositions. A *model* for CTL* is a tuple $M = (L, S, s^0, \rightarrow, V)$, where L is a set of labels, S is a set of states, $s^0 \in S$ is the initial state, $\rightarrow \subseteq S \times L \times S$ is a total successor relation[1], and $V : S \longrightarrow 2^{PV}$

---

[1] Totality means that $(\forall s \in S)(\exists s' \in S)\ s \rightarrow s'$.

is a valuation function. For $s, s' \in S$ the notation $s \to s'$ means that there is $l \in L$ such that $s \xrightarrow{l} s'$. Moreover, for $s_0 \in S$ a *path* $\pi = (s_0, s_1, \ldots)$ is an infinite sequence of states in S starting at s_0, where $s_i \to s_{i+1}$ for all $i \geq 0$, $\pi_i = (s_i, s_{i+1}, \ldots)$ is the i-th suffix of π, and $\pi(i) = s_i$.

Given a model M, a state s, and a path π of M, by $M, s \models \varphi$ $(M, \pi \models \varphi)$ we mean that φ holds in the state s (along the path π, respectively) of the model M. The model is sometimes omitted if it is clear from the context. The relation $\models$ is defined inductively as follows:

$$
\begin{aligned}
M, s &\models \wp & &\text{iff } \wp \in V(s), \text{ for } \wp \in PV, \\
M, s &\models \neg \wp & &\text{iff } M, s \not\models \wp, \text{ for } \wp \in PV, \\
M, x &\models \varphi \wedge \psi & &\text{iff } M, x \models \varphi \text{ and } M, x \models \psi, \text{ for } x \in \{s, \pi\}, \\
M, x &\models \varphi \vee \psi & &\text{iff } M, x \models \varphi \text{ or } M, x \models \psi, \text{ for } x \in \{s, \pi\}, \\
M, s &\models A\varphi & &\text{iff } M, \pi \models \varphi \text{ for each path } \pi \text{ starting at } s, \\
M, s &\models E\varphi & &\text{iff } M, \pi \models \varphi \text{ for some path } \pi \text{ starting at } s, \\
M, \pi &\models \varphi & &\text{iff } M, \pi(0) \models \varphi, \text{ for a state formula } \varphi, \\
M, \pi &\models X\varphi & &\text{iff } M, \pi_1 \models \varphi, \\
M, \pi &\models \varphi U\psi & &\text{iff } (\exists j \geq 0)\big(M, \pi_j \models \psi \text{ and } (\forall 0 \leq i < j)\, M, \pi_i \models \varphi\big), \\
M, \pi &\models \varphi R\psi & &\text{iff } (\forall j \geq 0)\big(M, \pi_j \models \psi \text{ or } (\exists 0 \leq i < j)\, M, \pi_i \models \varphi\big).
\end{aligned}
$$

Moreover, we assume $M \models \varphi$ iff $M, s^0 \models \varphi$, where s^0 is the initial state of M.

4.3 Equivalence Preserving ACTL* and ECTL*

Let $M = (L, S, s_0, \to, V)$ and $M' = (L', S', s_0', \to', V')$ be two models.

Definition 2 ([4]). *A relation* $\leadsto_{sim} \subseteq S' \times S$ *is a* simulation *from M' to M if the following conditions hold:*

- $s_0' \leadsto_{sim} s_0$,
- *for each $s \in S$ and $s' \in S'$, if $s' \leadsto_{sim} s$, then $V(s) = V'(s')$, and for every $s_1 \in S$ such that $s \xrightarrow{l} s_1$ for some $l \in L$, there is $s_1' \in S'$ such that $s' \xrightarrow{l'} s_1'$ for some $l' \in L'$ and $s_1' \leadsto_{sim} s_1$.*

The model M' simulates M ($M' \leadsto_{sim} M$) if there is a simulation from M' to M. The models M, M' are simulation equivalent *iff $M \leadsto_{sim}^1 M'$ and $M' \leadsto_{sim}^2 M$ for some simulations $\leadsto_{sim}^1 \subseteq S \times S'$ and $\leadsto_{sim}^2 \subseteq S' \times S$. Two models M and M' are called* bisimulation equivalent *if $M' \leadsto_{sim} M$ and $M(\leadsto_{sim})^{-1}M'$, where $(\leadsto_{sim})^{-1}$ is the inverse of $\leadsto_{sim}$.*

The following theorem holds:

Theorem 1 ([4]). *Let M, M' be two simulation equivalent models, where the range of the valuation functions V, V' is 2^{PV}. Then, $M, s_0 \models \varphi$ iff $M', s_0' \models \varphi$, for any formula φ over PV such that $\varphi \in$ ACTL* $\cup$ ECTL*.*

5 Discrete- vs. Dense-Time Verification for ACTL* and ECTL*

It is easy to see that the models $M_r(\mathcal{N})$ and $M_n(\mathcal{N})$ can be used in ACTL* and ECTL* verification for a net $\mathcal{N}$ with the semantics the model corresponds to (as both the models meet the definition of a model for CTL*). However, it is also not difficult to see that the second model is smaller and less prone to the state explosion problem. The aim of our work is then to show that both the models are equivalent w.r.t. checking ACTL* and ECTL* properties of time Petri nets. In our proof we make use of the approach of Popova presented in the paper [8].

Consider the dense concrete model $M_r(\mathcal{N}) = (T \cup \mathbb{R}_+, \Sigma, \sigma^0, \rightarrow_r, V)$ of a TPN $\mathcal{N}$. A state $\sigma = (m, clock) \in \Sigma$ is called an *integer-state* if $clock(t) \in \mathbb{N}$ for all $t \in T$. An *integer σ-run* of $\mathcal{N}$ is a sequence of states $\sigma_0 \xrightarrow{a_0}_r \sigma_1 \xrightarrow{a_1}_r \sigma_2 \xrightarrow{a_2}_r \ldots$, where $\sigma_0 = \sigma \in \Sigma$ and $a_i \in T \cup \mathbb{N}$ for each $i \geq 0$. Note that all the states of an integer-run starting at an integer-state are integer-states as well. Thus, it is easy to see that the following holds:

Lemma 1. *For a given time Petri net $\mathcal{N}$ the model $M_r(\mathcal{N})$ reduced to the integer-states and the transition relation between them is equal to $M_n(\mathcal{N})$.*

Due to the above fact, the transition relation in integer runs will be denoted either by $\rightarrow_r$ or by $\rightarrow_n$, depending on the context.

Given a real number $x \in \mathbb{R}_+$, let $\lfloor x \rfloor$ denote the *floor* of x, i.e., the greatest $a \in \mathbb{N}$ such that $a \leq x$, and let $\lceil x \rceil$ denote the *ceiling* of x, i.e., the smallest $a \in \mathbb{N}$ such that $x \leq a$. Moreover, let $fire(\sigma)$ denote a set of the transitions that are ready to fire in the state $\sigma \in \Sigma$, i.e., $fire(\sigma) = \{t \in en(m) \mid clock(t) \in [Eft(t), Lft(t)]\}$. We define the integer-states to be *neighbour states* of real-valued ones as follows:

Definition 3 (Neighbour States). *Let $\sigma = (m, clock)$ be a state of a TPN $\mathcal{N}$. An integer-state $\sigma' = (m', clock')$ is a* neighbour state *of σ (denoted $\sigma' \sim_n \sigma$) iff*

- *$m' = m$,*
- *for each $t \in en(m)$, $\lfloor clock(t) \rfloor \leq clock'(t) \leq \lceil clock(t) \rceil$.*

Intuitively, a neighbour state of σ is an integer-state of the same marking, and such that the values of its clocks, for all the enabled transitions, are "in a neighbourhood" of these of σ. However, it is easy to see that these values can be such that they make more transitions ready to fire than the corresponding values in σ do: each transition t which can be fired at a given value of $clock(t)$ can be fired both at $\lfloor clock(t) \rfloor$ and at $\lceil clock(t) \rceil$ since all these three values are either equal if $clock(t)$ is a natural number, or belong to the same (integer-bounded) interval $[Eft(t), Lft(t)]$ if $clock(t) \notin \mathbb{N}$; on the other hand, a transition t' which is not ready to fire at $clock(t')$ can be firable at $\lceil clock(t') \rceil$ if $\lceil clock(t') \rceil = Eft(t')$. This implies $fire(\sigma) \subseteq fire(\sigma')$.

Let $\pi := \sigma_0 \overset{a_0}{\to}_r \sigma_1 \overset{a_1}{\to}_r \ldots$ be a σ^0-run in $M_r(\mathcal{N})$. By $\pi_{[k]}$, for $k \in \mathbb{N}$, we denote the prefix $\sigma_0 \overset{a_0}{\to}_r \sigma_1 \overset{a_1}{\to}_r \ldots \overset{a_{k-1}}{\to}_r \sigma_k$ of π, and by $\pi(k)$ - the k-th state of π, i.e., σ_k. Moreover, we assign a time δ_i to each step $\sigma_i \overset{a_i}{\to}_r \sigma_{i+1}$ in the run, i.e., define $\delta_i = a_i$ if $a_i \in \mathbb{R}$, and $\delta_i = 0$ otherwise. By $\Delta_G(\sigma_i, \pi)$, for $i \in \mathbb{N}$, we denote the value $\Sigma_{j=0}^{i-1} \delta_j$ (i.e., the time passed along π before reaching its i-th state). Moreover, given $k \in \mathbb{N}$ and a $\pi(k)$-run $\rho := \sigma_k \overset{b_0}{\to}_r \beta_1 \overset{b_1}{\to}_r \beta_2 \overset{b_2}{\to}_r \ldots$, by $\pi_{[k]} \cdot \rho$ we denote the run $\sigma_0 \overset{a_0}{\to}_r \sigma_1 \overset{a_1}{\to}_r \ldots \overset{a_{k-1}}{\to}_r \sigma_k \overset{b_0}{\to}_r \beta_1 \overset{b_1}{\to}_r \beta_2 \overset{b_2}{\to}_r \ldots$ (i.e, the run obtained by "joining" $\pi_{[k]}$ and ρ). The above definitions apply to discrete runs in the analogous way. Next, we introduce the following definition (see also Fig. 2):

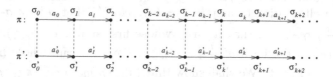

Fig. 2. Neighbour prefix of $\pi_{[k]}$ (denoted $\pi'_{[k]}$). If $a_i \in T$, then $a'_i = a_i$; the states of $\pi_{[k]}$ and $\pi'_{[k]}$ linked by dashed lines are related by $\sim_n$.

Definition 4 (Neighbour Prefix). *Let* $\pi := \sigma_0 \overset{a_0}{\to}_r \sigma_1 \overset{a_1}{\to}_r \ldots$ *be a run in* $M_r(\mathcal{N})$, *and let* $\pi' := \sigma'_0 \overset{a'_0}{\to}_r \sigma'_1 \overset{a'_1}{\to}_r \ldots$ *be an integer run. For* $k \in \mathbb{N}$, *the prefix* $\pi'_{[k]}$ *is a* neighbour prefix *of* $\pi_{[k]}$ *(denoted* $\pi'_{[k]} \sim_n \pi_{[k]}$*) iff for each* $i = 0, \ldots, k$ *we have:*

- $\sigma'_i \sim_n \sigma_i$, *and*
- $a_i \in T$ *iff* $a'_i \in T$, *and if* $a_i, a'_i \in T$ *then* $a'_i = a_i$.

Intuitively, a neighbour prefix "visits" neighbour states of these in $\pi_{[k]}$, and the corresponding steps of these prefixes are either both firings of the same transition, or both passages of time (possibly of different lengths).

In order to show that $M_n(\mathcal{N})$ can replace $M_r(\mathcal{N})$ in ACTL*/ECTL* verification we shall prove the following lemma:

Lemma 2. *The models* $M_r(\mathcal{N})$ *and* $M_n(\mathcal{N})$ *are simulation equivalent.*

Proof. It is obvious from Lemma 1 that $M_r(\mathcal{N})$ simulates $M_n(\mathcal{N})$, where a simulation relation $\mathcal{R}_1 \subseteq \Sigma \times \Sigma_n$ is defined as $\mathcal{R}_1 = \{(\sigma, \sigma') \mid \sigma = \sigma'\}$.

Let $R_r(\mathcal{N})$ and $R_n(\mathcal{N})$ denote respectively the sets of all the dense σ^0-runs (discrete σ_n^0-runs) of the net $\mathcal{N}$. In order to prove that $M_n(\mathcal{N}) \leadsto_{sim} M_r(\mathcal{N})$ we shall show that the relation $\mathcal{R} \subseteq \Sigma_n \times \Sigma$ given by

$$\mathcal{R} = \{(\sigma', \sigma) \mid \exists \pi \in R_r(\mathcal{N}) \, \exists \pi' \in R_n(\mathcal{N}) \, \exists k \in \mathbb{N} \text{ s.t.}$$

$$\sigma = \pi(k) \wedge \sigma' = \pi'(k) \wedge \pi'_{[k]} \sim_n \pi_{[k]} \wedge \forall_{j \leq k} \, \Delta_G(\sigma'_j, \pi') = \lfloor \Delta_G(\sigma_j, \pi) \rfloor\}$$

is a simulation from $M_n(\mathcal{N})$ to $M_r(\mathcal{N})$. Intuitively, the states σ, σ' are related by $\mathcal{R}$ if they both are reachable from the initial state of $\mathcal{N}$ in k steps for some natural k, on runs π, π' such that $\pi'_{[k]}$ is a neighbour prefix of $\pi_{[k]}$ and for each $j \leq k$ the total time passed along $\pi'_{[j]}$ is the floor of that passed along $\pi_{[j]}$.

It is obvious that $(\sigma_n^0, \sigma^0) \in \mathcal{R}$ due to equality of these states. Next, consider σ, σ' such that $(\sigma', \sigma) \in \mathcal{R}$. Assume that the runs "justifying" this relation (for some k) are of the form $\pi := \sigma_0 \xrightarrow{a_0}_r \sigma_1 \xrightarrow{a_1}_r \ldots$ and $\pi' := \sigma_n^0 = \sigma_0' \xrightarrow{a_0'}_n \sigma_1' \xrightarrow{a_1'}_n \ldots$ respectively, and that $\sigma_i = (m_i, clock_i)$, $\sigma_i' = (m_i', clock_i')$ for each $i \in \mathbb{N}$ (which implies also the notation $\sigma = (m_k, clock_k)$ and $\sigma' = (m_k', clock_k')$ used below).

- if $\sigma \xrightarrow{t}_r \gamma$ for a transition $t \in T$ and a state $\gamma = (m_\gamma, clock_\gamma)$, then from $\sigma' \sim_n \sigma$ (and therefore $fire(\sigma) \subseteq fire(\sigma')$) the transition t can be fired at σ' as well, leading to a state $\xi = (m_\xi, clock_\xi')$. Let ρ be a σ-run of the form $\sigma \xrightarrow{t}_r \gamma \rightarrow_r \ldots$ (i.e., a σ-run whose first step is $\sigma \xrightarrow{t}_r \gamma$), and let ρ' be a σ'-run of the form $\sigma' \xrightarrow{t}_n \xi \rightarrow_n \ldots$ (i.e., a σ'-run whose first step is $\sigma' \xrightarrow{t}_n \xi$; see Fig. 3). We shall show that $(\pi'_{[k]} \cdot \rho')_{[k+1]} \sim_n (\pi_{[k]} \cdot \rho)_{[k+1]}$ and that $\Delta_G(\xi, \pi'_{[k]} \cdot \rho') = \lfloor \Delta_G(\gamma, \pi_{[k]} \cdot \rho) \rfloor$.

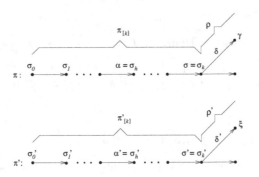

Fig. 3. Relation between π, π', ρ and ρ' in the proof of Lemma 2

- In order to prove $(\pi'_{[k]} \cdot \rho')_{[k+1]} \sim_n (\pi_{[k]} \cdot \rho)_{[k+1]}$ it is sufficient to show that $\xi \sim_n \gamma$. It is obvious that the markings m_γ and m_ξ are equal, and that $newly\_en(m_k, t) = newly\_en(m_k', t)$. Next, consider $t' \in en(m_\gamma)$. If $t' \notin newly\_en(m_k, t)$ then the value of its clock in γ is the same as in σ (since firing of t does not influence the value of the clock of t'). In turn, if $t' \in newly\_en(m_k, t)$ then the values of its clock in γ and in ξ are equal to 0. Thus, from the fact that for σ, σ' we have $\lfloor clock_k(t) \rfloor \leq clock_k'(t) \leq \lceil clock_k(t) \rceil$ we have also $\lfloor clock_\gamma(t) \rfloor \leq clock_\xi'(t) \leq \lceil clock_\gamma(t) \rceil$, which implies $\xi \sim_n \gamma$.
- the condition $\Delta_G(\xi, \pi'_{[k]} \cdot \rho') = \lfloor \Delta_G(\gamma, \pi_{[k]} \cdot \rho) \rfloor$ holds in an obvious way $(\Delta_G(\xi, \pi'_{[k]} \cdot \rho') = \Delta_G(\sigma', \pi') = \lfloor \Delta_G(\sigma, \pi) \rfloor = \lfloor \Delta_G(\gamma, \pi_{[k]} \cdot \rho) \rfloor$ as the step consisting in firing a transition is assigned the time 0).

− if $\sigma \xrightarrow{\delta}_r \gamma$ for a time $\delta \in \mathbb{R}_+$ and a state $\gamma = (m_\gamma, clock_\gamma)$, then let ρ be a σ-run $\sigma \xrightarrow{\delta}_r \gamma \xrightarrow{\cdot}_r \dots$ (i.e., a σ-run with the first step $\sigma \xrightarrow{\delta}_r \gamma$; see Fig. 3), and let $\pi_{[k]} \cdot \rho$ denote the run $\sigma_0 \xrightarrow{a_0}_r \sigma_1 \xrightarrow{a_1}_r \dots \xrightarrow{a_{k-1}}_r \sigma_k \xrightarrow{\delta}_r \gamma \xrightarrow{\cdot}_r \dots$ (i.e, the run obtained by "joining" $\pi_{[k]}$ and ρ). Next, let

$$\delta' = \lfloor \Delta_G(\gamma, \pi_{[k]} \cdot \rho) \rfloor - \Delta_G(\sigma', \pi')$$

(which is an integer value due to $\Delta_G(\sigma', \pi') \in \mathbb{N}$). We shall show first that the time δ' can pass at σ', leading to a state $\xi = (m_\xi, clock'_\xi)$.

- To show that δ' can pass at σ' notice that

$$\delta = \Delta_G(\gamma, \pi_{[k]} \cdot \rho) - \Delta_G(\sigma, \pi_{[k]} \cdot \rho),$$

and that

$$\Delta_G(\sigma_i, \pi) = \Delta_G(\sigma_i, \pi_{[k]} \cdot \rho) \text{ for each } i = 0, \dots, k.$$

Moreover, we have that $clock_\gamma(t) = clock_k(t) + \delta \leq Lft(t)$ for each $t \in en(m_k)$.

Consider a transition $t \in en(m'_k)$ (where $en(m'_k) = en(m_k) = en(m_\gamma)$). Let h be an index along $\pi_{[k]}$ pointing to a state (denoted α) at which t became enabled most recently, and let h' be an index along $\pi'_{[k]}$ pointing to a state (denoted α') at which t became enabled most recently. From the fact that $\pi'_{[k]} \sim_n \pi_{[k]}$ we have $h = h'$ (for each $j \leq k - 1$ the corresponding j-th steps of $\pi_{[k]}$ and $\pi'_{[k]}$ are either both firings of the same transition or both time passings, which implies that for each $i \leq k$ a transition t becomes enabled in $\pi(i)$ iff it becomes enabled in $\pi'(i)$). From the definitions of $clock$ and $clock'$, it is easy to see that

$$clock_k(t) = \Delta_G(\sigma, \pi) - \Delta_G(\alpha, \pi),$$

$$clock_\gamma(t) = \Delta_G(\gamma, \pi_{[k]} \cdot \rho) - \Delta_G(\alpha, \pi)$$

and

$$clock'_k(t) = \Delta_G(\sigma', \pi') - \Delta_G(\alpha', \pi')$$

Moreover, we have
$clock'_k(t) + \delta' = \Delta_G(\sigma', \pi') - \Delta_G(\alpha', \pi') + \delta' =$
$\Delta_G(\sigma', \pi') - \Delta_G(\alpha', \pi') + \lfloor \Delta_G(\gamma, \pi_{[k]} \cdot \rho) \rfloor - \Delta_G(\sigma', \pi') =$
$\lfloor \Delta_G(\gamma, \pi_{[k]} \cdot \rho) \rfloor - \Delta_G(\alpha', \pi') \stackrel{def.\ of\ \mathcal{R}\ and\ h=h'}{=}$
$\lfloor \Delta_G(\gamma, \pi_{[k]} \cdot \rho) \rfloor - \lfloor \Delta_G(\alpha, \pi) \rfloor.$

From $clock_\gamma(t) \leq Lft(t)$ we have $\lceil clock_\gamma(t) \rceil \leq Lft(t)$, and from the property $\lfloor a \rfloor - \lfloor b \rfloor \leq \lceil a - b \rceil$ we get
$clock'_k(t) + \delta' = \lfloor \Delta_G(\gamma, \pi_{[k]} \cdot \rho) \rfloor - \lfloor \Delta_G(\alpha, \pi) \rfloor \leq$
$\lceil \Delta_G(\gamma, \pi_{[k]} \cdot \rho) - \Delta_G(\alpha, \pi) \rceil = \lceil clock_\gamma(t) \rceil \leq Lft(t).$
Thus, we have that $clock'_k(t) + \delta' \leq Lft(t)$ for each $t \in en(m'_k)$, and therefore the time δ' can pass at σ'.

Next, let ρ' be a σ'-run of the form $\sigma' \xrightarrow{\delta'}_n \xi \rightarrow_n \ldots$. We shall show that $(\pi'_{[k]} \cdot \rho')_{[k+1]} \sim_n (\pi_{[k]} \cdot \rho)_{[k+1]}$ and that $\Delta_G(\xi, \pi'_{[k]} \cdot \rho') = \lfloor \Delta_G(\gamma, \pi_{[k]} \cdot \rho) \rfloor$.

- In order to prove $(\pi'_{[k]} \cdot \rho')_{[k+1]} \sim_n (\pi_{[k]} \cdot \rho)_{[k+1]}$ it is sufficient to show that $\xi \sim_n \gamma$. It is obvious that the markings of these states are equal. Consider $t \in en(m)$. We show that $\lfloor clock_\gamma(t) \rfloor \leq clock'_\xi(t) \leq \lceil clock_\gamma(t) \rceil$. Let α, α', h, h' be defined as in the previous part of the proof (see the 8th line of the previous item). Similarly as before, from the definitions of $clock$, $clock'$ we have that

$$clock_\gamma(t) = \Delta_G(\gamma, \pi_{[k]} \cdot \rho) - \Delta_G(\alpha, \pi),$$

and that

$$clock'_\xi(t) = \Delta_G(\sigma', \pi') + \delta' - \Delta_G(\alpha', \pi').$$

* From the property $\lfloor a - b \rfloor \leq \lfloor a \rfloor - \lfloor b \rfloor$ (for $a, b \in \mathbb{R}_+$ with $a \geq b$) we have
$$\lfloor clock_\gamma(t) \rfloor = \lfloor \Delta_G(\gamma, \pi_{[k]} \cdot \rho) - \Delta_G(\alpha, \pi) \rfloor \leq$$
$$\lfloor \Delta_G(\gamma, \pi_{[k]} \cdot \rho) \rfloor - \lfloor \Delta_G(\alpha, \pi) \rfloor \overset{h = h' \text{and def. of } \mathcal{R}}{=}$$
$$\lfloor \Delta_G(\gamma, \pi_{[k]} \cdot \rho) - \Delta_G(\sigma', \pi') + \Delta_G(\sigma', \pi') \rfloor - \Delta_G(\alpha', \pi') =$$

$$\lfloor \Delta_G(\gamma, \pi_{[k]} \cdot \rho) \rfloor - \Delta_G(\sigma', \pi') + \Delta_G(\sigma', \pi') - \Delta_G(\alpha', \pi') =$$

$$\delta' + \Delta_G(\sigma', \pi') - \Delta_G(\alpha', \pi') = clock'_\xi(t).$$
* From the property $\lfloor a \rfloor - \lfloor b \rfloor \leq \lceil a - b \rceil$ we have
$$clock'_k(t) + \delta' = \lfloor \Delta_G(\gamma, \pi_{[k]} \cdot \rho) \rfloor - \lfloor \Delta_G(\alpha, \pi) \rfloor \leq$$
$$\lceil \Delta_G(\gamma, \pi_{[k]} \cdot \rho) - \Delta_G(\alpha, \pi) \rceil = \lceil clock_\gamma(t) \rceil$$

- Next, we have
$$\Delta_G(\xi, \pi'_{[k]} \cdot \rho') = \Delta_G(\sigma', \pi') + \delta' =$$
$$\Delta_G(\sigma', \pi') + \lfloor \Delta_G(\gamma, \pi_{[k]} \cdot \rho) \rfloor - \Delta_G(\sigma', \pi') = \lfloor \Delta_G(\gamma, \pi_{[k]} \cdot \rho) \rfloor,$$
which ends the proof.

Therefore, we can formulate the following theorem:

Theorem 2. *Let $M_r(\mathcal{N})$ and $M_n(\mathcal{N})$ be respectively a dense and a discrete model for a time Petri net $\mathcal{N}$, and let φ be an ACTL* (ECTL*) formula. The following condition holds:*

$$M_r(\mathcal{N}) \models \varphi \text{ iff } M_n(\mathcal{N}) \models \varphi.$$

Proof. Follows from Theorem 1 and Lemma 2 in a straightforward way.

It should also be explained that in the case of timed systems (and therefore also TPNs) with the dense-time semantics, logics without the next-step operator are usually used, due to problems with interpreting the "next" step in the case of continuous time. However, Theorem 2 considers more general logics, in case one would interpret the next-step operator over an arbitrary passage of time (i.e., to consider each time successor of a state as a "next" one).

Fig. 4. A net

It should be noticed that the relation $\mathcal{R}$ used in our proof cannot be used to prove bisimulation between the models, i.e., their equivalence w.r.t. the CTL* properties, since the integer run π' "justifying" $\sigma'\mathcal{R}\sigma$ and the dense run π occurring in the relation do not need to "branch" in the same way. Thus, although one can prove that each transition t which can be fired at σ can be fired at σ' as well, the reverse does not hold. To see an example of the above consider the net shown in Fig. 4 and its runs:

– the dense one:
$$\pi := (p1, (0,0)) \xrightarrow{0.5}_r (p1, (0.5, 0)) \xrightarrow{t1}_r (p2, (0,0)) \xrightarrow{0.6}_r (p2, (0, 0.6)) \rightarrow_r \ldots$$
– and the discrete one (denoted π'), built in the way shown in [8] and used in our proof in the definition of $\mathcal{R}$ (i.e., satisfying $\pi'_{[3]} \sim_n \pi_{[3]}$ and $\Delta_G(\sigma'_j, \pi') = \lfloor \Delta_G(\sigma_j, \pi) \rfloor$ for each $j \leq 3$):
$$\pi' := (p1, (0,0)) \xrightarrow{0}_n (p1, (0,0)) \xrightarrow{t1}_n (p2, (0,0)) \xrightarrow{1}_n (p2, (0,1)) \rightarrow_n \ldots.$$

It is easy to see that in $\pi(3)$ we have $clock(t2) = 0.6$, which means that $t2$ cannot be fired at this state, while in $\pi'(3)$ we have $clock(t2) = 1$, which means that the transition $t2$ is firable.

6 Experimental Results

In order to show that using discrete-time models instead of the dense ones can be profitable, we have performed some tests, using the implementation of SAT-based bounded model checking (BMC) for distributed TPNs with the discrete-time semantics [6] and the logic ACTL$_{-X}$ as well as its modification for the dense-time case prepared for this paper. BMC is a technique applied mainly to searching for counterexamples for universal properties, using a model truncated up to some specific depth k. The formulas used by the method are then negations of these expressing properties to be tested. So, in our case they are formulas of ECTL$_{-X}$.

The first system we consider is the Generic Pipeline Paradigm [7] Petri net model (GTPP) shown in Fig. 5. It consists of three parts: Producer producing data (*ProdReady*) or being inactive, Consumer receiving data (*ConsReady*) or being inactive, and a chain of n intermediate Nodes which can be ready for receiving data (*Node$_i$Ready*), processing data (*Node$_i$Proc*), or sending data (*Node$_i$Send*). The example can be scaled by adding more intermediate nodes. The parameters a, b, c, d, e, f are used to adjust the time properties of Producer, Consumer, and of the intermediate Nodes. The formulas considered are EGEF*ConsReceived*, EG(*ProdReady* ∨ *ConsReady*) and EF*Node$_1$Send*.

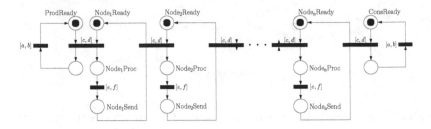

Fig. 5. A net for Generic Timed Pipeline Paradigm

The next system tested is the standard *Fischer's mutual exclusion protocol* (Mutex) [1]. The system consists of n time Petri nets, each one modelling a process, plus one additional net used to coordinate the access of the processes to the critical sections. A TPN modelling the system for $n = 2$ is presented in Fig. 6. In this case we have tested the formula $\mathrm{EGEF}(crit_1 \vee \ldots \vee crit_n)$.

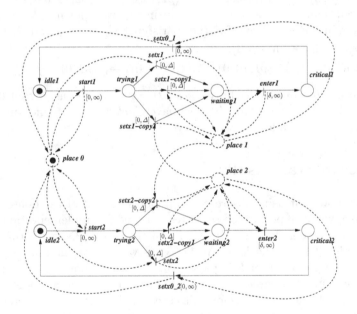

Fig. 6. A net for Fischer's mutual exclusion protocol for $n = 2$

The results are presented in Fig. 7–9 for GTPP, and in Fig. 10 for Mutex. It can be seen that in all the cases we are able to verify systems containing more components (indicated in the column n) when discrete models are used (the "−" signs in the tables mean that the limit on the runtime was exceeded), and the total time ($bmcT + satT$) and the memory required ($\max(bmcM, satM)$) are usually smaller for the discrete-time case (the columns with "IN :"). In some cases the differences are quite substantial, but there are also examples in which

n	k	LL	ℝ:		ℕ:	
			bmcT+satT	max(bmcM,satM)	bmcT+satT	max(bmcM,satM)
1	5	7	1.41	12.00	0.20	8.00
2	7	9	9.94	25.00	1.15	12.00
3	9	11	49.45	60.00	3.55	21.00
4	11	13	154.70	146.00	9.94	38.00
5	13	15	310.18	243.00	20.90	61.00
6	15	17	708.66	313.00	41.43	94.00
7	17	19	1934.63	818.00	76.81	145.00
8	19	21	4121.60	1071.00	131.98	215.00
9	21	23	6819.25	1640.00	237.21	314.00
10	23	25	20519.20	3455.00	361.03	377.00
11	25	27	-	-	562.15	552.00

Fig. 7. Comparison of the results for GTPP and the formula EGEF*ConsReceived*

n	k	LL	ℝ:		ℕ:	
			bmcT+satT	max(bmcM,satM)	bmcT+satT	max(bmcM,satM)
1	5	1	0.41	7.00	0.17	7.00
2	7	1	4.14	12.00	0.76	8.00
3	9	1	32.27	29.00	2.20	9.00
4	11	1	63.28	52.00	8.57	12.00
5	13	1	200.14	151.00	21.14	17.00
6	15	1	488.59	165.00	43.18	24.00
7	17	1	870.21	342.00	105.18	38.00
8	19	1	1870.65	415.00	234.00	54.00
9	21	1	3745.33	658.00	763.84	139.00
10	23	1	7097.01	1364.00	1696.58	283.00
11	25	1	-	-	3013.98	306.00

Fig. 8. Comparison of the results: GTPP, the formula EG(*ProdReady* ∨ *ConsReady*)

n	k	LL	ℝ:		ℕ:	
			bmcT+satT	max(bmcM,satM)	bmcT+satT	max(bmcM,satM)
100	2	1	2.02	23.00	1.60	19.00
200	2	1	7.04	76.00	5.74	51.00
300	2	1	15.03	153.00	12.15	102.00
400	2	1	26.30	270.00	18.59	179.00
500	2	1	40.50	412.00	28.47	273.00
600	2	1	58.71	563.00	40.45	397.00
700	2	1	79.71	738.00	54.69	537.00
800	2	1	104.84	992.00	72.06	654.00
900	2	1	133.78	1173.00	90.48	854.00
1000	2	1	169.19	1528.00	114.86	1005.00
1100	2	1	211.16	1772.00	140.22	1168.00
1200	2	1	-	-	168.86	1506.00
1300	2	1	-	-	203.24	1604.00

Fig. 9. Comparison of the results: GTPP, the formula EF*Node1Send*

the time and the memory used are similar for both the semantics. However, one can see that the noticeable differences occur in the cases in which the length of the witness for the formula (k) or the number of paths required to check this formula (LL) grow together with the size of the system, making the verification more expensive.

n	k	LL	IR:		IN:	
			bmcT+satT	max(bmcM,satM)	bmcT+satT	max(bmcM,satM)
2	4	5	1.04	11.00	0.74	10.00
3	4	5	1.77	13.00	1.10	12.00
4	4	5	1.83	15.00	1.63	14.00
5	4	5	3.18	17.00	2.41	16.00
10	4	5	9.15	40.00	7.20	31.00
20	4	5	26.14	90.00	18.76	86.00
30	4	5	74.70	177.00	58.56	161.00
40	4	5	258.34	330.00	108.34	320.00
50	4	5	265.06	419.00	170.93	358.00
60	4	5	710.11	732.00	442.42	713.00
70	4	5	701.81	1092.00	728.20	1073.00
80	4	5	919.34	1001.00	2288.34	1349.00
90	4	5	780.89	1161.00	934.72	1140.00
100	4	5	4566.16	3181.00	4230.64	4549.00
110	4	5	4260.76	3414.00	4956.38	3237.00
120	4	5	-	-	4217.44	3238.00
130	4	5	-	-	2155.04	2571.00
140	4	5	-	-	5087.76	3603.00

Fig. 10. Comparison of the results: mutex, the formula $\mathrm{EGEF}(crit_1 \vee \ldots \vee crit_n)$ The abnormalities in the increase of some values follow from the non-deterministic behaviour of the SAT-solver (in some cases searching for an appropriate valuation can take more or less resources than one would expect).

7   Conclusions and Further Work

We have shown that the result of Popova, stating that integer time steps are sufficient to test reachability of markings in time Petri nets, can be extended to testing the ECTL* and ACTL* properties. We have focused on 1-safe TPNs for simplicity of the presentation, but it is easy to see that the result applies also to "general" time Petri nets: neither the definitions of a marking and of enabledness of a transition, nor the way multiple enabledness of transitions is handled (see [2]) do influence the proof.

Our experimental results show that considering the discrete semantics while verifying properties of dense-time nets can be profitable. Due to this, in our further work we are going to check whether discrete-time semantics can be used when testing other classes of properties of the dense-time Petri net systems (e.g., CTL*).

References

1. Abadi, M., Lamport, L.: An old-fashioned recipe for real time. In: Huizing, C., de Bakker, J.W., Rozenberg, G., de Roever, W.-P. (eds.) REX 1991. LNCS, vol. 600, pp. 1–27. Springer, Heidelberg (1992)
2. Boyer, M., Diaz, M.: Multiple enabledness in Petri nets with time. In: Proc. of the 9th Int. Workshop on Petri Nets and Performance Models (PNPM 2001), pp. 219–228 (2001)
3. Goltz, U., Kuiper, R., Penczek, W.: Propositional temporal logics and equivalences. In: Cleaveland, W.R. (ed.) CONCUR 1992. LNCS, vol. 630, pp. 222–236. Springer, Heidelberg (1992)
4. Grumberg, O., Long, D.E.: Model checking and modular verification. In: Groote, J.F., Baeten, J.C.M. (eds.) CONCUR 1991. LNCS, vol. 527, pp. 250–265. Springer, Heidelberg (1991)
5. Janowska, A., Penczek, W., Półrola, A., Zbrzezny, A.: Towards discrete-time verification of time Petri nets with dense-time semantics. In: Proc. of the Int. Workshop on Concurrency, Specification and Programming (CS&P 2011), pp. 215–228. Bialystok University of Technology (2011)
6. Męski, A., Penczek, W., Półrola, A., Woźna-Szcześniak, B., Zbrzezny, A.: Bounded model checking approaches for verificaton of distributed time Petri nets. In: Proc. of the Int. Workshop on Petri Nets and Software Engineering (PNSE 2011), pp. 72–91. University of Hamburg (2011)
7. Peled, D.: All from one, one for all: On model checking using representatives. In: Courcoubetis, C. (ed.) CAV 1993. LNCS, vol. 697, pp. 409–423. Springer, Heidelberg (1993)
8. Popova, L.: On time Petri nets. Elektronische Informationsverarbeitung und Kybernetik 27(4), 227–244 (1991)
9. Popova-Zeugmann, L.: Essential states in time Petri nets. Informatik-Bericht 96, Humboldt University (1998)
10. Popova-Zeugmann, L.: Time Petri nets state space reduction using dynamic programming. Journal of Control and Cybernetics 35(3), 721–748 (2006)
11. Popova-Zeugmann, L., Schlatter, D.: Analyzing paths in time Petri nets. Fundamenta Informaticae 37(3), 311–327 (1999)

When Can We Trust a Third Party?

A Soundness Perspective

Kees M. van Hee, Natalia Sidorova, and Jan Martijn E.M. van der Werf*

Department of Mathematics and Computer Science
Technische Universiteit Eindhoven
P.O. Box 513, 5600 MB Eindhoven, The Netherlands
{k.m.v.hee,n.sidorova,j.m.e.m.v.d.werf}@tue.nl

Abstract. Organizations often do not want to reveal the way a product is created or a service is delivered. As a consequence, if two organizations want to cooperate, they contact a trusted third party. Each specifies how it wants to communicate with the other party. The trusted third party then needs to assure that the two organizations cooperate correctly. In this paper, we study requirements on trusted third parties to ensure correct cooperation between the different organizations.

1 Introduction

Organizations need to anticipate on the increasing dynamicity and complexity of business markets. Therefore, organizations focus more and more on their core activities. As a result, organizations need to cooperate in large networks. The organizations in the network have as common goal the delivery of their services. Such a network is called a *virtual enterprise* [14].

Communication between the organizations is asynchronous by nature: an organization sends some data, like an inquiry, to some other organization, and eventually the latter organization sends a response. Therefore, we use Petri nets to model organizations using *components*. Components can be composed into networks of components. Such a network is again a component. A component has an initial state and a desired final state. We say that a component, or a network of components communicates correctly if (1) it is *weakly terminating*, i.e., if in all its reachable states the component is always able to eventually reach the desired final state, and (2) it is *properly completing*, i.e., there are no pending messages if the component is in the final state. If a component is working correctly, we call it *sound*.

Trust is an important property in a network of cooperating organizations: organizations share business knowledge and intellectual property with other organizations within the network in order to organize the component network properly and achieve desired goals. At the same time, organizations often want

* Supported by the PoSecCo project (project no. 257129), partially co-funded by the European Union under the Information and Communication Technologies (ICT) theme of the 7th Framework Programme for R&D (FP7).

M. Koutny et al. (Eds.): ToPNoC VIII, LNCS 8100, pp. 106–122, 2013.

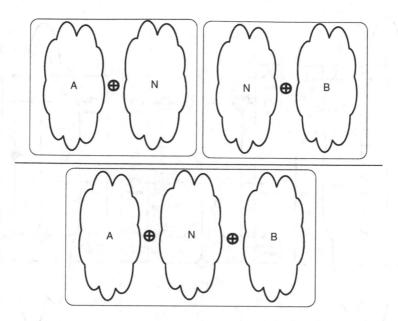

Fig. 1. If the notary N communicates correctly with A and B individually, we want to conclude correctness of the network of A, B and N

to keep some intellectual property within their organization and avoid sharing it for clear reasons. A common approach used in real life is the use of trusted third parties. It becomes nowadays also quite common in the virtual world. In this paper, we consider the use of a *third party*, also called a *notary*, that is trusted by all the organizations in the network. By using a notary, each of the organizations explains to the notary the way it wants to conduct business, and the notary will assure that the organizations can do business together. This requires the notary to ensure that it communicates correctly with each of the organizations, i.e., that the notary with each of the individual organizations can reach the common goals, and secondly, that the complete network with all the organizations together can reach its common goals. If this is the case, we call the notary *trusted*.

In this paper we limit ourselves to the cooperation between two organizations using a notary. Rather than to use verification to check whether the communication between the notary and the two organizations is correct, we search for conditions such that if the communication between the notary and each of the individual organizations is correct, we can automatically conclude that the communication between the three parties is correct, as depicted in Fig. 1.

This paper is structured as follows. Sec. 2 presents an illustrative example of a trusted third party. Sec. 3 introduces the basic notions needed throughout the paper. Next, Sec. 4 explains the concept of components and their composition. In Sec. 5 we study the conditions under which the notary is guaranteed to ensure soundness of the composition of the three parties. Sec. 6 concludes the paper.

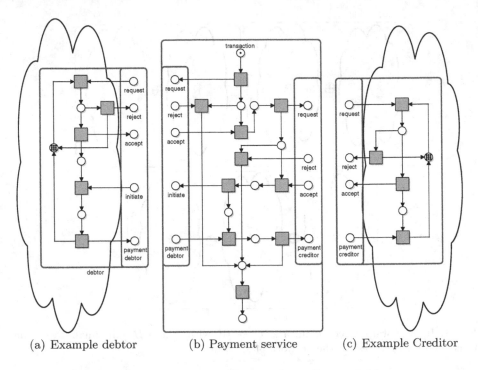

(a) Example debtor   (b) Payment service   (c) Example Creditor

Fig. 2. Payment service with example creditor and debtor

2   Illustrative Example

Trusted third parties are often used in sercive oriented architectures. For example, if multiple parties each delivers the same service, the trusted third party can serve as a gateway [9].

An example of such a trusted third party is the payment service, for example the protocol agreed upon in iDEAL and the European SEPA standard. On the one hand, the payment service serves as a single interface for the different payment methods for web sites. In this way, a web site only needs to implement a single interface to offer a plethora of payment methods. On the other hand, the payment service ensures the communication with the different payment providers, like banks and credit card organizations.

The payment service is shown in Fig. 2(b). It initiates a transaction on request, e.g. for some web shop. The payment service then sends a request to the bank of the debtor.

In case the debtor rejects the payment via its bank, the transaction is cancelled. Otherwise, the payment service contacts the bank of the creditor. The creditor's bank then checks whether the account fulfills the criteria for this type of transactions. If this is not the case, the transaction will be rejected. Otherwise, the payment service initiates the payment at the debtor's bank, and the payment is passed to the webshop's bank.

In the mean time, the payment service logs the payment, so that it can send regularly reports to its customers, such as statistics about accepted and rejected transactions, and lists of accepted transactions.

In order to cooperate, banks or other payment organizations, like credit card companies, need to implement the debtor and creditor interfaces to cooperate with this payment service. However, banks have similar, but not equivalent implementations of the debtor and creditor interfaces. Fig. 2 depicts two sample implementations of a debtor (Fig. 2(a)) and a creditor (Fig. 2(c)).

In this example is easy to check that (1) the debtor implementation shown in Fig. 2(a) works correctly with the payment service, (2) that the payment service works correctly with the creditor implementation (Fig. 2(c)), and (3) that these three services together work correctly. However, the payment service needs to ensure that if it works correctly with some debtor implementation, it works correctly also when it is connected to a different creditor, and vice versa.

When implementing the payment service, it needs to administer for each transaction which specific creditor and debtor from a set of possible organizations are selected. To model this explicitly, Petri nets with identifiers [10,12,17,18] can be used. However, as each transaction is independent, i.e. communication is only within a single transaction and not between different transactions, identities can be abstracted from. Therefore, we choose to model the components implementing these services with classical, uncolored, Petri nets.

In the remainder of this paper, we show that by the structure of the trusted third party, in this example the payment service, is sound in any composition with an implemented debtor and creditor, provided that each implementation individually is sound in a composition with the payment service.

3 Preliminaries

Let S be a set. The powerset of S is denoted by $\mathcal{P}(S) = \{S' \mid S' \subseteq S\}$. We use $|S|$ for the number of elements in S. Two sets S and T are *disjoint* if $S \cap T = \emptyset$.

A *bag* m over S is a function $m : S \to \mathbb{N}$, where $\mathbb{N} = \{0, 1, \ldots\}$ denotes the set of natural numbers. We denote e.g. the bag m with an element a occurring once, b occurring three times and c occurring twice by $m = [a, b^3, c^2]$. The set of all bags over S is denoted by $\mathbb{N}^S$. Sets can be seen as a special kind of bag where all elements occur only once; we interpret sets in this way whenever we use them in operations on bags. We use $+$ and $-$ for the sum and difference of two bags, and $=, <, >, \leq, \geq$ for the comparison of two bags, which are defined in a standard way. The projection of a bag $m \in \mathbb{N}^S$ on some set U is a bag defined by $m_{|U}(s) = m(s)$ if $s \in U$ and $m_{|U}(s) = 0$ otherwise.

A *sequence* over S of length $n \in \mathbb{N}$ is a function $\sigma : \{1, \ldots, n\} \to S$. If $n > 0$ and $\sigma(i) = a_i$ for $i \in \{1, \ldots, n\}$, we write $\sigma = \langle a_1, \ldots, a_n \rangle$. The length of a sequence is denoted by $|\sigma|$. The sequence of length 0 is called the *empty sequence*, and is denoted by ϵ. The set of all finite sequences over S is denoted by S^*. We write $a \in \sigma$ if $\sigma(i) = a$ for some $1 \leq i \leq |\sigma|$. *Concatenation* of two sequences $\nu, \gamma \in S^*$, denoted by $\sigma = \nu; \gamma$, is a sequence defined by $\sigma :$

$\{1, \ldots, |\nu| + |\gamma|\} \to S$, such that $\sigma(i) = \nu(i)$ for $1 \le i \le |\nu|$, and $\sigma(i) = \gamma(i - |\nu|)$ for $|\nu| + 1 \le i \le |\nu| + |\gamma|$. We inductively define the projection of $\sigma \in S^*$ on some set U by $a; \sigma'|_U = \langle a \rangle; \sigma'|_U$ if $a \in U$ and $a; \sigma'|_U = \sigma'|_U$ otherwise.

Definition 1 (Petri Net [16]). *A Petri net N is a tuple (P, T, F) where (1) P and T are two disjoint sets of* places *and* transitions *respectively, we call an element of the set $(P \cup T)$ a* node *of N; and (2) $F \subseteq (P \times T) \cup (T \times P)$ is the* flow relation. *An element of F is called an* arc.

Two Petri nets (P, T, F) and (P', T', F') are called disjoint if both P and P', and T and T' are disjoint. Let $N = (P, T, F)$ be a Petri net. Given a node $n \in (P \cup T)$, we define its preset by ${}_N^\bullet n = \{x \mid (x, n) \in F\}$, and its postset by $n_N^\bullet = \{x \mid (n, x) \in F\}$. We omit the subscript if the context is clear.

A subnet $N' = (P', T', F')$ is a subnet of a Petri net $N = (P, T, F)$ if $P' \subseteq P, T' \subseteq T$ and $F' = F \cap ((P' \times T') \cup (T' \times P'))$.

Let $N = (P, T, F)$ be a Petri net. A path from a node $n \in P \cup T$ to a node $m \in P \cup T$ is a sequence $\pi \in (P \cup T)^*$ such that $(\pi(i - 1), \pi(i)) \in F$ for all $1 < i < |\pi|$. The set of all paths from n to m is denoted by $\Pi(n, m)$. A path is called *cyclic* if there exists a non-empty path π, i.e., $|\pi| > 0$, such that $\pi(1) = \pi(|\pi|)$. If N has a cyclic path, the net is called *cyclic*. If no such cycle exists, it is called *acyclic*.

To describe the semantics of a Petri net, we use *markings*. A *marking* of N is a bag $m \in \mathbb{N}^P$, where $m(p)$ denotes the number of *tokens* in place $p \in P$. If $m(p) > 0$, place p is called *marked* in marking m. A Petri net N with a marking m is written as (N, m) and is called a *marked Petri net*.

Given a marked Petri net (N, m) with $N = (P, T, F)$, a transition $t \in T$ is *enabled*, denoted by $(N : m \xrightarrow{t})$, if ${}^\bullet t \le m$. If a transition is enabled in (N, m), it can *fire*. A transition firing, denoted by $(N : m \xrightarrow{t} m')$, results in a new marking $m' = m - {}^\bullet t + t^\bullet$. We lift the firing to sequences of transitions in the standard way. A sequence $\sigma \in T^*$ of length n is a *firing sequence* from m_0 to m_n, if there exist markings $m_i, m_{i+1} \in \mathbb{N}^P$ such that $(N : m_i \xrightarrow{\sigma(i)} m_{i+1})$ for all $0 \le i < n$. The set of reachable markings from a given marking m is denoted as $\mathcal{R}(N, m) = \{m' \mid \exists \sigma \in T^* : (N : m \xrightarrow{\sigma} m')\}$. We lift the set of reachable markings from a single marking to a set of markings in a standard way, i.e., given a set $M \subseteq \mathbb{N}^P$, $\mathcal{R}(N, M) = \bigcup_{m \in M} \mathcal{R}(N, m)$.

Given a marked Petri net (N, m_0) with $N = (P, T, F)$, a place $p \in P$ is called *k-bounded* for some $k \in \mathbb{N}$ if $m(p) \le k$ for all markings $m \in \mathcal{R}(N, m_0)$. If all places are k-bounded, we call (N, m_0) k-bounded. A transition $t \in T$ is called *live* if for all markings $m \in \mathcal{R}(N, m_0)$ there exist a firing sequence $\sigma \in T^*$ and a marking $m' \in \mathcal{R}(N, m)$ such that $(N : m \xrightarrow{\sigma} m' \xrightarrow{t})$. If all transitions of (N, m_0) are live, (N, m_0) is called live. A transition $t \in T$ is called *quasi-live* if there exists a marking $m \in \mathcal{R}(N, m_0)$ such that $(N : m \xrightarrow{t})$. If all transitions of (N, m_0) are quasi-live, the marked Petri net is called quasi-live. A marking $m \in \mathcal{R}(N, m_0)$ is called a *home marking* if $m \in \mathcal{R}(N, m')$ for all $m' \in \mathcal{R}(N, m_0)$. A reachable marking $m \in \mathcal{R}(N, m_0)$ is called a *deadlock* of (N, m_0) if there is no transition $t \in T$ with $(N : m \xrightarrow{t})$. Given a desired marking $f \in \mathcal{R}(N, m_0)$, a non-empty subset of markings $L \subseteq \mathcal{R}(N, m_0)$ is called a *live-lock* w.r.t f if (1) $f \notin \mathcal{R}(N, L)$, (2) no marking in L is a deadlock, and (3) $L = \mathcal{R}(N, L)$, i.e., from L the desired marking is not reachable, and no other marking than a marking in L can be reached from L.

For Petri nets, we define two classes based on their structure: S-Nets, also called state machines, and workflow nets. A Petri net $N = (P, T, F)$ is a *S-net* if $|{}^\bullet t| = 1$ and $|t^\bullet| = 1$ for all transitions $t \in T$.

Definition 2 (Workflow Net, Closure). *Let $N = (P, T, F)$ be a Petri net. It is a* workflow net *(WFN) if there exist two places $i \in P$ and $f \in P$, called the* initial place *and* final place *respectively, such that ${}^\bullet i = f^\bullet = \emptyset$, and all nodes of N are on a path from i to f. Its* closure *is the net $N^* = (P, T \cup \{t^*\}, F \cup \{(t^*, i), (f, t^*)\}$, where $t^* \notin T$.*

A workflow net is called *sound* if (1) it is weakly terminating, i.e., it always has the option to reach the final marking in which only the final place is marked, (2) it is properly completing, i.e., if in a marking the final place is marked, it is the only place marked, and (3) all transitions have a function, i.e., for every transition a reachable marking exists that enables the transition. Note that we use the classical soundness definition [1, 2].

Definition 3 (Soundness). *A workflow net $N = (P, T, F)$ with initial place i and final place f is called* sound *if (1) $[f]$ is a home marking of $(N, [i])$, (2) for any reachable marking $m \in \mathcal{R}(N, [i])$, if $m \geq [f]$ then $m = [f]$, and (3) $(N, [i])$ is quasi live.*

A WFN $N = (P, T, F)$ with initial place i is sound if and only if the marked Petri net $(N^*, [i])$ is live and bounded [1].

If we give a tuple a name, we subscript the elements with the name of the tuple, e.g. for $N = (A, B, C)$ we refer to its elements by A_N, B_N, and C_N. If the context is clear, we omit the subscript.

4   Components and Their Composition

In this paper, we use asynchronously communicating components [5,7]. We therefore model our components using Petri nets with interface places, called *open Petri nets* (OPNs). An OPN [3, 13] has two types of places: *internal places* for the inner control of the component, and *interface places* to communicate with its environment. An interface place is either an output place, i.e., it sends a message to the environment, or an input place, i.e., it requires a message from the environment. Further, a component has an initial and a final marking, defining the desired begin and end markings of the component.

Definition 4 (Component, Open Petri net, Skeleton, Open Workflow Net [3]). *An* open Petri net *(OPN), also called a* component, *is a 6-tuple (P, I, O, T, F, i, f) where*

- $((P \cup I \cup O, T, F), i)$ *is a marked Petri net;*
- P *is a set of* internal places;
- I *is a set of* input places, *and* $^{\bullet}I = \emptyset$;
- O *is a set of* output places, *and* $O^{\bullet} = \emptyset$;
- P, I *and* O *are pairwise disjoint;*
- $\forall t \in T : |(^{\bullet}t \cup t^{\bullet}) \cap (I \cup O)| \leq 1$; *and*
- $i \in \mathbb{N}^P$ *is the* initial marking; *and*
- $f \in \mathbb{N}^P$ *is the* final marking.

We call the set $I \cup O$ *the* interface places *of the OPN. We lift the notion of subnets to OPNs in the standard way. Two OPNs* N *and* M *are called* disjoint *if* $(P_N \cup I_N \cup O_N \cup T_N) \cap (P_M \cup I_M \cup O_M \cup T_M) = \emptyset$. *An OPN* N *is called* closed *if* $I_N = O_N = \emptyset$. *We write* $\mathcal{R}(N, m)$ *for* $\mathcal{R}((P_N \cup I_N \cup O_N, T_N, F_N), m)$ *for* $m \in \mathbb{N}^{P_N \cup I_N \cup O_N}$.

The skeleton *of* N *is defined as the Petri net* $\mathcal{S}(N) = (P_N, T_N, F)$ *with* $F = F_N \cap ((P_N \times T_N) \cup (T_N \times P_N))$. *For nodes* $n \in (P_N \cup T_N)$, *we write* $_N^{\circ}n$ *and* t_N° *as a shorthand for* $_{\mathcal{S}(N)}^{\bullet}t$ *and* $t_{\mathcal{S}(N)}^{\bullet}$, *respectively.*

If $\mathcal{S}(N)$ *is a workflow net with initial place* s *and final place* o, $i = [s]$ *and* $f = [o]$, N *is called an* open workflow net.

OPNs are composed with each other to build networks of communicating components. As a network of components can be used as a component again, the result of the composition is a component too. We say two OPNs are *composable* if the only elements shared between the two OPNs are their interface places, such that input places of the one are output places of the other and vice versa. Composition is then defined as the union of the two OPNs.

Definition 5 (Composition of OPNs [3]). *Two OPNs* A *and* B *are* composable, *denoted by* $A \oplus B$, *if and only if* $(P_A \cup I_A \cup O_A \cup T_A) \cap (P_B \cup I_B \cup O_B \cup T_B) = (O_A \cap I_B) \cup (I_A \cap O_B)$.

If A *and* B *are composable, their* composition *results in an OPN* $A \oplus B = (P_A \cup P_B \cup H, (I_A \cup I_B) \setminus H, (O_A \cup O_B) \setminus H, T_A \cup T_B, F_A \cup F_B, i_A + i_B, f_A + f_B)$ *with* $H = (O_A \cap I_B) \cup (I_A \cap O_B)$.

Note that two disjoint OPNs are composable by definition. Two important properties of composition are commutativity and projection, as shown in [18].

Corollary 6 (Commutativity, Projection Property [18]). *Let* A *and* B *be two composable OPNs. Then* $N = A \oplus B = B \oplus A$, *and* $(\mathcal{S}(A) : m_{|P_A} \xrightarrow{\sigma_{|T_A}} m'_{|P_A})$ *for any firing sequence* $\sigma \in T_N^*$ *and markings* $m, m' \in \mathbb{N}^{P_N}$ *such that* $(\mathcal{S}(N) : m \xrightarrow{\sigma} m')$.

The composition operator allows to create arbitrary networks of communicating components. As long as the interface places match, it is allowed to compose the components. However, it does not guarantee that the components communicate correctly. Composition is thus a syntactic check whether components are able to communicate.

Components communicate correctly if all components in the network are able to reach their desired final marking, and no messages are pending in one of the interface places. Further, we do not want to have transitions that are unreachable in the composition. To express this property, we use the notion of *soundness* for components: a component is sound if, ignoring the communication with other components in the network, (1) all components can reach their final marking, and (2) if all components reach their final marking, no tokens are left in the network.

Definition 7 (Soundness). *An OPN N is* sound *if:*

1. $\forall m \in \mathcal{R}(\mathcal{S}(N), i_N) : f_N \in \mathcal{R}(\mathcal{S}(N), m)$ *(weak termination); and*
2. $\forall m \in \mathcal{R}(\mathcal{S}(N), i_N) : m \geq f_N \implies m = f_N$ *(proper completion).*

Note that this soundness definition is stronger than the soundness notion used in [3,18], where soundness has been defined as weak termination of the skeleton.

A direct consequence of the projection property and soundness is that if in a composition between A, B and C, such that A and C are disjoint, and A and B are composable, as well as B and C, and B is in its final marking, then the other two components can reach their final marking as well.

Lemma 8. *Let A, B and C be three pairwise composable OPNs such that A and C are disjoint, and $A \oplus B$ and $B \oplus C$ are sound. Define $M = A \oplus B \oplus C$. Then $f_M \in \mathcal{R}(\mathcal{S}(M), m)$ for all markings $m \in \mathcal{R}(\mathcal{S}(M), i_M)$ such that $f_B \leq m$.*

Proof. Define $K = A \oplus B$ and $H = (I_A \cap O_B) \cup (I_B \cap O_A)$. Let $\sigma \in T_M^*$ such that $(\mathcal{S}(M) : i_M \xrightarrow{\sigma} m)$. By the projection property, $(\mathcal{S}(K) : i_K \xrightarrow{\sigma|_{T_K}} m_{|P_K})$. Since $f_B \leq m$, and by the weak termination property of K, there exists a firing sequence $\mu \in T_A^*$ such that $(\mathcal{S}(K) : m_{|P_K} \xrightarrow{\mu} f_K)$, and, by the proper completion of K, $f_{K|H} = \emptyset$. By the firing rule of Petri nets, also $(\mathcal{S}(M) : m \xrightarrow{\mu} m')$ for some $m' \in \mathbb{N}^{P_M}$ with $m'_{|P_K} = f_K$ and $m'_{|H} = \emptyset$.

Now, apply the same argument to m' and $L = B \oplus C$, which results in a firing sequence $\nu \in T_B^*$ and a marking $m'' \in \mathbb{N}^{P_M}$ such that $(\mathcal{S}(M) : m \xrightarrow{\mu} m' \xrightarrow{\nu} m'')$, $m''_{|P_L} = f_L$ and $m''_{|P_K} = f_K$. Hence $m'' = f_M$, which proves the statement. $\qquad\square$

5 Soundness Using Trusted Third Parties

Organizations have to cooperate more and more in order to do their business. However, they often do not want to share the way they operate, for example to hide internal business knowledge or intellectual property. An often proposed solution is a third party that is trusted by all organizations within the network. This third party, the notary, needs to ensure that it knows how the organizations within the network want to operate. On the one hand the notary needs to ensure that it works correctly with each individual organization, and on the other hand, that the network of all organizations, including the notary, is correct.

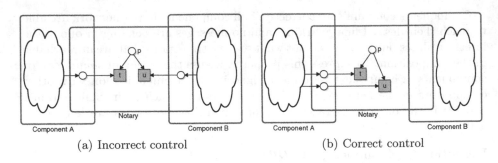

(a) Incorrect control   (b) Correct control

Fig. 3. Conflicts in a notary

As the main purpose of a notary is to ensure correct behavior of the communication between the two organizations that want to cooperate, we model the notary by an OWN. The main actions of the notary are the sending and receiving of messages of the different components. Therefore, each transition that is communicating is labeled with the sending or receiving of a message, or as silent if the transition represents an internal step of the notary. We restrict the notary to state machines, i.e., each notary is sound by its structure [11].

Definition 9 (Notary). *Let A and B be two disjoint OPNs. A notary, between A and B is an OWN N such that (1) both A and N, as well as B and N are composable, (2) $\mathcal{S}(N)$ is an S-net, (3) each transition is connected to at most one interface place, i.e., $|({}^\bullet t \cup t^\bullet) \cap (I \cup O)| \leq 1$ for all $t \in T$, and, (4) each interface place is connected to exactly one transition, i.e., $|{}^\bullet x \cup x^\bullet| = 1$ for all $x \in I \cup O$.*

As each transition is connected to at most one component, we introduce the communication function $C_N : T \to \{A, B, \tau\}$ by $C_N(t) = X$ iff ${}^\bullet t \cap O_X \neq \emptyset$ for $X \in \{A, B\}$ and $C_N(t) = \tau$ otherwise.

The composition of a notary between two parties A and B, is not directly sound if the compositions of the notary with A and of the notary with B are sound. One source of possible erroneous behavior lies in the control of conflicts: if in a notary two transitions share a place in their presets, then the transitions should either be both controlled by the same component, or by the notary.

Consider the examples of Fig. 3. Taking the composition $A \oplus N$ of Fig. 3(a), then transition u is always enabled if transition t is enabled, whereas in Fig. 3(b), component A controls the conflict in the composition of A and N.

To prevent this type of miscommunication, we introduce the *control conflict pattern*. A subnet within some OPN follows the control conflict pattern if all transitions of that subnet that are quasi-live in the OPN are controlled by the same component.

Definition 10 (Conflict Control Pattern). *Let N be an OPN. A subnet M of N follows the* conflict control pattern *if ${}^\circ t \leq m$ and ${}^\circ t \cap {}^\circ u \neq \emptyset$, then $C_N(t) = C_N(u)$ for all markings $m \in \mathcal{R}(\mathcal{S}(N), i_N)$ and transitions $t, u \in T_M$.*

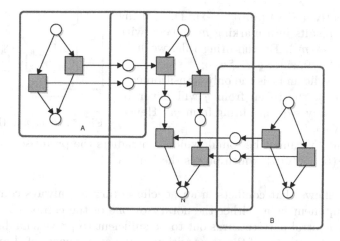

Fig. 4. Although N fulfills the control of conflict pattern, $A \oplus N \oplus B$ is not sound

In the remainder of this section, we will focus on two subclasses of notaries that ensure soundness: acyclic and simple-cyclic notaries.

5.1 Acyclic Notaries

The structural requirement imposed by the control of conflict pattern is not sufficient to conclude soundness. Consider for example the composition depicted in Fig. 4. Although all choices fulfill the conflict control pattern, the composition of $A \oplus N \oplus B$ is not sound. This problem is resolved by the additional requirement that both $A \oplus N$ and $N \oplus B$ have to be sound: as in the example the latter is not sound, the premisses are not satisfied.

For acyclic notaries, a stronger statement can be made: if for an acyclic notary N between components A and B both $A \oplus N$ and $N \oplus B$ are sound, then the notary follows the control conflict pattern.

Lemma 11 (Conflict Control). *Let A and B be two OPNs, and let N be an acyclic notary between A and B, such that $A \oplus N$ and $N \oplus B$ are sound. Then N follows the control conflict pattern in both $A \oplus N$ and $N \oplus B$.*

Proof. Define $K = X \oplus N$ with $X \in \{A, B\}$.

Let $m \in \mathcal{R}(\mathcal{S}(K), i_K)$ be a reachable marking that enables some transition $t \in T_N$ with ${}^\bullet t \cap I_N \neq \emptyset$, and let $u \in T_N$ such that ${}_N^\circ t = {}_N^\circ u$.

Define $q \in {}^\bullet t \cap I_N$. Then $m(q) > 0$. Suppose N does not follow the control conflict pattern, i.e., $C_N(t) \neq C_N(u)$. Then ${}_K^\circ u \subset {}_K^\circ t$ (see Fig. 5).

Consequently, $(\mathcal{S}(K) : m_{|P_K} \xrightarrow{u})$. Thus, firing transition u results in a marking $m' \in \mathbb{N}^{P_K}$ with $(\mathcal{S}(K) : m \xrightarrow{u} m')$. By the firing rule, we have $\bar{m}'(q) = m(q) > 0$, since $q \notin {}_K^{\circ}u$.

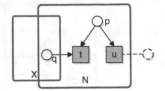

As N is acyclic and t is the only transition consuming from q, the token from q will never be consumed by any sequence firing from m'. Hence, $f_K \notin \mathcal{R}(\mathcal{S}(K), m')$.

Fig. 5. Place p in the OPN K

As a result, K cannot be sound, which contradicts the premises, and hence, we have $C_N(t) = C_N(u)$, which proves the lemma. □

The lemma shows that conflicts in an acyclic notary are always controlled by a single component being either the notary or one of the components A or B. The conflict control pattern turns out to be sufficient to prove soundness of the composition of the three, if the composition of the components of A and B with N individually is sound, as proven in the next theorem.

Theorem 12. *Let A and B be two OPNs such that A and B are disjoint. Let N be an acyclic notary between A and B. If $A \oplus N$ and $N \oplus B$ are sound, then $A \oplus N \oplus B$ is sound.*

Proof. Suppose $M = A \oplus N \oplus B$ is not sound. As notary N is acyclic, there exists a reachable marking $m \in \mathcal{R}(\mathcal{S}(M), i_M)$ with firing sequence $\sigma \in T_L^*$ such that (i) $(\mathcal{S}(M) : i_M \xrightarrow{\sigma} m)$, (ii) $f_M \notin \mathcal{R}(\mathcal{S}(M), m)$, and (iii) all firing sequences from $(\mathcal{S}(M), m)$ contain no transitions of T_N, i.e., for all firing sequences $\gamma \in T_M^*$ with $(\mathcal{S}(M) : m \xrightarrow{\gamma})$, we have $\gamma_{|T_N} = \emptyset$. Now there are two possible cases: either

1. Notary N is in its final place in this marking m, i.e. $m \geq f_N$, but A or B are not in their final markings; or
2. Notary N is not in its final marking, i.e., $m(f_N) = 0$.

The first case contradicts Lm. 8.

Consider the second case. As $m(f_N) = 0$ and $\mathcal{S}(N)$ is an S-net, there is a place $p \in P_N$ of the notary such that $m(p) > 0$. No transition of N will ever be enabled in any marking reachable from $(\mathcal{S}(M), m)$, and N is not in its final marking. By (iii), $p^\bullet$ cannot contain any transition t with $C_N(t) = \tau$. Due to Lm. 11, an $X \in \{A, B\}$ exists such that $C_N(u) = X$ for all transitions $u \in t^\bullet$.

Since the OPN $K = X \oplus N$ is sound, it is weakly terminating, Thus, there exists a firing sequence $\sigma \in T_X^*$, a marking $\bar{m}' \in \mathcal{R}(\mathcal{S}(K), m_{|P_K})$ and a transition $t \in p^\bullet$ such that $(\mathcal{S}(K) : m_{|P_K} \xrightarrow{\sigma} \bar{m}' \xrightarrow{t})$. Let q be the interface place connected to transition t, i.e., $q \in {}_N^\bullet t \cap I_N$. Then, $\bar{m}'(q) > 0$.

As $\sigma \in T_X^*$, it is also a firing sequence of $(\mathcal{S}(M), m)$. Thus, $(\mathcal{S}(M) : m \xrightarrow{\sigma} m')$ for some $m' \in \mathcal{R}(\mathcal{S}(M), m)$ and $m'_{|P_K} = \bar{m}'$. Hence, $m'(q) = \bar{m}'(q) > 0$. But then, transition $t \in T_N$ is enabled in $(\mathcal{S}(M), m')$, which contradicts the statement that no transition from T_N can fire starting from m in $(\mathcal{S}(M), m)$.

Therefore, $A \oplus N \oplus B$ is sound. □

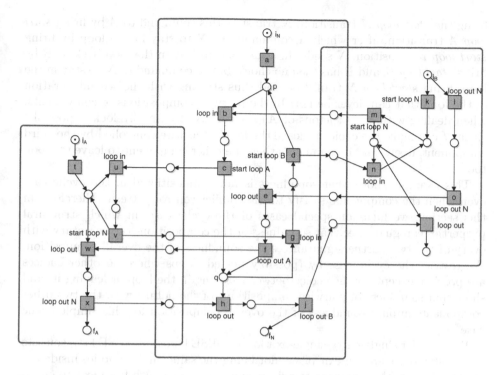

Fig. 6. Although the cyclic notary N satisfies the control of conflict pattern, $A \oplus N \oplus B$ is not sound

Returning to the payment service introduced in Sec. 2, this theorem shows that if the payment service works correctly with some debtor implementation, and if the service works correctly with some creditor implementation, i.e., the composition of the payment service with the debtor implementation and the composition of the payment service with the debtor implementation are sound, then the composition of the debtor implementation, the creditor implementation and the payment service is sound.

5.2 Simple Cyclic Notaries

Acyclic notaries ensure the correctness of the composition of two components if these components communicate correctly with the notary. Often, cyclic behavior between components is needed. For example, in order to agree on some quote, several cycles may be involved.

While in the acyclic case deadlock was the only kind of unsound behaviour, the cyclic case introduces a danger of obtaining livelocks in the compositions of components. Fig. 6 shows three components whose composition $A \oplus N \oplus B$ is not sound, while their pairwise compositions $A \oplus N$ and $N \oplus B$ are sound, and moreover, every conflict is resolved by one of the components, thus satisfying the conflict control pattern. If B chooses to start a loop resulting in a livelock by firing the *start loop N* transition, N transfers this command to A by firing *start loop A* transition, after which A commands to N to stay in the loop by firing *start loop N* transition. N sends the command to stay in the loop back to B by firing *start loop B*, and B has then no choice but to command to N to stay in the loop, firing *start loop N* transition and thus starting with the second iteration of the loop that can never be left. In the pairwise compositions of components, when dealing with the skeletons of $A \oplus N$ and $N \oplus B$, no livelock is possible, since N can make the choice to leave the loop, otherwise controlled by the third component, freely, and it commands then the other component to leave the loop too.

This example shows that soundness is not compositional in the cyclic case even when the components satisfy to the conflict control pattern. Therefore, in this section, we focus on special cases of the cyclic case, in which structural properties can guarantee that soundness of the compositions of the notary with every of the two partners guarantees the soundness of the overall composition. We restrict the cyclic case by (possibly nested) loops where no other choices are possible except for the choice between staying in the loop or leaving it, and show that soundness of pairwise compositions of the notary with the two other components implies soundness of the overall composition for this simple cyclic case.

We consider single-entry-single-exit loops (SESE loops). A SESE loop consists of an entry place and an exit place, not being the same, and all nodes inside the loop are on a path from entry to exit or vice versa, on a path from exit to entry. Furthermore, we require each place in the loop to have exactly one transition in its preset and one in its postset, except for the entry and exit place. An example of a SESE loop is depicted in Fig. 7(b).

In simple cyclic nets, each loop can be replaced by a place, which results in an acyclic S-net (see Fig. 7).

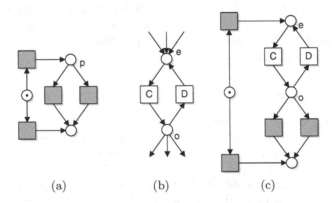

(a)   (b)   (c)

Fig. 7. An acyclic S-net (a), a single-entry-single-exit loop (b), and the refinement of place p in (a) with loop (b)

Definition 13 (SESE Loop). *A single-entry-single-exit loop (SESE loop) is a triple (L, e, o) where L is a strongly-connected S-net with $|P_L| > 1$ and $|{}^\bullet p| = |p^\bullet| = 1$ for all places $p \in P_L$; $e, o \in P_L$, with $e \neq o$, are the entry point and exit point, respectively, of the SESE loop.*

Definition 14 (Simple-cyclic S-net). *We define the class of simple cyclic nets (SCS nets) $\mathcal{N}$ inductively as follows:*

- *if N is an acyclic S-net, then $N \in \mathcal{N}$;*
- *Given an SCS-net $N \in \mathcal{N}$, a place $p \in P_N$ not being the entry or exit point of some loop, a SESE loop (L, e, o) such that L and N are disjoint. Then $(P, T, F) \in \mathcal{N}$, with $P = P_L \cup P_N \setminus \{p\}$, $T = T_N \cup T_L$, and $F = (F_N \setminus (({}^\bullet p \times \{p\}) \cup (\{p\} \times p^\bullet))) \cup F_L \cup ({}_N^\bullet p \times \{e\}) \cup (\{o\} \times p_N^\bullet).$*

By the definition of the SESE loop, if a node contains multiple elements in its preset or postset, it is either the entry or the exit of some (nested) loop. As a consequence, all SESE loops are simple: there is a unique acyclic path from the entry to the exit and a unique acyclic path from the exit to the entry. The basis of an SCS-net is an acyclic S-net.

Taking into account the lesson learnt from the acyclic case, we introduce a requirement with respect to the conflict control at the exits of loop:

Definition 15 (Loop Control Pattern). *Let N be a simple cyclic net. It satisfies the loop control pattern, if for every exit e of a SESE loop of N, for every $t, u \in e^\bullet : C_N(t) = C_N(u).$*

The net from Fig. 8 does not satisfy this pattern since $C_N(t) = A$, $C_N(u) = B$ and $C_N(v) = \tau$.

Similarly to the acyclic case, if the skeleton of a notary is a simple-cyclic S-net, soundness of the three parties is assured if the notary composed with each of the organizations individually is sound. As a consequence of the cyclic behaviour, we need not only to show that no deadlocks are possible but also that livelocks, like the one shown in Fig. 6 are not possible for simple-cyclic S-nets.

Theorem 16. *Let A and B be two disjoint OPNs and let N be a simple-cyclic S-net notary satisfying the loop control pattern. Then $A \oplus N \oplus B$ is sound if $A \oplus N$ and of $N \oplus B$ are sound.*

Proof. Define $K = A \oplus N$, $L = N \oplus B$ and $M = A \oplus N \oplus B$. Suppose M is not sound. Then there exists a marking $m \in \mathcal{R}(\mathcal{S}(M), i_M)$ such that $f_M \notin \mathcal{R}(\mathcal{S}(M), m)$. Lm. 8 implies that the final place f_N of notary N is not marked in m, i.e. $m(f_N) = 0$. By the definition of soundness, all the firing sequences from m lead either to a deadlock different from the desired final marking, or to a livelock.

First we prove that M has no deadlock. Suppose, some deadlock marking m' is reachable. By the projection property, $m'|_{P_K} \in \mathcal{R}(\mathcal{S}(K), i_K)$ and $m'|_{P_L} \in \mathcal{R}(\mathcal{S}(L), i_L)$. As K is sound, there exists a transition $u \in T_K$ such that $(\mathcal{S}(K) : m'|_{P_K} \xrightarrow{u})$. If $u \in T_A$ or $u \in T_N$ with $C_N(u) = \tau$, then transition u would also

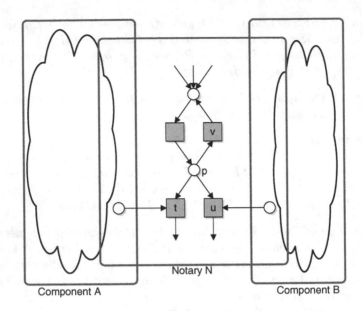

Fig. 8. Conflicts like the one between t, u and v are forbidden in a simple-cyclic notary satisfying the loop control pattern

be enabled in $(\mathcal{S}(M), m')$, hence, $u \in T_N$ with $C_N(u) = B$. Similarly, as L is sound, a transition $t \in T_N$ with $C_N(t) = A$ has to exist. This contradicts to the fact that N satisfies the loop control pattern. Thus, M has no deadlock.

Now, we prove that M has no livelock. Suppose that there is a livelock in M, meaning that there exists a non-empty subset of markings $X \subseteq \mathcal{R}(M, i_M)$ such that (1) $f \notin \mathcal{R}(M, X)$, (2) no marking in X is a deadlock, and (3) $X = \mathcal{R}(N, X)$, i.e., from X the desired marking is not reachable, and no other marking then a marking in X can be reached from X.

By the definition of simple-cyclic S-nets, we can conclude that the projection of X on P_N will give us singleton markings with tokens on the places of one or several SESE-loops. X contains thus a marking m with a token on the exit of some loop, let it be place $x \in P_N$. Since N satisfies the loop control pattern, we know that for the SESE-loop transition $t \in x^\bullet$ and any transition u leaving the SESE-loop from x, $C_N(t) = C_N(u)$. These transitions cannot be controlled by N, since otherwise u would be enabled whenever t is enabled. Thus they are controlled either by A or by B.

Since both K and L are sound and X is a livelock, we conclude that if these transitions are controlled by A, then B allows for any number of iterations on t, and another way around: if these transitions are controlled by B, then A allows for any number of iterations on t.

Finally, note that by the definition of SESE-loops no branching is possible within SESE-loops except for branching when choosing to re-iterate or to exit the loop. Then by combining the choices of A in $A \oplus N$ and of B in $N \oplus B$

on the number of iterations towards enabling u, we obtain the firing sequence in $A \oplus N \oplus B$ resulting in enabling transition u and thus leaving X, which contradicts the assumption that X is a livelock, which completes the proof.   □

6   Conclusions

We studied in this paper the problem of ensuring correctness of networks of co-operating organizations. By introducing a trusted third party, called a notary, organizations do not need to share their knowledge with the other organizations within the network. The notary needs to ensure that firstly it works correctly with each of the organizations individually, and secondly that all organizations in the network, including the notary itself, work correctly together. In this paper, we showed for two organizations and a notary that if the notary is an acyclic state machine, or if it contains only single-entry-single-exit (SESE) loops, then the notary ensures soundness if it is sound with each of the organizations individually.

Different approaches exist in literature. For example, in the approach of [4], the authors use contracts, implemented as public views. Organizations then need to implement their public views as a private view. If each of the private views agrees on the public view, the network is guaranteed to be correct. In [8], an interactive Petri net is designed, modeling the communication between different organizations.

The disadvantage of these approaches is that each of the organizations need to implement a private view, whereas often organizations already have existing components. In these approaches, the organizations have to re-engineer the existing components, and prove that these re-engineered components adhere to the views defined in the contract using e.g. accordance [15] or contract theory [6]. In the approach described in this paper, organizations can reuse existing components, as the approach requires an organization to cooperate correctly with the notary.

The setting in this paper is comparable with the more general setting of decentralized controllability [19], which is shown to be undecidable [20]. We limited ourselves to two organizations with a notary which is either acyclic or only contains SESE loops. Although these requirements are quite strong, they are needed to ensure soundness. Future work will be to search for more liberal notaries and to extend the results to service trees [3]. As shown in [18], soundness is not compositional, and additional requirements are needed.

References

1. van der Aalst, W.M.P.: Verification of Workflow Nets. In: Azéma, P., Balbo, G. (eds.) ICATPN 1997. LNCS, vol. 1248, pp. 407–426. Springer, Heidelberg (1997)
2. van der Aalst, W.M.P., van Hee, K.M., ter Hofstede, A.H.M., Sidorova, N., Verbeek, H.M.W., Voorhoeve, M., Wynn, M.T.: Soundness of workflow nets: classification, decidability, and analysis. Formal Aspects of Computing, 1–31 (2010)

3. van der Aalst, W.M.P., van Hee, K.M., Massuthe, P., Sidorova, N., van der Werf, J.M.E.M.: Compositional Service Trees. In: Franceschinis, G., Wolf, K. (eds.) PETRI NETS 2009. LNCS, vol. 5606, pp. 283–302. Springer, Heidelberg (2009)
4. van der Aalst, W.M.P., Lohmann, N., Massuthe, P., Stahl, C., Wolf, K.: Multi-party Contracts: Agreeing and Implementing Interorganizational Processes. The Computer Journal 53(1), 90–106 (2010)
5. Alonso, G., Casati, F., Kuno, H., Machiraju, V.: Web Services – Concepts, Architectures and Applications. Springer, Heidelberg (2004)
6. Bauer, S.S., David, A., Hennicker, R., Guldstrand Larsen, K., Legay, A., Nyman, U., Wąsowski, A.: Moving from specifications to contracts in component-based design. In: de Lara, J., Zisman, A. (eds.) Fundamental Approaches to Software Engineering. LNCS, vol. 7212, pp. 43–58. Springer, Heidelberg (2012)
7. Beisiegel, M., Khand, K., Karmarkar, A., Patil, S., Rowley, M.: Service Component Architecture Assembly Model Specification Version 1.1 (2010)
8. Decker, G., Weske, M.: Local Enforceability in Interaction Petri Nets. In: Alonso, G., Dadam, P., Rosemann, M. (eds.) BPM 2007. LNCS, vol. 4714, pp. 305–319. Springer, Heidelberg (2007)
9. Gamma, E., Helm, R., Johnson, R., Vlissides, J.: Design Patterns: Elements of Reusable Object-Oriented Software. Addison-Wesley (1994)
10. van Hee, K.M., Keiren, J., Post, R., Sidorova, N., van der Werf, J.M.E.M.: Designing case handling systems. In: Jensen, K., van der Aalst, W.M.P., Billington, J. (eds.) Transactions on Petri Nets and Other Models of Concurrency I. LNCS, vol. 5100, pp. 119–133. Springer, Heidelberg (2008)
11. van Hee, K.M., Sidorova, N., Voorhoeve, M.: Soundness and Separability of Workflow Nets in the Stepwise Refinement Approach. In: van der Aalst, W.M.P., Best, E. (eds.) ICATPN 2003. LNCS, vol. 2679, pp. 337–356. Springer, Heidelberg (2003)
12. van Hee, K.M., Sidorova, N., Voorhoeve, M., van der Werf, J.M.E.M.: Generation of database transactions with petri nets. Fundamenta Informaticae 93(1-3), 171–184 (2009)
13. Massuthe, P., Reisig, W., Schmidt, K.: An Operating Guideline Approach to the SOA. Annals of Mathematics, Computing & Teleinformatics 1(3), 35–43 (2005)
14. Mehandjiev, N., Grefen, P.W.P.J. (eds.): Dynamic Business Process Formation for Instant Virtual Enterprises. Springer, Berlin (2010)
15. Mooij, A.j., Stahl, C., Voorhoeve, M.: Relating fair testing and accordance for service replaceability. J. Log. Algebr. Program. 79(3-5), 233–244 (2010)
16. Reisig, W.: Petri Nets: An Introduction. Monographs in Theoretical Computer Science: An EATCS Series, vol. 4. Springer, Berlin (1985)
17. Rosa-Velardo, F., de Frutos-Escrig, D., Marroquín-Alonso, O.: On the expressiveness of Mobile Synchronizing Petri nets. In: Proceedings of the International Workshop on Security and Concurrency (SecCo 2005). ENTCS, vol. 1, pp. 77–94. Elsevier (2007)
18. van der Werf, J.M.E.M.: Compositional design and verification of component-based information systems. PhD thesis, Technische Universiteit Eindhoven (2011)
19. Wolf, K.: Does My Service Have Partners? In: Jensen, K., van der Aalst, W.M.P. (eds.) Transactions on Petri Nets and Other Models of Concurrency II. LNCS, vol. 5460, pp. 152–171. Springer, Heidelberg (2009)
20. Wolf, K.: Decidability Issues for Decentralized Controllability of Open Nets. In: 17th German Workshop on Algorithms and Tools for Petri Nets, vol. 643, pp. 124–129. CEUR-WS (2010)

Hybrid Petri Nets
for Modelling the Eukaryotic Cell Cycle

Mostafa Herajy[1], Martin Schwarick[2], and Monika Heiner[2]

[1] Port Said University, Faculty of Science,
Department of Mathematics and Computer Science,
42521 - Port Said, Egypt
[2] Brandenburg University of Technology at Cottbus,
Computer Science Institute,
Data Structures and Software Dependability,
Postbox 10 13 44, 03044 Cottbus, Germany
http://www-dssz.informatik.tu-cottbus.de/

Abstract. System level understanding of the repetitive cycle of cell growth and division is crucial for disclosing many unknown principles of biological organisms. The deterministic or stochastic approach – when deployed separately – are not sufficient to study such cell regulation due to the complexity of the reaction network and the existence of reactions at different time scales. Thus, an integration of both approaches is advisable to study such biochemical networks. In this paper we show how Generalised Hybrid Petri Nets can be used to intuitively represent and simulate the eukaryotic cell cycle. Our model captures intrinsic as well as extrinsic noise and deploys stochastic as well as deterministic reactions. Additionally, marking-dependent arc weights are biologically motivated and introduced to Snoopy – a tool for animating and simulating Petri nets in various paradigms.

Keywords: Generalised hybrid Petri nets, hybrid modelling, eukaryotic cell cycle, Snoopy, marking-dependent arc weight.

1 Introduction

The reproduction of eukaryotic cells is controlled by a complex regulatory network of reactions known as cell cycle [19,20,24]. During a cell cycle, cells grow, replicate and divide into two daughter cells [13,21]. This regulation cycle consists of four phases: S phase (synthesis) and M phase (mitosis) separated by two gap phases: G1 and G2 [24]. During the S phase, the cell replicates all of its components, while it divides each component more or less evenly between the two daughter cells at the end of the M phase [13]. After the S phase, there is a gap (G2) where the cell ensures that the duplication of DNA has been completed and prepares itself for mitosis. Newborn cells are not immediately replicated, instead they are located at the G1 gap. The processes of synthesis and mitosis alternate during the reproduction process; see Figure 1 for a graphical illustration of the cell cycle regulation process. Please note that the phases G1, S, and

M. Koutny et al. (Eds.): ToPNoC VIII, LNCS 8100, pp. 123–141, 2013.

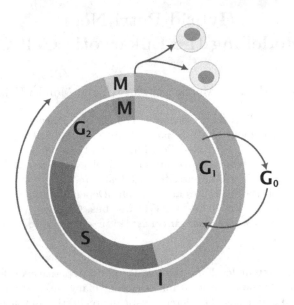

Fig. 1. Graphical illustration of the cell cycle [27]. The cell cycle consists of four distinct phases: G_1, synthesis (S), G_2, and mitosis (M), respectively. The first three phases are known as interphase (referred to by the outer ring). Cells that have stopped dividing enter the G_0 phase.

G2 are commonly subsumed as interphase as indicated by the outer cycle in that figure. Understanding such control cycles is crucial for revealing defects in cell growth that underlies many human diseases (e.g., cancer) [25].

In the eukaryotic cell cycle, the alternation between the S and the M phase as well as the balance of growth and division is governed by the activity of a family of cyclin-dependent protein kinases (CDK) [24]. Therefore, many computational models have been constructed to study the control system of CDK (e.g., in [1,13,19,20,24]). Some of these models are based on the deterministic approach which represents changes of species concentrations as continuous variables which evolve deterministically and continuously with respect to time (in the following called *continuous simulation*). However, an important requirement of the cell cycle model is to capture the variability of the cellular volume to reproduce the "in vivo" experiment results. Unfortunately, the deterministic approach cannot capture such cellular volume variability [20]. Motivated by this argument, a number of stochastic models have been created and simulated using either a stochastic simulation algorithm (e.g., [13]) or by introducing noise to the model through Langevin equation [22]. However, the stochastic approach is computationally expensive, particularly when the model under study contains reactions with high rates and/or species with large numbers of molecules.

The eukaryotic cell cycle model does indeed exhibit high rates of some reactions, while some other reactions have low rates, which are responsible for the intrinsic noise due to molecular fluctuations [13]. Similarly, the model contains some species with a large number of molecules, while some other species have a few number of molecules. The existence of reactions at different time scales (fast and slow) suggests a simulation using a hybrid approach.

Generalised Hybrid Petri Nets ($\mathcal{GHPN}_{bio}$) have been introduced in [10], [11] and [12], to represent and simulate stiff biochemical networks where fast reactions are represented and simulated continuously, while slow reactions are carried out stochastically. $\mathcal{GHPN}_{bio}$ provide rich modelling and simulation functionalities by combining all features of Continuous Petri Nets [3] and Extended Stochastic Petri Nets [16], including three types of deterministic transitions. Moreover, the partitioning of reaction networks (i.e., the assignment of each reaction to either the stochastic or the continuous paradigm) can either be done off-line (statically, i.e., before the simulation starts) or on-line (dynamically, i.e., while the simulation is in progress). The implementation of $\mathcal{GHPN}_{bio}$ is available as part of Snoopy [7] - a tool to design and animate or simulate hierarchical graphs, among them qualitative, stochastic, continuous and hybrid Petri nets. Indeed, the cell cycle model turns out to be an ideal case study where the majority of the $\mathcal{GHPN}_{bio}$ features can be demonstrated. Moreover, it makes a strong case for the introduction of marking-dependent arc weights.

Another hybrid net class which provides functionalities related to $\mathcal{GHPN}_{bio}$ is known as Hybrid Functional Petri nets (HFPN) [18]. However, HFPN have been developed to focus on hybrid (discrete/continuous) model construction where stochastic transitions are not required. Moreover, modelling features like logical nodes, hierarchy, and modifier arcs, which are imperative when considering larger models, are not supported [7].

In this paper we present another argument to motivate hybrid simulation of the cell cycle control system. The cell cycle model contains some reactions which would be better represented as continuous processes, specifically the growth of the cellular volume needs to be treated continuously, while other reactions of low rates have to be considered as stochastic processes. For instance, Mura and Csikasz-Nagy constructed in [19] a stochastic version of the model in [1] using stochastic Petri nets. However, they could not intuitively represent the cell growth process which evolves continuously and exponentially with respect to time using stochastic Petri net primitives only. Indeed, cell growth is a typical example where continuous transitions are an appropriate means.

This paper is organised as follows: we start off by pinpointing some related work. After that, a brief introduction of Generalised Hybrid Petri Nets is presented. To conveniently model the cell cycle regulation behaviour, we extend the formal definition of $\mathcal{GHPN}_{bio}$, as they have been introduced in [10], to include marking-dependent arc weights. Next, we discuss a hybrid Petri net model of the eukaryotic cell cycle and discuss in detail some of its key modelling components. In Section 5 we show the simulation results produced by Snoopy's hybrid simulation engine and compare them to the continuous and stochastic ones. Finally, we sum up with conclusions and outlook.

2   Related Work

Mura and Csikasz-Nagy converted the deterministic model of Chen et al. [1] into a stochastic Petri net [19] to study the effect of noise on cell cycle progression. However, some components could not intuitively be modelled using stochastic Petri net primitives only (e.g., cell growth). Moreover, their model is based on phenomenological rate laws (e.g., Michaelis-Menten) which do not work well with stochastic simulation algorithms [13]. Sabouri-Ghomi et al. [20], and Kar et al. [13] asserted that applying Gillespie's stochastic simulation algorithm [4,5] directly to phenomenological rate laws might produce incorrect results. Therefore, they unpacked the deterministic model of Tyson-Novak [24] (who use non-elementary reaction kinetics, e.g., Michaelis Menten and Hill functions) to express it completely in terms of elementary mass-action kinetics. The Tyson-Novak model is based on a bistable switch between the complex CycB-Cdk1 (denoted by variable X) and the complex Cdh1-APC (denoted by the variable Y). CycB-Cdk1 phosphorylates Cdh1-APC and free Cdh1-APC catalyses the degradation of CycB-Cdk1. Figure 2 presents a continuous Petri net representation of the Tyson-Novak model. To model a complete cell cycle, Kar et al. [13] unpacked the effect of Cdc20 and Cdc14 which are lumped in the variable Z in the Tyson-Novak model. High activity of CycB-Cdk1 promotes the synthesis of Cdc20 which activates Cdc14. Finally the dephosphorylated Cdc14 activates Cdh1-APC. The Kar et al. model accounts for both intrinsic and extrinsic noise. Intrinsic noise is due to the fluctuation of species with low numbers of molecules, while extrinsic noise is due to the unequal division of the cell between the two daughter cells [13].

In [2] and [17], two detailed HFPN models are constructed for the Fission yeast and Xenopus cell cycles, respectively. However, intrinsic noise, which is necessary for reproducing the variability of the cellular volume, is not captured because HFPN do not support the (full) interplay between stochastic and continuous regimes. Thus, these models are built using the hybrid (discrete/continuous) paradigm.

In [21], a hybrid model, which combines ordinary differential equations (ODEs) and discrete boolean networks, has been constructed to integrate quantitative as well as qualitative parts in one model. The latter approach requires less knowledge of realistic kinetic rate constants. Liu et al. [15] simulate the stochastic model of [13] using the Haseltine and Rawlings approach [6]. However, such models cannot be represented structurally or graphically which makes their maintenance and extension more difficult.

In this paper a hybrid Petri net model of the eukaryotic cell cycle is presented as a sophisticated example for the kind of hybrid models that can be constructed using $\mathcal{GHPN}_{bio}$. The model is hybrid in the sense that it combines continuous, stochastic and immediate transitions to represent deterministic, stochastic and control behaviour. Our main goal is to show how such a class of models is intuitively represented and executed using hybrid Petri net primitives. Besides, Petri nets analysis tools can be applied to the constructed models as well [8]. Using Snoopy's simulator, cell cycle models incorporating continuous net components can be simulated using either the continuous or hybrid engine.

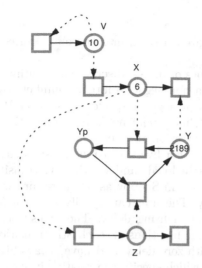

Fig. 2. A continuous Petri net representation of the Tyson-Novak model [24]: X (*CycB-Cdk1*) phosphorylates Y (*Cdh1-APC*) and free Y catalyses the degradation of X. Z denotes the effects of *Cdc20* and *Cdc14*. High activity of X promotes the synthesis of *Cdc20* which activates *Cdc14*. The dephosphorylated *Cdc14* activates Y. This behaviour results in a bistable switch that is responsible for the transitions between *G1* and *S-G2-M* states.

3   Generalised Hybrid Petri Nets

To model stiff biochemical networks, $\mathcal{GHPN}_{bio}$ [10] combine both stochastic and continuous elements in one and the same model. Indeed, continuous and stochastic Petri nets complement each other. Fluctuation and discreteness can conveniently be modelled and simulated in the stochastic paradigm and at the same time, the computational expensive parts can be simulated deterministically via ODE solvers. Modelling and efficient simulation of stiff biochemical networks (i.e., networks that contain reactions at more than one time scale) are helpful functionalities that $\mathcal{GHPN}_{bio}$ provide for systems biology.

Generally speaking, biochemical systems can involve reactions from more than one type of biological networks, for instance gene regulation, metabolic pathways or signal transduction pathways. Incorporating reactions which belong to distinct (biological) network types, tends to result into stiff systems. This follows from the fact that, e.g., species in gene regulation networks may contain few numbers of molecules, while species in metabolic networks often contain large numbers of molecules [14].

In the rest of this section, we will give a brief introduction of $\mathcal{GHPN}_{bio}$ in terms of the graphical representation of its elements as well as the firing rule and connectivity between the continuous and stochastic net parts. The formal semantics is given in [10].

3.1 Elements

The $\mathcal{GHPN}_{bio}$ elements are classified into three categories: places, transitions, and arcs.

$\mathcal{GHPN}_{bio}$ offer two types of places: discrete and continuous. A discrete place (single line circle) holds a non-negative integer number which represents, e.g., the number of molecules of a given species (tokens in Petri net notions). A continuous place (shaded line circle) holds a non-negative real number which represents, e.g., the concentration of a given species.

Furthermore, $\mathcal{GHPN}_{bio}$ offer five transition types: stochastic, immediate, deterministically delayed, scheduled, and continuous transitions [8]. Stochastic transitions, which are drawn in Snoopy as a square, fire with an exponentially distributed random delay. The user can specify a set of firing rate functions, which determine the random firing delay. The transitions' pre-places can be used to define the firing rate functions of stochastic transitions. Immediate transitions (black bar) fire with zero delay, and have always highest priority to fire. They may carry weights which specify the relative firing frequency in the case of conflicts between immediate transitions. Deterministically delayed transitions (black square) fire after a specified constant time delay. Scheduled transitions (grey square) fire at user-specified absolute time points. Continuous transitions (shaded line square) fire continuously in the same way like in continuous Petri nets. Their semantics is governed by ODEs which define the continuous change in the transitions' pre- and post-places. More details about the biochemical interpretation of deterministically delayed, scheduled, and immediate transitions can be found in [9] and [16]. To simplify the presentation, we occasionally refer to stochastic, immediate, deterministically delayed or scheduled transitions as discrete transitions.

The connection between those two types of nodes (places and transitions) takes place using a set of different arcs (edges). $\mathcal{GHPN}_{bio}$ offer six types of arcs: standard, inhibitor, read, equal, reset and modifier arcs. Standard arcs connect transitions with places or vice versa. They can be discrete, i.e., carry non-negative integer-valued weights (stoichiometry in the biochemical context), or continuous, i.e., carry non-negative real-valued weights. In addition to their influence on the enabling of transitions, they also affect the place marking when a transition fires by removing (adding) tokens from (to) the transition's pre-places (post-places).

Extended arcs like inhibitor, read, equal, reset, and modifier arcs can only be used to connect places with transitions, but not vice versa. A transition connected with an inhibitor arc is enabled (with respect to this pre-place) if the marking of the pre-place is less than the arc weight. Contrary, a transition connected with a read arc is enabled if the marking of the pre-place is greater than or equal to the arc weight. Similarly, a transition connected using an equal arc is enabled if the marking of the pre-place is equal to the arc weight.

The other two remaining arcs do not affect the enabling of transitions. A reset arc is used to reset a place marking to zero when the corresponding transition fires. Modifier arcs permit to include any place in the transitions' rate functions and simultaneously preserve the net structure restriction.

Places

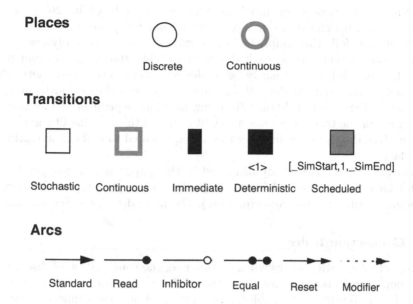

Transitions

Arcs

Fig. 3. Graphical representation of the $\mathcal{GHPN}_{bio}$ elements. Places are classified as discrete and continuous, transitions as stochastic, continuous, immediate, deterministically delayed, and scheduled, and arcs as standard, inhibitor, read, equal, reset, and modifier.

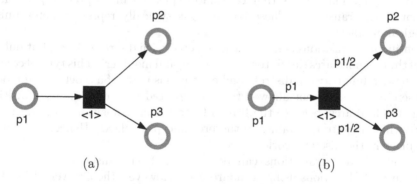

Fig. 4. Marking-dependent arc weights illustrated by a simple biological example. (a) cell division cannot be modelled, (b) cell division can intuitively be modelled. The numbers between angle brackets are the delays of the deterministically delayed transitions. Later we will assume that cell division does not consume time.

The connection rules and their underlying formal semantics are discussed in more details below. Figure 3 provides a graphical illustration of all elements. Although this graphical notation is the default one, it can easily be customised using Snoopy, the Petri nets editing tool. To support special modelling requirements of some biological models (e.g., the cell cycle model), we extended $\mathcal{GHPN}_{bio}$ to permit pre-places of a transition as arc weight, similar to the idea of self-modifying nets which has been originally introduced in [26], or even a function which is defined in terms of a transition's pre-places [18].

Consider the following simple biological example. When a cell divides its mass between two daughter cells, each daughter obtains approximately half of the mass. This example cannot easily be modelled using discrete Petri nets. Moreover, there is no way to model it if the mass is represented by a continuous place as shown in Figure 4a. In Figure 4b, using marking-dependent arc weights; the ingoing arc of the transition t has a weight equal to the marking of the place p_1, while each of the two outgoing arcs has a weight equal to half of the marking of that place.

Motivated by the case study discussed in this paper, marking-dependent arc weights have been introduced for the majority of arc types supported by Snoopy (standard, read, inhibitor, and equal arc). For more details see Section 4.2.

3.2   Connection Rules

An important question arises when considering the combination of discrete and continuous elements: how are these two different parts connected with each other? Figure 5 provides a graphical illustration of how the connection between different elements of $\mathcal{GHPN}_{bio}$ takes place.

First, we will consider the connection between continuous transitions and the other elements of $\mathcal{GHPN}_{bio}$. Continuous transitions can be connected with continuous places in both directions using continuous arcs (i.e., arcs with real-valued weight). This means that continuous places can be pre- or post-places of continuous transitions. These connections typically represent deterministic biological interactions.

Continuous transitions can also be connected with discrete places, but only by one of the extended arcs (inhibitor, read, equal, and modifier). This type of connection allows a link between discrete and continuous parts of a biochemical model.

Discrete places are not allowed to be connected with continuous transitions using standard arcs, because the firing of continuous transitions is governed by ODEs which require real values in the pre- and post-places. Hence, this cannot take place in the discrete world.

Second, discrete transitions can be connected with discrete or continuous places in both directions using standard arcs. However, the arc weight needs to be considered. The connection between discrete transitions and discrete places takes place using arcs with non-negative integer numbers, while the connection between continuous places and discrete transitions is weighted by non-negative real numbers. The general rule to determine the weight type of arcs is to follow the type of the connected place.

3.3   Formal Definition

In this section, the syntax of $\mathcal{GHPN}_{bio}$ is formally defined to include the making-dependent arc weight. The formal semantics including the enabling and firing rules as well as the conflict resolution are given in [10].

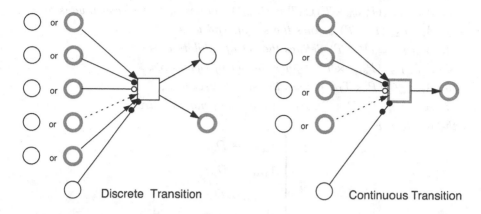

Fig. 5. Possible connections between $\mathcal{GHPN}_{bio}$ elements. The restrictions are: discrete places cannot be connected with continuous transitions using standard arcs, continuous places cannot be tested with equal arcs, and continuous transitions cannot use reset arcs.

Definition 1 (Generalised Hybrid Petri Nets). *A Generalised Hybrid Petri Net is a 6-tuple $\mathcal{GHPN}_{bio} = [P, T, A, F, V, m_0]$, where P, T are finite, non-empty and disjoint sets. P is the set of places, and T is the set of transitions with:*

- *$P = P_{disc} \cup P_{cont}$ whereby P_{disc} is the set of discrete places to which non-negative integer values are assigned, and P_{cont} is the set of continuous places to which non-negative real values are assigned.*
- *$T = T_D \cup T_{cont}$,*
  $T_D = T_{stoch} \cup T_{im} \cup T_{timed} \cup T_{scheduled}$ with:
  1. *T_{stoch} is the set of stochastic transitions, which fire randomly after exponentially distributed waiting time.*
  2. *T_{im} is the set of immediate transitions, which fire with waiting time zero; they have higher priority compared with other transitions.*
  3. *T_{timed} is the set of deterministically delayed transitions, which fire after a deterministic time delay.*
  4. *$T_{scheduled}$ is the set of scheduled transitions, which fire at predefined time points.*
  5. *T_{cont} is the set of continuous transitions, which fire continuously over time.*
- *$A = A_{disc} \cup A_{cont} \cup A_{inhibit} \cup A_{read} \cup A_{equal} \cup A_{reset} \cup A_{modifier}$ is the set of directed arcs, with:*
  1. *$A_{disc} \subseteq ((P \times T) \cup (T \times P))$ defines the set of discrete arcs.*

2. $A_{cont} \subseteq ((P_{cont} \times T) \cup (T \times P_{cont}))$ *defines the set of continuous arcs.*
3. $A_{read} \subseteq (P \times T)$ *defines the set of read arcs.*
4. $A_{inhibit} \subseteq (P \times T)$ *defines the set of inhibits arcs.*
5. $A_{equal} \subseteq (P_{disc} \times T)$ *defines the set of equal arcs.*
6. $A_{reset} \subseteq (P \times T_D)$ *defines the set of reset arcs,*
7. $A_{modifier} \subseteq (P \times T)$ *defines the set of modifier arcs.*

— *the function F*

$$
F : \begin{cases}
A_{cont} \to D_q, \\[4pt]
A_{disc} \to D_n, \\[4pt]
A_{read} \to D_q, \\[4pt]
A_{inhibit} \to D_q, \\[4pt]
A_{equal} \to D_n, \\[4pt]
A_{reset} \to \{1\}, \\[4pt]
A_{modifier} \to \{1\}.
\end{cases}
$$

assigns a marking-dependent function to each arc, where D_n and D_q are sets of functions defined as follows:

$$
D_n = \{d_n | d_n : \mathbb{N}_0^{|{}^{\bullet}t_j|} \to \mathbb{N}, t_j \in T\},
$$

$$
D_q = \{d_q | d_q : \mathbb{R}_0^{|{}^{\bullet}t_j|} \to \mathbb{Q}^+, t_j \in T\}.
$$

— *V is a set of functions $V = \{g, d, w, f\}$ where :*
1. $g : T_{stoch} \to H_s$ *is a function which assigns a stochastic hazard function h_{s_t} to each transition $t_j \in T_{stoch}$, whereby $H_s = \{h_{s_t} | h_{s_t} : \mathbb{R}_0^{|{}^{\bullet}t_j|} \to \mathbb{R}_0^+, t_j \in T_{stoch}\}$ is the set of all stochastic hazard functions, and $g(t_j) = h_{s_t}, \forall t_j \in T_{stoch}$.*
2. $w : T_{im} \to H_w$ *is a function which assigns a weight function h_w to each immediate transition $t_j \in T_{im}$, such that $H_w = \{h_{w_t} | h_{w_t} : \mathbb{R}_0^{|{}^{\bullet}t_j|} \to \mathbb{R}_0^+, t_j \in T_{im}\}$ is the set of all weight functions, and $w(t_j) = h_{w_t}, \forall t_j \in T_{im}$.*
3. $d : T_{timed} \cup T_{scheduled} \to \mathbb{R}_0^+$, *is a function which assigns a constant time to each deterministically delayed and scheduled transition representing the (relative or absolute) waiting time.*
4. $f : T_{cont} \to H_c$ *is a function which assigns a rate function h_c to each continuous transition $t_j \in T_{cont}$, such that $H_c = \{h_{c_t} | h_{c_t} : \mathbb{R}_0^{|{}^{\bullet}t_j|} \to \mathbb{R}_0^+, t_j \in T_{cont}\}$ is the set of all rates functions and $f(t_j) = h_{c_t}, \forall t_j \in T_{cont}$.*

– $m_0 = m_{disc} \cup m_{cont}$ *is the initial marking for both the continuous and discrete places, whereby* $m_{cont} \in \mathbb{R}_0^{|P_{cont}|}$, $m_{disc} \in \mathbb{N}_0^{|P_{disc}|}$.

Here, $\mathbb{N}$ *denotes the set of natural numbers excluding 0,* $\mathbb{N}_0$ *denotes the set of non-negative integer numbers,* $\mathbb{R}_0$ *denotes the set of non-negative real numbers,* $\mathbb{Q}^+$ *denotes the set of positive rational numbers, and* $^\bullet t_j$ *denotes the set of pre-places of a transition* t_j.

$\square$

A distinguishing feature of $\mathcal{GHPN}_{bio}$ compared with other hybrid Petri net classes is its support of the full interplay between stochastic and continuous transitions. Such interplay is implemented by updating and monitoring the rates of stochastic transitions while numerically solving the set of ODEs induced by the continuous transitions (For more details see [10]). By this way, accurate results are obtained during simulation.

4 The Model

Figure 6 shows the hybrid Petri net model which has been developed based on the previous one introduced by Kar et al. in [13]. Proteins, genes, and mRNAs are represented by places, reactions by transitions. We use the same kinetic parameters and initial values as in [13]. For the sake of space we do not repeat the kinetic parameters, but the initial marking is shown on the places. Moreover, we use Snoopy's logical node feature to simplify the connections between nodes. For example, place X and Y are involved in many reactions which decreases the network's readability. We repeat those nodes multiple times with the same names to keep the model understandable (logical places). Likewise, the transition *divide* is a logical transition. Furthermore, the increase of the cellular volume is intuitively represented using a continuous transition with a rate $\mu \cdot V$, where μ is the growth factor and V is the cellular volume, modelled as a continuous place.

The model contains three different transition types: continuous, stochastic, and immediate. Continuous transitions simulate the corresponding reactions deterministically, while stochastic transitions carry them out stochastically. The latter transitions are responsible for molecular fluctuations. Immediate transitions monitor the model evolution and perform the division when the free number of molecules of $Cdh1\_APC$ reaches a certain threshold ($\hat{Y} = Y + Y\_X + X\_Y$).

In the sequel we discuss in more detail some of the model's key components and the corresponding $\mathcal{GHPN}_{bio}$ representations.

4.1 Decision to Perform Division

In this section we consider the process of division in more detail. When the number of molecules of $\hat{Y}$ becomes greater than a certain threshold (in our case

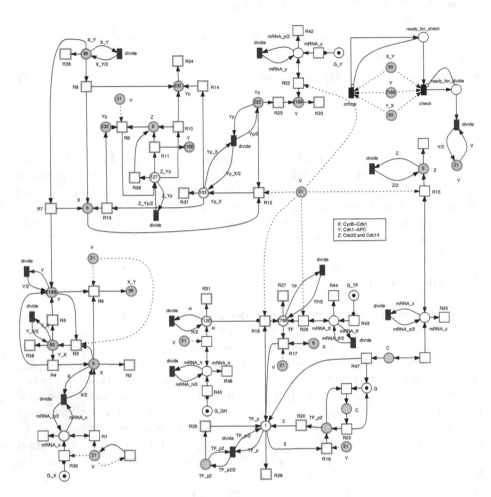

Fig. 6. A $\mathcal{GHPN}_{bio}$ representation of the eukaryotic cell cycle. The model employs different types of transitions: continuous, stochastic and immediate. All reactions affecting mRNAs are represented and simulated stochastically. Repetitive nodes (places and transitions) with same names are logical nodes. When the immediate transition *divide* fires, it divides the current place marking more or less equally. Equal division means that the cellular volume of the daughter cell is always half of its parent. This model could be easily extended to permit unequal division, where a random variation in the cellular volume is possible, by having arc weights with random functions. The unequal division type will reproduce extrinsic noise. The type of division (equal, or unequal) depends on the outgoing arc weight and its effect is implemented by marking-dependent arc weights.

1200), the cell divides the cellular volume and other components (e.g., mRNAs) between the two daughter cells. In Figure 7a, this process is represented by the immediate transition *check* with a weight defined by the Boolean expression $\hat{Y} > threshold$ (the weight is 0 if the Boolean expression yields false, and 1 for the result true). Recall that weights of immediate transitions determine the firing frequencies of immediate transitions in the case of conflicts. A weight of zero means that a transition cannot fire at all. However, when the transition *check* has a weight of one, it adds a token to the place *ready_to_divide* which triggers the transition *divide* to carry out the division. To give the transition *divide* a chance to fire before re-checking the value of $\hat{Y}$, an inhibitor arc is used as constraint. Please note that the transitions *critical* and *check* need the current marking of the places X_Y, Y, and Y_X only to calculate the term $\hat{Y}$ in the transitions' weight. Therefore, modifier arcs are used to fulfil this requirement.

An interesting characteristics of the model is the division process. Although the division can take place when the value of $\hat{Y}$ is greater than a certain threshold, it does not do that all the times. For example, at the beginning of the simulation, the initial value of $\hat{Y}$ satisfies the division criteria. However; the cell should not divide because it is still at G1 phase which means that it has to replicate itself before it can divide. We model these cases by adding a new immediate transition which detects the critical value of $\hat{Y}$, before checking for division. Therefore the transition *critical* monitors the value of $\hat{Y}$. When the value of $\hat{Y}$ goes below a certain threshold, it enables the division process.

4.2   Cell Division and Marking-Dependent Arc Weights

When a cell divides, it splits all of its components more or less evenly between the two daughter cells. This is most naturally expressed with marking-dependent arc weights [26]. In Figure 7a, when the transition *divide* fires, it removes all of the current marking of the place V and adds $V/2$ to it. To permit uneven division of the cell volume and other components, arc weights can be a function which operates on the current place marking [18]. However, we restrict the places used in arc weights to a transition's pre-places to keep the locality principle Petri nets are famous for.

Figure 7b illustrates the process of cell division graphically by showing a simulation trace.

Moreover, all proteins and mRNAs have to undergo such division. This means the transition *divide* has to be connected with each place in the net that represents a protein or mRNA. The ingoing arc weight of such a connection is equal to the pre-place's current marking, while the outgoing arc weight is equal to half of the pre-place's current marking. Furthermore, the markings of discrete places are rounded after the division process to preserve the discrete representation of the molecular species.

4.3   Transition Partitioning

The model in Figure 6 contains transitions which fire at different rates. For instance, transition R_3 fires more frequently than R_1 as illustrated in Figure

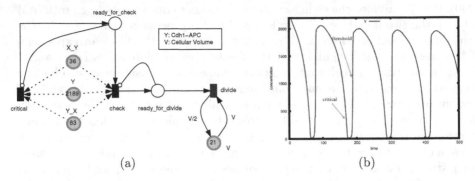

(a)   (b)

Fig. 7. Cell Division (a) A sub-net for modelling the decision of the division process (see also upper right corner of Figure 6). The transition *critical* monitors the value of $\hat{Y}$ and adds a token to *ready_for_check* when $\hat{Y} < 300$. Later, when the value of $\hat{Y}$ increases and becomes greater than a certain threshold (1200), the transition *check* fires and adds a token to *ready_for_divide* which signals the transition *divide* to perform the division. Inhibitor arcs are used as checkpoints for the sequence of events: critical → check → divide. (b) Hybrid simulation trace of cell division.

8a. Slow transitions should be simulated stochastically to account for molecular fluctuations, while fast transitions need to be simulated continuously for the sake of numerical efficiency. Indeed, transitions of the latter type consume the majority of computational resources.

In this model, transitions are statically partitioned before the simulation starts. The transition type is determined by executing a single run and analysing the results as shown in Figure 8. Increasing (decreasing) the accuracy of the simulation results involves converting more continuous (stochastic) transitions into stochastic (continuous) ones.

Another approach for partitioning is to perform it dynamically during the simulation. Using this technique, a transition changes its type from stochastic to continuous or vice versa according to the current firing rate. $\mathcal{GHPN}_{bio}$ provide the user with a trade-off between efficiency and accuracy by permitting the user to specify two thresholds: $a_{0_{min}}$ and $a_{0_{max}}$, the minimum and maximum cumulative propensity (i.e., the total rates of stochastic transitions), respectively. Moreover, two other thresholds are required to perform dynamic partitioning: the place marking threshold and the transition rate threshold. The former is used to ensure that species concentrations are large enough to be simulated continuously, while the latter is used to partition transitions into fast and slow based on their rates. A transition is simulated continuously, if its rate exceeds the rate threshold and the marking of all its pre-place is greater than the marking threshold.

Nevertheless, cell growth has to be represented and simulated continuously in both partitioning approaches. Using off-line partitioning, this can be easily communicated to the simulator by drawing a continuous transition. However, in the case of dynamic partitioning, the transition rate threshold had to be set less than the smallest expected rate of cell growth which makes the latter approach unsuitable for the cell cycle model.

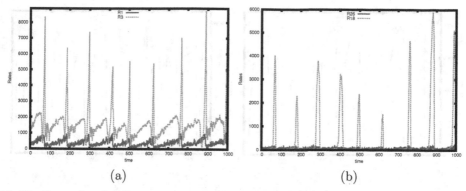

(a)   (b)

Fig. 8. Example of different transition firing rates. (a) transition R_3 fires more frequently than the transition R_1, and (b) transition R_{18} fires much more often than R_{26}.

5   Simulation Results

In this section we show some simulation results of the model in Figure 6 using Snoopy's hybrid simulator. Figures 9 - 12 present time course simulation results of some model species of continuous and hybrid trajectories.

In the hybrid setting, species of low numbers of molecules are simulated using the stochastic regime, e.g., $mRNA_x$ and $mRNA_z$; thus, their numbers of molecules show variability. Such variability is due to the intrinsic noise which is captured by the stochastic simulation algorithm.

Figure 12 compares continuous and hybrid simulation results of the cellular volume (V). Using continuous simulation, parent cells divide all the time equally, and the model does not produce variability in its volume size. Contrary, hybrid simulation does show variability in the cellular volume because species of low numbers of molecules (e.g., mRNAs) are simulated stochastically.

The variability behaviour in the cellular volume, which is produced by the hybrid simulation, is close to the biological model behaviour. For example, the Fission yeast cells have at division a Coefficient of Variation (CV) of the cellular volume of about 6% [13]. The CV is a normalised measure of dispersion of a probability distribution. It is used to judge the variability of a result and it is defined as the ratio of the standard deviation σ to the mean μ, i.e, $CV = \frac{\sigma}{\mu}$.

Table 1 compares the CV and mean values of the deterministic, stochastic, and hybrid simulation results as well as the experimental data of the Fission yeast (wild-type). The continuous and hybrid results are computed by exporting the Snoopy simulation output to a comma-separated values format (CSV). Then a tiny script extracts the different statistics, i.e., μ and CV.

As expected, the CVs of continuous simulation results are zero. This means that continuous simulation does not exhibit any variability in the cellular volume. Moreover, the stochastic and hybrid statistics are similar, but not the same. The variability of cellular volumes of cells simulated via the hybrid version is slightly less than the corresponding stochastic simulation. However, this is an expected behaviour since some of the transitions are continuously simulated.

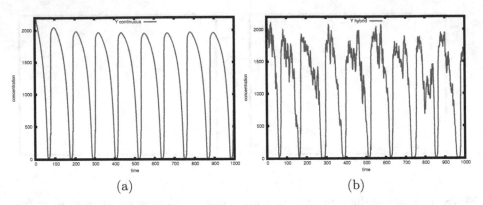

(a)   (b)

Fig. 9. Time course result of Y; (a) continuous, and (b) hybrid

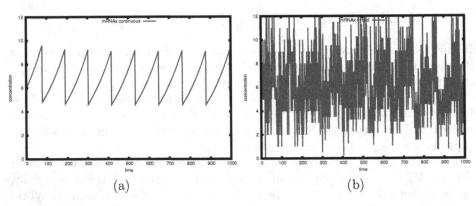

(a)   (b)

Fig. 10. Time course result of $mRNAx$; (a) continuous, and (b) hybrid

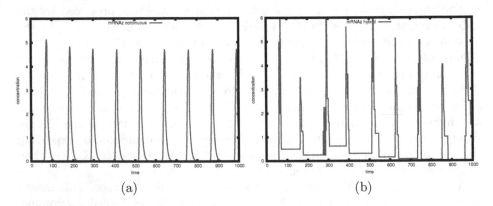

(a)   (b)

Fig. 11. Time course result of mRNAz; (a) continuos, and (b) hybrid

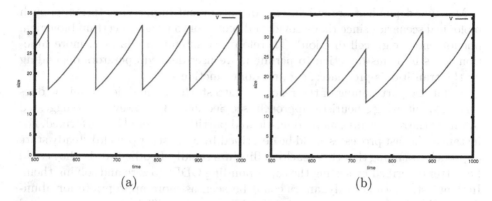

Fig. 12. Time course results of the cellular volume (V); (a) continuous, and (b) hybrid simulation

Table 1. Comparison of the continuous, stochastic, and hybrid simulation results of the model in Figure 6. The volume size is given in fl (femtolitre).

No.	simulator	cell age, min		size at division, fl		size at birth, fl		reference
		mean	CV%	mean	CV %	mean	CV%	
1	Fission yeast	148	10.8	14.4	5.9	8.2	6.3	[23]
2	deterministic	115.9	0	30.9	0	15.9	0	-
3	stochastic	115.5	13	29.1	8.2	14.5	8.2	[13]
4	hybrid	115.5	12	29.9	7.4	15	7.4	-

6   Conclusions and Outlook

In this paper we have shown a class of biological models that can appropriately be modelled using hybrid Petri nets. As an example we have presented and discussed a hybrid Petri net model of the eukaryotic cell cycle. This specific model can be executed using either continuous or hybrid simulators. It employs continuous, stochastic and immediate transitions to intuitively represent the entire model logic. Generally, depending on the type of model, a $\mathcal{GHPN}_{bio}$ model can be simulated continuously, stochastically or in a hybrid way.

The model is implemented using Snoopy. The model itself and the tool are available at http://www-dssz.informatik.tu-cottbus.de/. Marking-dependent arc weights are a new feature recently added to Snoopy which is currently not available in the official Snoopy release. However, the under-development version is freely available on request.

Comparing the simulation results we notice that hybrid simulation produces results close to the stochastic ones (in terms of the resulting CVs), while simulation efficiency could be preserved. Indeed, the reactions of this model can easily be split into slow and fast reactions, which makes it an ideal case study for hybrid simulation algorithms.

Marking-dependent arc weights are of paramount importance to model such biological scenarios since they provide a direct tool to program certain biological phenomenon (e.g., cell division). Therefore, we intend to add even more functionalities into this direction to permit more user-defined operators depending on the transition's pre-places, e.g., random function.

So far the partitioning of the reactions into stochastic and deterministic ones is carried out using a heuristic approach (see Section 4.3). However, (as suggested by one of the reviewers) a more sophisticated partitioning could be performed. For instance, the fast processes could be described by a quasi (or pseudo) steady state approach, assuming that they reach equilibrium rapidly. In other words, they could be better described by setting the corresponding ODEs to zero and solving them. In contrast, continuous dynamics could be seen as more appropriate for abundant molecules whose concentration display a small coefficient of variation, and stochastic dynamics for those molecules evolving at low copy numbers.

Finally, the model presented in this paper could be viewed as a sub-net in a bigger network of reactions (e.g., modelling budding yeast cell cycle or Fission yeast cells). Snoopy's hierarchical nodes might simplify such task as they provide an easy tool to insert a sub-net into a bigger one.

Acknowledgements. This work was done during the stay of Mostafa Herajy at the Brandenburg University of Technology at Cottbus, Germany, supported by the GERLS (German Egyptian Research Long Term Scholarships) program, which is administered by the DAAD in close cooperation with the MHESR and German universities.

References

1. Chen, K., Calzone, L., Csikasz-Nagy, A., Cross, F., Novak, B., Tyson, J.: Integrative analysis of cell cycle control in budding yeast. Mol. Biol. Cel. 5(8), 3841–3862 (2004)
2. Fujita, S., Matsui, M., Matsuno, H., Miyano, S.: Modeling and simulation of fission yeast cell cycle on hybrid functional Petri net. IEICE Transactions on Fundamentals of Electronics, Communications and Computer Sciences E87-A(11), 2919–2927 (2004)
3. Gilbert, D., Heiner, M.: From Petri nets to differential equations - an integrative approach for biochemical network analysis. In: Donatelli, S., Thiagarajan, P.S. (eds.) ICATPN 2006. LNCS, vol. 4024, pp. 181–200. Springer, Heidelberg (2006)
4. Gillespie, D.: A general method for numerically simulating the stochastic time evolution of coupled chemical reactions. J. Comput. Phys. 22(4), 403–434 (1976)
5. Gillespie, D.: Stochastic simulation of chemical kinetics. Annual Review of Physical Chemistry 58(1), 35–55 (2007)
6. Haseltine, E., Rawlings, J.: Approximate simulation of coupled fast and slow reactions for stochastic chemical kinetics. J. Chem. Phys. 117(15), 6959–6969 (2002)
7. Heiner, M., Herajy, M., Liu, F., Rohr, C., Schwarick, M.: Snoopy – a unifying Petri net tool. In: Haddad, S., Pomello, L. (eds.) PETRI NETS 2012. LNCS, vol. 7347, pp. 398–407. Springer, Heidelberg (2012)
8. Heiner, M., Gilbert, D., Donaldson, R.: Petri nets for systems and synthetic biology. In: Bernardo, M., Degano, P., Zavattaro, G. (eds.) SFM 2008. LNCS, vol. 5016, pp. 215–264. Springer, Heidelberg (2008)

9. Heiner, M., Lehrack, S., Gilbert, D., Marwan, W.: Extended stochastic Petri nets for model-based design of wetlab experiments. In: Priami, C., Back, R.-J., Petre, I. (eds.) Transactions on Computational Systems Biology XI. LNCS, vol. 5750, pp. 138–163. Springer, Heidelberg (2009)
10. Herajy, M., Heiner, M.: Hybrid representation and simulation of stiff biochemical networks. Nonlinear Analysis: Hybrid Systems 6(4), 942–959 (2012)
11. Herajy, M.: Computational Steering of Multi-Scale Biochemical Reaction Networks. Ph.D. thesis, Brandenburg University of Technology Cottbus - Computer Science Institute (2013)
12. Herajy, M., Heiner, M.: Hybrid representation and simulation of stiff biochemical networks through generalised hybrid Petri nets. Tech. Rep. 02/2011, Brandenburg University of Technology Cottbus, Dept. of CS (2011)
13. Kar, S., Baumann, W.T., Paul, M.R., Tyson, J.J.: Exploring the roles of noise in the eukaryotic cell cycle. Proceedings of the National Academy of Sciences of the United States of America 106(16), 6471–6476 (2009)
14. Kiehl, T., Mattheyses, R., Simmons, M.: Hybrid simulation of cellular behavior. Bioinformatics 20, 316–322 (2004)
15. Liu, Z., Pu, Y., Li, F., Shaffer, C., Hoops, S., Tyson, J., Cao, Y.: Hybrid modeling and simulation of stochastic effects on progression through the eukaryotic cell cycle. J. Chem. Phys. 136(34105) (2012)
16. Marwan, W., Rohr, C., Heiner, M.: Petri nets in Snoopy: A unifying framework for the graphical display, computational modelling, and simulation of bacterial regulatory networks. Methods in Molecular Biology, ch. 21, vol. 804, pp. 409–437. Humana Press (2012)
17. Matsui, M., Fujita, S., Suzuki, S., Matsuno, H., Miyano, S.: Simulated cell division processes of the xenopus cell cycle pathway by genomic object net. Journal of Integrative Bioinformatics, 0001 (2004)
18. Matsuno, H., Tanaka, Y., Aoshima, H., Doi, A., Matsui, M., Miyano, S.: Biopathways representation and simulation on hybrid functional Petri net. Silico Biology 3(3) (2003)
19. Mura, I., Csikász-Nagy, A.: Stochastic Petri net extension of a yeast cell cycle model. Journal of Theoretical Biology 254(4), 850–860 (2008)
20. Sabouri-Ghomi, M., Ciliberto, A., Kar, S., Novak, B., Tyson, J.J.: Antagonism and bistability in protein interaction networks. Journal of Theoretical Biology 250(1), 209–218 (2008)
21. Singhania, R., Sramkoski, R.M., Jacobberger, J.W., Tyson, J.J.: A hybrid model of mammalian cell cycle regulation. PLoS Comput. Biol. 7(2), e1001077 (2011)
22. Steuer, R.: Effects of stochasticity in models of the cell cycle: from quantized cycle times to noise-induced oscillations. Journal of Theoretical Biology 228(3), 293–301 (2004)
23. Sveiczer, Á., Novák, B., Mitchison, J.: The size control of fission yeast revisited. J. Cell Sci. 109, 2947–2957 (1996)
24. Tyson, J., Novak, B.: Regulation of the eukaryotic cell cycle: Molecular antagonism, hysteresis, and irreversible transitions. Journal of Theoretical Biology 210(2), 249–263 (2001)
25. Tyson, J., Novak, B.: A Systems Biology View of the Cell Cycle Control Mechanisms. Elsevier, San Diego (2011)
26. Valk, R.: Self-modifying nets, a natural extension of Petri nets. In: Ausiello, G., Böhm, C. (eds.) Proceedings of the Fifth Colloquium on Automata, Languages and Programming, vol. 62, pp. 464–476. Springer, Heidelburg (1978)
27. Wikipedia: Wikipedia website (2012), http://www.wikipedia.org/ (accessed: September 20, 2012)

Simulative Model Checking of Steady State and Time-Unbounded Temporal Operators

Christian Rohr

Brandenburg University of Technology Cottbus,
Chair of Data Structures and Software Dependability,
Postbox 10 13 44, D-03013 Cottbus, Germany
rohrch@tu-cottbus.de
http://www-dssz.informatik.tu-cottbus.de

Abstract. When working with large stochastic models simulation remains the only possible analysis technique. Therefore, simulative model checking is the way to go. While finite time horizon algorithms are well known for probabilistic linear-time temporal logic, we provide an infinite time horizon procedure as well as steady state computation, based on exact stochastic simulation algorithms. All presented algorithms are implemented in our advanced model checking tool MARCIE. We demonstrate the approach on models of the RKIP inhibited ERK pathway and angiogenetic process.

Keywords: simulative model checking, stochastic Petri net, steady state, unbounded temporal operator, probabilistic linear-time temporal logic.

1 Introduction

Stochastic modelling of biochemical reaction networks is getting more and more popular. This also increases the demand for efficient analysis of such models. While small and medium-sized models can be analysed numerically, we focus on large or unbounded models. Therefore we use stochastic simulation to overcome the problem of state space explosion.

We use stochastic Petri nets ($\mathcal{SPN}$) [1] as modelling paradigm, which gives us a complete formalised and standardised framework, as well as an intuitive way of modelling concurrent behaviour. A number of biochemical species N involved in the biological model are represented as places $p_1 \dots p_N$, and the reactions between them refer to the transitions $t_1 \dots t_M$. The kinetics of a reaction is defined as possibly state-dependent rate function h_t assigned to the transition. Places and transitions are connected via directed arcs. Each arc contains the stoichiometric value of the associated species. The initial marking m_0 of a $\mathcal{SPN}$ specifies the amount of tokens on each place. The semantics of such a $\mathcal{SPN}$ is defined as continuous-time Markov chain (CTMC) with an initial state $s_0 = m_0$.

The dynamic behaviour of stochastic models can be analysed in different ways. We showed in [2] that numerical analysis is currently efficient up to 1×10^9 states. Beyond this limit, stochastic simulation remains the only possible technique.

M. Koutny et al. (Eds.): ToPNoC VIII, LNCS 8100, pp. 142–158, 2013.

Stochastic simulation may be performed with approximate or exact methods. An approximate method is τ-leaping [3], which generates an approximate realisation of the stochastic process. Its advantage is the ability to jump over several transitions and thus be more efficient in trace generation than exact methods. But for simulative model checking, we need to know the exact occurrences of each transition, that means the simulation has to compute real (exact) paths through the state space of the net. Therefore, only exact simulation algorithms are suitable for the purpose of simulative model checking, like Gillespie's direct method [4] or the next reaction method [5] by Gibson & Bruck.

Simulative model checking of time-bounded temporal formulas is well known and produces reasonable results and performs well in comparison to numerical methods [2]. The main problem in verifying time-unbounded formulas is: "When to stop the simulation trace?" Naive solutions like a fixed, large number of simulation steps or a fixed, long end time for the simulation trace, are not suitable.

In this paper, we extend the finite time horizon model checking algorithm of probabilistic linear-time temporal logic to an infinite time horizon and provide an algorithm to compute simulatively steady state formulas.

2   Stochastic Simulation

In biochemical reaction networks (with n molecular species and k reactions), the molecular reactions between the species are random processes, because it is impossible to predict the time at which the next reaction will occur. Stochastic modelling has therefore become an important tool to fully understand the system behaviour of such reaction networks.

The stochasticity can be described in a time-dependent manner by the Chemical Master Equation. In probability theory, this identifies the evolution as a continuous-time Markov chain (CTMC), with the integrated master equation obeying a Chapman-Kolmogorov equation. When working with biological systems, it may be infeasible to set up the CTMC as the state space $\mathcal{X} \subseteq \mathbb{N}^n$ can be very large or even infinite. The largeness of CTMCs makes simulation an important analysis technique: instead of computing the CTMC directly, simulation aims at imitating the CTMC by generating different paths of the CTMC, i.e., a sequence of discrete random variable $X_l(t)$. The discrete random variable $X_l(t)$ describes the number of molecules of species S_l, $l \in \{1, \ldots, n\}$ present at time t. The system state at time t is thus a discrete n-dimensional random vector $X(t) = (X_1(t), \ldots, X_n(t)) \in \mathcal{X}$. Given the system is in state $X(t)$, the probability that a transition/reaction of type $j \in \{1, \ldots, k\}$ will occur in the infinitesimal time interval $[t + \tau, t + \tau + d\tau)$ is given by:

$$P(t + \tau, j | X(t))d\tau = a_j(X(t)) \exp\left(-a_0(X(t))\tau\right) d\tau$$

For each reaction j, the rate is given by the propensity function a_j, where $a_j(x)d\tau$ is the conditional probability that a reaction of type j occurs in the infinitesimal time interval $[t, t + d\tau)$, given state $X(t)$ at time t. The sum of the propensities of all possible transitions in the current state $X(t)$ is given by $a_0(X)$. Thus, the different (enabled) transitions in the net compete in a race condition and the fastest one determines next state and the time elapsed. In the new state, the race condition is started anew.

To analyse or understand the behaviour of a biochemical reaction network, many trajectories need to be simulated for a good approximation of the underlying CTMC. Although in principle known a long time before, Gillespie was the first who developed a supporting theory for a stochastic simulation of chemical kinetics [4]. He presented the Stochastic Simulation Algorithm (SSA; often also called Gillespie's algorithm), which is a Monte Carlo procedure for numerically generating CTMC. Since Gillespie's seminal work, several variants and different implementations and optimisations of the SSA have been proposed. Basically, each variant performs the following steps:

1. Initialise time $t = t_0$ and the system's state X at time t_0.
2. Repeat:
   (a) determine time increment $\tau \in \mathbb{R}$
   (b) select next reaction type j depending on the current state $X(t)$
   (c) perform state transition imposed by reaction of type j and update state vector X
   (d) update time $t = t + \tau$.
   until simulation time is reached.

The SSA simulates every state transition event, one at a time, and updates the system after each state transition. To determine the time increment τ and to select the next reaction requires to generate random numbers. Different realisations of the CTMC are obtained by different initialisations of the random number generator. Since reliable statements about the system behaviour (variance) can only be made based on many simulations, the usefulness of the simulation approach depends on the simulation time for each individual trajectory. Accelerating simulations is therefore desirable without changing the basic ideas of the algorithm.

Many variants of the SSA aim at reducing the computational cost of selecting the next reaction that will occur. Cao et al. [6] keep the reactions with larger propensities at the beginning of the list. The position of each reaction in the list is thereby determined after some pre-simulations. McCollum et al. [7] maintain a loosely sorted order of the reactions as the simulation proceeds. Instead of arranging the reactions in a linear list, Gibson & Bruck [5] propose to use advanced data structures (trees) to speed up the search for the next reaction that will occur. However, the time to manage the advanced data structures partially compensates the speed-up due to faster search [8].

Further performance increases of the SSA are obtained if only those propensities are recalculated that actually have changed after a state transition, whereas all others are reused (e.g. [8,5]).

An additional speed-up to the SSA is provided by the approximate method τ-leaping [3], in which time t is advanced by a preselected amount τ and the numbers of firings of the individual transitions during the time interval $[t, t + \tau)$ are approximated by Poisson random numbers. Thus, instead of (sequentially) tracing every single state transition, several reactions are executed in parallel. With τ-leaping, it is assumed that all propensity functions are approximately constant in $[t, t + \tau)$, which is referred to as the leap condition. To ensure this, it is important to select τ sufficiently small, but also large enough to accelerate simulation.

3   Model Checking

Model checking is an advanced analysis technique to check whether a model of a system satisfies some properties or specifications. Therefor temporal logics are used to specify the properties of interest, e.g. the Computational Tree Logic (CTL) [9], the Linear-time Temporal Logic (LTL) [10] or their probabilistic extensions Probabilistic CTL (PCTL) [11], Continuous Stochastic Logic (CSL) [12] and Probabilistic LTL (PLTL) [13].

For the specification of temporal formulas we use PLTL, because it reasons over paths through the state space of the model and stochastic simulation produces traces through the state space of the model. We define the probabilistic extension of the Linear-time Temporal Logic with numerical constraints [14], which is called Probabilistic Linear-time Temporal Logic with numerical constraints (PLTLc) [15]. The grammar of all PLTLc formulas is given in Definition 1.

Definition 1. *Probabilistic Linear-time Temporal Logic with Constraints*

$$\psi := \mathcal{P}_{\bowtie x}\left[\phi\right] \mid \mathcal{P}_{=?}\left[\phi\right]$$
$$\bowtie \in \{<, \leq, \geq, >\}, \ x \in [0, 1]$$
$$\phi := \mathbf{X}^I \phi \mid \mathbf{F}^I \phi \mid \mathbf{G}^I \phi \mid \phi \ \mathbf{U}^I \phi \mid \neg\phi \mid \phi \wedge \phi \mid \phi \vee \phi \mid \sigma$$
$$I := [x_1, x_2] = \left\{x \in \mathbb{R}^+ \mid x_1 \leq x \leq x_2\right\}, \ omit \ I = [0, \infty)$$
$$\sigma := \neg\sigma \mid \sigma \wedge \sigma \mid \sigma \vee \sigma \mid value \trianglelefteq value \mid true \mid false$$
$$\trianglelefteq \in \{<, \leq, \geq, >, =, \neq\}$$
$$value := value \sim value \mid Place \mid \$Variable \mid Int \mid Real \mid function$$
$$\sim \in \{+, -, *, /\}$$

The probability operator $\mathcal{P}$ has two different modes. If it is used with the question mark as $\mathcal{P}_{=?}\left[\phi\right]$ then it will return the probability $Pr(\phi)$ that ϕ is true. In the second case, $\mathcal{P}_{\bowtie x}\left[\phi\right]$ returns *true*, if $Pr(\phi) \bowtie x$ is fulfilled, *false* otherwise. In simulative model checking we compute a confidence interval (*c.i.*); in consequence of that, we have to introduce an additional return value in the second case. For simplicity, we assume the *c.i.* to have a lower and an upper bound $B_l, B_u \in \mathbb{R}_{\geq 0}$, such that the probability $Pr(\phi)$, which is not known in our case, is $B_l \leq Pr(\phi) \leq B_u$.

$$\mathcal{P}_{\bowtie x}[\phi] = \begin{cases} true & \text{if } x \bowtie [B_l, B_u] \wedge x \notin [B_l, B_u] \\ false & \text{if } x \not\bowtie [B_l, B_u] \wedge x \notin [B_l, B_u] \\ unknown & \text{if } x \in [B_l, B_u] \end{cases}$$

The operators $\neg$, $\wedge$, $\vee$ are the standard boolean operators *not, and, or*. Whereas X, F, G, U denote the temporal operators *NEXT, FINALLY, GLOBALLY* and *UNTIL*. The *NEXT* operator ($X^I \phi$) refers to *true* in the next state and within the time interval I. The *UNTIL* operator ($\phi_1 U^I \phi_2$) indicates that a state where ϕ_2 holds is eventually reached within the time interval I, while ϕ_1 continuously holds. The *FINALLY* operator ($F^I \phi$) means that at some point within the time interval I a state where ϕ holds is eventually reached. Whereas the *GLOBALLY* operator ($G^I \phi$) refers to the condition ϕ continuously holding true within the time interval I. The latter two are syntactic sugar, as they rely on the equivalences $F \phi \equiv true \, U \phi$ and $G \phi \equiv \neg F \neg \phi$.

A trace T fulfils a linear-time temporal logic formula ϕ if the following $\models$ relations hold:

$$T \models X \phi \iff T^{(1)} \models \phi$$

$$T \models F \phi \iff \exists i \in \mathbb{N} : T^{(i)} \models \phi$$

$$T \models G \phi \iff \forall i \in \mathbb{N} : T^{(i)} \models \phi$$

$$T \models \phi_1 U \phi_2 \iff \exists i \in \mathbb{N} : T^{(i)} \models \phi_2 \text{ and } \forall j \in \mathbb{N} \wedge j < i : T^{(j)} \models \phi_1$$

$$T \models \neg \phi \iff T \not\models \phi$$

$$T \models \phi_1 \wedge \phi_2 \iff T \models \phi_1 \wedge T \models \phi_2$$

$$T \models \phi_1 \vee \phi_2 \iff T \models \phi_1 \vee T \models \phi_2$$

$$T \models v_1 \trianglelefteq v_2 \iff evalState(v_1, T^{(0)}) \trianglelefteq evalState(v_2, T^{(0)})$$

The function $evalState(v, T^{(i)})$ assigns a numerical value to the expression v by looking up the tokens that each place $x \in P(v)$ has in state $T^{(i)}$ of trace T.

In the next sections we present an algorithm to compute time-unbounded temporal operators in a simulative manner, and afterwards an algorithm to compute steady state formulas. Time-bounded algorithms for simulative model checking are well known, e.g., [14].

3.1   Verification of Time-Unbounded Until

Verifying time-unbounded until formulas $\mathcal{P}_{=?} [\phi_1 U \phi_2]$ is done by creating a trace T and checking if $T \models \phi_1 U \phi_2$. Therefore we extend T until a state is reached where $T^{(i)} \not\models \phi_1$, so that trace T does not fulfil our formula, or $T^{(i)} \models \phi_2$, that means trace T satisfies our formula. This approach works fine for time-bounded until formulas, because it is guaranteed to terminate with a probability of 1. It either terminates on a positive or negative observation of our formula or at the end of the time interval associated with the until operator. But there is no finite time bound in the case of time-unbounded until formulas, so the algorithm does not eventually terminate.

The stochastic Petri net in Fig. 1 demonstrates the problem of not terminating while verifying time-unbounded until formulas.

Consider, for example, the formula

$$\mathcal{P}_{=?} [true \, U \, p3 = 1] \ .$$

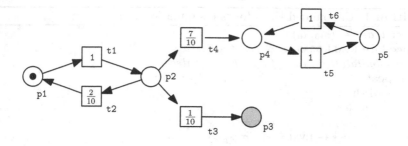

Fig. 1. Example of a stochastic Petri Net

The corresponding CTMC of the $\mathcal{SPN}$ in Fig. 1 has only one state that satisfies the formula. But any trace T starting in s_0 (Fig. 1), that does not fulfil the formula is of infinite length. For this net, the probability of reaching the satisfying state starting from state s_0 and time 0 can be computed as follows:

$$Pr\left(true \,\mathsf{U}\, p3 = 1\right) = \frac{1}{10} \cdot \sum_{n=0}^{\infty} \left(\frac{2}{10}\right)^n = \frac{1}{8}\,.$$

Using the algorithm for time-bounded until formulas does not work, because it will not terminate with a probability of $\frac{7}{8}$. We need another stopping criteria to solve this problem.

In Algorithm 1 we present the algorithm for checking time-unbounded until formulas. It is nearly the same as for time-bounded formulas except that one has to stop the simulation trace at some time point. The decision of doing that is the crucial part of the algorithm. We assume that reaching the steady state is a reasonable stopping criteria (line 38). A system in a steady state has numerous properties that are unchanging in time. This implies that for any property p of the system, the partial derivative with respect to time is zero:

$$\frac{\partial p}{\partial t} = 0$$

If a system is in steady state, then the recently observed behaviour of the system will continue into the future. In stochastic systems, the probabilities that various states will be repeated will remain constant. But, if the system does not have a steady state, e.g. it oscillates, the algorithm will run forever or until the user stops the program.

3.2   Steady State Computation

In steady state simulation, the measures of interest are defined as limits, as the length of the simulation goes to infinity. There is no natural event to terminate the simulation, so the length of the simulation is made large enough to get "good" estimates of the quantities of interest. Steady-state simulation generally poses two problems:

Algorithm 1. Unbounded Until for one simulation run

Require: $trace \leftarrow (m_0, t_0)$
1: **procedure** EVALFORMULA(ϕ, pos, $trace$)
2:     $steadyStateReached \leftarrow false$, $res \leftarrow false$
3:     **repeat**
4:         switch ϕ
5:             case σ :
6:                 $(s_{pos}, t_{pos}) \leftarrow trace^{(pos)}$
7:                 $res \leftarrow$ EVALSTATE(σ, s_{pos})
8:                 **return** (pos, res)
9:             case $\neg\phi_1$:
10:                 $(pos_1, res_1) \leftarrow$ EVALFORMULA(ϕ_1, pos, $trace$)
11:                 **return** $(pos_1, \neg res_1)$
12:             case $\phi_1 \wedge \phi_2$:
13:                 $(pos_1, res_1) \leftarrow$ EVALFORMULA(ϕ_1, pos, $trace$)
14:                 $(pos_2, res_2) \leftarrow$ EVALFORMULA(ϕ_2, pos, $trace$)
15:                 **return** $(min(pos_1, pos_2), res_1 \wedge res_2)$
16:             case $\phi_1 \vee \phi_2$:
17:                 $(pos_1, res_1) \leftarrow$ EVALFORMULA(ϕ_1, pos, $trace$)
18:                 $(pos_2, res_2) \leftarrow$ EVALFORMULA(ϕ_2, pos, $trace$)
19:                 **return** $(max(pos_1, pos_2), res_1 \vee res_2)$
20:             case $X\phi_1$:
21:                 **if** $pos = |trace|$ **then**
22:                     $trace \leftarrow trace +$ NEXTSTATE($trace^{(pos)}$)
23:                 **end if**
24:                 $pos \leftarrow pos + 1$
25:                 $(pos_1, res_1) \leftarrow$ EVALFORMULA(ϕ_1, pos, $trace$)
26:                 **return** (pos_1, res_1)
27:             case $\phi_1 U \phi_2$:
28:                 $(pos_2, res_2) \leftarrow$ EVALFORMULA(ϕ_2, pos, $trace$)
29:                 **if** $res_2 = true$ **then**
30:                     **return** (pos_2, res_2)
31:                 **end if**
32:                 $(pos_1, res_1) \leftarrow$ EVALFORMULA(ϕ_1, pos, $trace$)
33:                 **if** $res_1 = false$ **then**
34:                     **return** (pos_1, res_1)
35:                 **end if**
36:                 $pos \leftarrow pos_1$
37:         end switch
38:         $steadyStateReached \leftarrow$ CHECKSTEADYSTATE($trace$)
39:         **if** $pos = |trace|$ **then**
40:             $trace \leftarrow trace +$ NEXTSTATE($trace^{(pos)}$)
41:         **end if**
42:         $pos \leftarrow pos + 1$
43:     **until** $steadyStateReached = true$
44:     **return** (pos, res)
45: **end procedure**

---

1. The existence of a transient phase may cause the estimate to be biased, because the initial conditions primarily affect data at the beginning of a run.
2. The simulation runs are long, and usually one cannot afford to carry out many independent simulations.

There are several methods that allow to cope with these problems to some extent. Among them are: the batch means method [16], the method of independent replicas [17], and the regeneration method [18]. Each of these methods has its advantages and disadvantages. In our implementation we use a sample batch means algorithm to compute the steady state.

We choose Skart [19], which is an automated sequential procedure for on-the-fly steady state simulation output analysis, because it is specifically designed to handle observation-based statistics and usually requires a smaller initial sample size compared with other well-known simulation analysis procedures [19]. This algorithm partitions a long simulation run into batches, computes an average statistics for each batch and constructs an interval estimate using the batch means. Based on this interval estimate Skart decides whether a steady state is reached or more samples were needed. A detailed description of the algorithm is given in [19].

We extend PLTLc with the steady state operator S. Definition 2 states the syntax of it. The return values are quite the same as for the probability operator $\mathcal{P}$. But inside of S only state formulas are allowed, i.e., no temporal operators.

Definition 2. *Extension of PLTLc with steady state operator S.*

$$\psi := \mathcal{P}_{\bowtie x}\,[\phi] \mid \mathcal{P}_{=?}\,[\phi] \mid S_{\bowtie x}\,[\sigma] \mid S_{=?}\,[\sigma]$$
$$\bowtie \in \{<, \leq, \geq, >\}, \ x \in [0, 1]$$

Steady-state formulas are computed with Algorithm 2. At first the simulation trace is created until the steady state is reached (line $4 - 8$). To get an unbiased result, we cut off the first n states, which bias the steady state (line 9). The remaining states are now checked whether the steady state property holds or not and the occupation time T_o of the fulfilling states and the simulation time T_s are summed up (line $11 - 19$). The steady state probability is now the ratio $\frac{T_o}{T_s}$ (line 19). But this gives correct results only for those Petri nets, where the reachability graph consists of only one strongly connected component (SCC). The complexity of this decision is the same as for constructing the reachability graph. In symbolic model checking the strongly connected components and the probabilities of reaching them are computed first. After that the probabilities within each SCC are computed and these are weighted with the probability of reaching the SCC. In that way the correct steady state probability is calculated. To solve this problem in simulative model checking, one has to make several simulation runs (steady state computations) and average the results. In that way the individual steady state estimates are weighted according to the strongly connected components.

Algorithm 2. Steady state computation for one simulation run

Require: $trace \leftarrow (m_0, t_0)$
1: **procedure** EVALSTEADYSTATE(σ)
2:     $steadyStateReached \leftarrow false$
3:     $pos \leftarrow 0$
4:     **repeat**
5:         $trace \leftarrow trace + $ NEXTSTATE($trace^{(pos)}$)
6:         $pos \leftarrow pos + 1$
7:         $steadyStateReached \leftarrow$ CHECKSTEADYSTATE($trace$)
8:     **until** $steadyStateReached = true$
9:     $cutOff \leftarrow$ GETSTEADYSTATECUTOFF
10:    $T_o \leftarrow 0,\ T_s \leftarrow 0$
11:    **for** $i \leftarrow cutOff, |trace|$ **do**
12:       $(s_i, t_i) \leftarrow trace^{(i)}$ $\triangleright$ state s_i, sojourn time t_i in s_i
13:       $T_s \leftarrow T_s + t_i$
14:       $res \leftarrow$ EVALSTATE(σ, s_i)
15:       **if** $res = true$ **then**
16:          $T_o \leftarrow T_o + t_i$
17:       **end if**
18:    **end for**
19:    **return** T_o/T_s
20: **end procedure**

---

4 MARCIE: An Implementation

MARCIE [20] is a tool for analysing generalised stochastic Petri nets ($\mathcal{GSPN}$), supporting qualitative and quantitative analyses including model checking capabilities. Particular features are symbolic state space analysis including efficient saturation-based state space generation, evaluation of standard Petri net properties as well as Computational Tree Logic model checking. Further it offers symbolic Continuous Stochastic Logic model checking and permits to compute expectations for rewards which can be added to the core $\mathcal{GSPN}$. Most of MARCIE's features are realised on top of an Interval Decision Diagram (IDD) implementation [21]. IDDs are used to efficiently encode interval logic functions representing marking sets of bounded Petri nets. Thus, MARCIE falls into the category of symbolic analysis tools.

However, it additionally comprises approximative and simulative engines, which work explicitly, to support also stochastic analysis of very large and unbounded nets. It includes two exact simulation algorithms, firstly Gillespie's direct method [4], and secondly the next reaction method by Gibson & Bruck [5]. The user can set the number of simulation runs directly when calling MARCIE or he can set the desired accuracy of the results and MARCIE computes the required number of simulation runs.

Parallelising the simulation is a good way to speed-up the computation. This is done via distribution of the simulation runs to the worker processes. Therefore the run-time decreases with the number of workers. We use the Message Passing

Interface (MPI) to develop a portable and scalable simulation tool for large-scale models. Moreover, MARCIE provides simulative PLTLc model checking as presented in this paper.

MARCIE is completely written in C++, and makes use of the libraries GMP, pthreads, flex/bison and boost. It comprises about 45,000 lines of source code. MARCIE is available for non-commercial use; we provide statically linked binaries for Linux and Mac OS X. The tool, the manual and a benchmark suite can be found on our website http://www-dssz.informatik.tu-cottbus.de/marcie.html. MARCIE itself comes with a textual user interface. Options and input files can also be specified by a generic Graphical User Interface (GUI), written in Java, which can be easily configured by means of a XML description. The GUI is part of our Petri net analyser Charlie [22].

5   Case Studies

In this section we demonstrate our approach on the models of the RKIP inhibited ERK pathway and angiogenetic process. All Petri nets were modelled with Snoopy [23] and analysed with MARCIE [20]. The experiments were carried out on a machine with 4x AMD Opteron^{TM} 6276 with 2.3 GHz and 256GB RAM running CentOS 6. All experiments were done with a maximum number of $6,634,234$ simulation runs.

5.1   RKIP Inhibited ERK Pathway

This model shows the influence of the Raf Kinase Inhibitor Protein (RKIP) on the Extracellular signal Regulated Kinase (ERK) signalling pathway. A model of non-linear ordinary differential equations was originally published in [24]. Later on, it was discussed as qualitative and continuous Petri nets in [25], and as stochastic Petri net in [26]. The stochastic Petri net SPN_{ERK} comprises 11 places and 11 transitions connected by 34 arcs and is shown in Fig. 2. All transition rate functions use mass action kinetics with the original parameter values from [24]. The model is scalable by the initial amount of tokens in the places RKIP, MEKpp, ERK and RP. The more initial tokens on each of these places, the bigger the state space of the Petri net. Table 1 shows the number of reachable states for different initial markings.

Table 1. The size of the state space for different initial markings of SPN_{ERK} computed with MARCIE's symbolic state space generation. All places which carry one token in Fig. 2 have now initially N tokens.

N	|states|	N	|states|	N	|states|	N	|states|
5	1,974	20	1,696,618	40	79,414,335	100	1.591×10^{10}
10	47,047	25	5,723,991	50	2.834×10^{8}	250	3.582×10^{12}
15	368,220	30	15,721,464	60	8.114×10^{8}	500	2.231×10^{14}

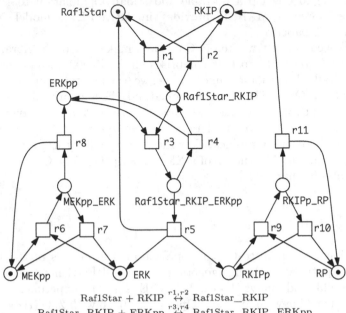

RaflStar + RKIP $\overset{r1,r2}{\leftrightarrow}$ RaflStar_RKIP
RaflStar_RKIP + ERKpp $\overset{r3,r4}{\leftrightarrow}$ RaflStar_RKIP_ERKpp
RaflStar_RKIP_ERKpp $\overset{r5}{\to}$ RaflStar + ERK + RKIPp
ERK + MEKpp $\overset{r6,r7}{\leftrightarrow}$ MEKpp_ERK $\overset{r8}{\to}$ ERKpp + MEKpp
RKIPp + RP $\overset{r9,r10}{\leftrightarrow}$ RKIPp_RP $\overset{r11}{\to}$ RKIP + RP

Fig. 2. Stochastic Petri net of the RKIP inhibited ERK pathway, including textual representation of the chemical reactions

In order to verify the correctness of our approach, we check the same properties as in [2]. We first check the reachability of a state at some time in the future, such that the number of tokens on place *MEKpp* is between 60% and 80% of N:

$$\mathcal{P}_{=?}\left[\text{F}\left[MEKpp \geq N \cdot 0.6 \wedge MEKpp \leq N \cdot 0.8\right]\right].$$

In any case such a state was reached, therefore the probability of the formula is 1, see Table 2.

Since we know now that such a state is eventually reached, we want to compute the steady state probability of being in such a state, where the number of tokens on place *MEKpp* is between 60% and 80% of N:

$$\mathcal{S}_{=?}\left[MEKpp \geq N \cdot 0.6 \wedge MEKpp \leq N \cdot 0.8\right].$$

The results in Table 3 show first that the resulting confidence interval covers the probability computed by the Jacobi method in [2]. Second the algorithm scales nearly linear with the number of worker processes. A very interesting behaviour regards the relationship between the state space size and the total run-time of the computation. One could expect an increase of the run-time, but it stays the same. This is a result of the level semantics described in [27], i.e., the rate

Table 2. Reachability analysis for different initial markings N of $\mathcal{SPN}_{ERK}$. The total time is given for different numbers of workers. The results are shown for the simulative engine and for the numerical engine using the Jacobi solver.

N	1	2	4	8	16	32	64	simulative	numerical
20	0m56s	0m28s	0m14s	0m7s	0m3s	0m2s	0m0s	[1,1]	1
30	1m17s	0m38s	0m19s	0m10s	0m4s	0m3s	0m1s	[1,1]	1
40	1m38s	0m48s	0m24s	0m12s	0m6s	0m3s	0m1s	[1,1]	1
50	1m57s	0m59s	0m30s	0m15s	0m7s	0m4s	0m2s	[1,1]	1
60	2m23s	1m9s	0m35s	0m17s	0m8s	0m5s	0m3s	[1,1]	1

functions are scaled by the initial number of tokens N. Therefore, the sojourn time of the transition remains the same, while the initial amount of tokens is increasing. In contrast to symbolic model checking, the stochastic rate functions are decisive for the run time of the algorithm and not the size of the state space.

Table 3. Steady state analysis for different initial markings N of $\mathcal{SPN}_{ERK}$. The total time is given for different numbers of workers. The results are shown for the simulative engine and for the numerical engine using the Jacobi solver.

N	1	2	4	8	16	32	64	simulative	numerical
20	7m31s	3m46s	1m53s	0m57s	0m27s	0m17s	0m10s	[0.77482, 0.77534]	0.77508
30	7m34s	3m43s	1m51s	0m57s	0m28s	0m17s	0m11s	[0.83277, 0.83325]	0.83297
40	7m40s	3m43s	1m56s	0m57s	0m28s	0m18s	0m11s	[0.87416, 0.87470]	0.87452
50	7m43s	3m57s	1m57s	1m0s	0m30s	0m17s	0m11s	[0.90437, 0.90486]	0.90465
60	7m53s	3m59s	1m56s	1m1s	0m28s	0m17s	0m12s	[0.92641, 0.92696]	0.92682

5.2   Angiogenesis

Angiogenesis is a complex phenomenon that goes from a molecular level to macroscopic events. This Petri net models a part of the signal transduction pathway involved in the angiogenetic process and was originally published in [28]. The stochastic Petri net $\mathcal{SPN}_{ANG}$ comprises 39 places and 64 transitions connected by 185 arcs.

The model is scalable by the initial amount of tokens in the places *Akt*, *DAG*, *Gab1*, *KdStar*, *Pip2*, *P3k*, *Pg* and *Pten*. The more initial tokens on each of these places, the bigger the state space of the Petri net. The number of reachable states for different initial markings are shown in Table 4. As in the previous case study we check for reachability first. Now we want to know the probability of eventually reaching a state where no tokens reside on place *Akt*:

$$\mathcal{P}_{=?}\,[\mathrm{F}\,[Akt = 0]].$$

Table 4. The size of the state space for different initial markings of SPN_{ANG} computed with MARCIE's symbolic state space generation. The places Akt, DAG, $Gab1$, $KdStar$, $Pip2$, $P3k$, Pg and $Pten$ carry initially N tokens.

N	|states|	N	|states|	N	|states|	N	|states|
1	96	4	2,413,480	7	2.181×10^9	10	4.537×10^{11}
2	5,384	5	29,224,050	8	1.464×10^{10}	15	5.207×10^{14}
3	144,188	6	277,789,578	9	8.623×10^{10}	20	1.428×10^{17}

Table 5. Reachability analysis for different initial markings N of SPN_{ANG}. The total time is given for different numbers of workers. The results are shown for the simulative engine and for the numerical engine using the Jacobi solver.

N	1	2	4	8	16	32	64	simulative	numerical
1	12m10s	6m13s	3m3s	1m29s	0m49s	0m25s	0m13s	[0.44642, 0.44742]	0.44670
2	60m19s	30m18s	14m47s	7m14s	3m36s	1m52s	1m17s	[0.81292, 0.81370]	0.81302
3	65m37s	35m41s	18m31s	8m20s	4m2s	2m1s	1m55s	[0.94249, 0.94365]	0.94272
4	74m43s	37m14s	19m52s	9m45s	4m58s	2m18s	3m0s	[0.98179, 0.98216]	0.98182
5	79m45s	38m37s	18m54s	9m20s	4m37s	2m22s	3m35s	[0.99360, 0.99396]	0.99379
6	79m37s	39m57s	19m50s	9m14s	4m34s	2m11s	3m3s	[0.99760, 0.99780]	0.99772

In contrast to SPN_{ERK}, Table 5 shows that the probability ranges from about $0.44 \, (N = 1)$ to $0.9 \, (N = 6)$. That means a state where no tokens lay on place Akt is not always reached, because the CTMC consists of several strongly connected components and in some of them such a state does not exist. Secondly we compute the steady state probability of being in a state that has no tokens on place Akt:

$$\mathcal{S}_{=?} \, [Akt = 0] \, .$$

The results in Table 6 show that the steady state probability is nearly the same as in the reachability case as the overall steady state probability consists of two parts, first the probability of reaching a strongly connected component and second the steady state probability inside these component. The result means the steady state probability inside a strongly connected component, where a state exists with $Akt = 0$, is almost 1. That's why the overall steady state probability almost coincides with the reachability probability.

6   Related Work

To compute the transient probability of the formula $\mathcal{P}_{=?}[\phi_1 \, \mathrm{U} \, \phi_2]$ in state s means to compute the probability distribution starting in s and making states absorbing, which satisfy $\neg\phi_1 \vee \phi_2$. The resulting linear system of equations can be solved numerically by iterative methods like Gauss-Seidel or Jacobi. There are several tools available that support such solvers, among them MARCIE [20].

Table 6. Steady state analysis for different initial markings N of $\mathcal{SPN}_{ANG}$. The total time is given for different numbers of workers. The results are shown for the simulative engine and for the numerical engine using the Jacobi solver. († = no result within 12h)

N	1	2	4	8	16	32	64	simulative	numerical
1	7m1s	3m17s	1m42s	0m47s	0m26s	0m13s	0m9s	[0.43773, 0.44771]	0.44141
2	28m25s	14m10s	6m54s	3m33s	1m34s	0m51s	0m36s	[0.80446, 0.81237]	0.80836
3	58m42s	30m19s	17m54s	7m32s	3m46s	2m30s	1m20s	[0.92772, 0.93284]	0.92899
4	94m27s	49m59s	24m39s	11m53s	6m11s	3m25s	2m11s	[0.97859, 0.98140]	0.97950
5	133m56s	66m44s	33m24s	17m22s	8mm44s	4m49s	3m12s	[0.98923, 0.99121]	†
6	170m57s	85m25s	42m54s	22m12s	11m13s	6m57s	3m30s	[0.99649, 0.99758]	†

The drawback of numerical solvers is their restriction to bounded CTMCs and their complexity is typically $O(n)$ and in worst case $O(n^2)$ with $n = |states|$. On the other hand they compute an "exact" result. The same methods were used to compute the steady state distribution of bounded CTMCs for computing the steady state probability of formulas like $\mathcal{S}_{=?}[\phi]$.

Statistical model checking [29,30,31] is a quite similar approach to simulative model checking, but differs in some details. Hypothesis testing, i.e., sequential probability ratio test (SPRT), has good performance compared to the computation of point estimates, but it can only check formulas like $\mathcal{P}_{\bowtie x}$. In the end, the user gets a result of *true* or *false* and has no idea of the scale of the estimated probability. COSMOS [32] is a statistical model checker for the Hybrid Automata Stochastic Logic and employs Linear Hybrid Automata. It analyses Discrete Event Stochastic Processes, a class of stochastic models which includes, but are not limited to, Markov chains. This approach looks promising but time-unbounded formulas are still an open problem.

Rabih et al. [33] developed a different simulation-based approach to verify time-unbounded Until formulas. Their algorithm is based on perfect simulation. The approach works well if the CTMC is monotone. In the other case the algorithm is practically useless. The authors don't show, how to determine, whether a CTMC is monotone or not. Therefore it's not clear whether this approach is generally applicable or not.

The on-the-fly probabilistic model checker MIRACH, developed by Koh et al. [34], implements simulation-based PLTL model checking of quantitative pathway models, defined in SBML [35]. The model checking capabilities are limited to an upper time bound, due to the requirement of specifying a time limit for the trace generation.

The Monte Carlo Model Checker MC2 [15] computes a point estimate of a Probabilistic LTL logic (with numerical constraints) formula to hold for a model. MC2 does not include any simulation engine but works offline by taking a set of sampled trajectories generated by any simulation or ODE solver software.

Last not least, a combination of simulation and reachability analysis were used to compute time-unbounded formulas in [29,36]. But this approach suffers from the same restrictions of bounded state spaces as the numerical methods.

7   Conclusions

In this paper we presented an infinite time horizon model checking algorithm plus steady state operator for probabilistic linear-time temporal logic. We verified the results of the simulative approach against the numerical solutions of the Jacobi and Gauss-Seidel methods. We proved the efficiency of our algorithm and the scalability by using several worker processes through MPI.

As our algorithm is based on stochastic simulation, its run-time does not directly depend on the size of the state space, as for the numerical methods, but on the rate functions of the transitions and the structural size of the Petri net. That is the greater the sum of the transitions rates, the smaller the time steps are, and the more simulation steps need to be done to reach a certain time point.

But the main drawback of simulation-based methods remains. The achieved accuracy depends on the number of simulation runs, i.e. the required number of simulation runs exponentially grows with the expected accuracy. Therefore numerical analysis methods should be used for bounded and medium-sized models, whereas simulation should be used for large-sized and unbounded models.

In the future, further steady state detection algorithms are examined for their suitability. Furthermore the potential of multi-core processors and GPGPUs be examined in order to speed up the computation.

References

1. Marsan, M.A., Balbo, G., Conte, G., Donatelli, S., Franceschinis, G.: Modelling with Generalized Stochastic Petri Nets. Wiley Series in Parallel Computing, 2nd edn. John Wiley and Sons (1995)
2. Heiner, M., Rohr, C., Schwarick, M., Streif, S.: A comparative study of stochastic analysis techniques. In: Proc. CMSB 2010, pp. 96–106. ACM (2010)
3. Gillespie, D.T.: Approximate accelerated stochastic simulation of chemically reacting systems. J. Chem. Phys. 115(4), 1716–1733 (2001)
4. Gillespie, D.T.: Exact stochastic simulation of coupled chemical reactions. J. Phys. Chem. 81(25), 2340–2361 (1977)
5. Gibson, M.A., Bruck, J.: Efficient exact stochastic simulation of chemical systems with many species and many channels. J. Phys. Chem. A 104, 1876–1889 (2000)
6. Cao, Y., Gillespie, D.T., Petzold, L.R.: Adaptive explicit-implicit tau-leaping method with automatic tau selection. J. Chem. Phys. 126(22), 224101 (2007)
7. McCollum, J.M., Peterson, G.D., Cox, C.D., Simpson, M.L., Samatova, N.F.: The sorting direct method for stochastic simulation of biochemical systems with varying reaction execution behavior. Comput. Biol. Chem. 30(1), 39–49 (2006)
8. Cao, Y., Li, H., Petzold, L.: Efficient formulation of the stochastic simulation algorithm for chemically reacting systems. J. Chem. Phys. 121(9), 4059–4067 (2004)
9. Clarke, E.M., Emerson, E.A.: Design and synthesis of synchronization skeletons using branching time temporal logic. In: Proceedings of the Workshop on Logics of Programs. LNCS, vol. 131, pp. 52–71. Springer (1981)
10. Pnueli, A.: The temporal logic of programs. In: Proc. 18th IEEE Symposium on the Foundations of Computer Science, pp. 46–57. IEEE Computer Society Press (1977)

11. Hansson, H., Jonsson, B.: A Logic for Reasoning about Time and Reliability. Formal Aspects of Computing 6(5), 512–535 (1994)
12. Aziz, A., Sanwal, K., Singhal, V., Brayton, R.: Model checking continuous-time Markov chains. ACM Trans. on Computational Logic 1(1), 162–170 (2000)
13. Baier, C.: On algorithmic verification methods for probabilistic systems. Habilitation thesis, University of Mannheim (1998)
14. Fages, F., Rizk, A.: On the analysis of numerical data time series in temporal logic. In: Calder, M., Gilmore, S. (eds.) CMSB 2007. LNCS (LNBI), vol. 4695, pp. 48–63. Springer, Heidelberg (2007)
15. Donaldson, R., Gilbert, D.: A Monte Carlo model checker for probabilistic LTL with numerical constraints. Technical report, University of Glasgow, Dep. of CS (2008)
16. Schmeiser, B.W.: Batch size effects in the analysis of simulation output. Operations Research 30, 556–568 (1982)
17. Welch, P.D.: The statistical analysis of simulation results. In: The Computer Performance Modeling Handbook, pp. 268–328. Academic Press, New York (1983)
18. Crane, M.A., Iglehart, D.L.: Simulating stable stochastic systems III: Regenerative processes and discrete-event simulations. Operations Research 23, 33–45 (1975)
19. Tafazzoli, A., Wilson, J.R., Lada, E.K., Steiger, N.M.: Skart: A skewness- and autoregression-adjusted batch-means procedure for simulation analysis. In: Winter Simulation Conference, pp. 387–395 (2008)
20. Schwarick, M., Rohr, C., Heiner, M.: MARCIE - Model checking and Reachability analysis done effiCIEntly. In: Proc. 8th International Conference on Quantitative Evaluation of SysTems (QEST 2011), pp. 91–100. IEEE CS Press (September 2011)
21. Tovchigrechko, A.: Model Checking Using Interval Decision Diagrams. PhD thesis, BTU Cottbus, Dep. of CS (2008)
22. Franzke, A.: A concept for redesigning Charlie. Technical report, BTU Cottbus, Dep. of CS (2008)
23. Rohr, C., Marwan, W., Heiner, M.: Snoopy–a unifying Petri net framework to investigate biomolecular networks. Bioinformatics 26(7), 974–975 (2010)
24. Cho, K.-H., Shin, S.-Y., Kim, H.-W., Wolkenhauer, O., McFerran, B., Kolch, W.: Mathematical modeling of the influence of RKIP on the ERK signaling pathway. In: Priami, C. (ed.) CMSB 2003. LNCS, vol. 2602, pp. 127–141. Springer, Heidelberg (2003)
25. Gilbert, D., Heiner, M.: From Petri nets to differential equations - an integrative approach for biochemical network analysis. In: Donatelli, S., Thiagarajan, P.S. (eds.) ICATPN 2006. LNCS, vol. 4024, pp. 181–200. Springer, Heidelberg (2006)
26. Heiner, M., Donaldson, R., Gilbert, D.: In: Iyengar, M.S. (ed.) Petri Nets for Systems Biology. Symbolic Systems Biology: Theory and Methods. Jones and Bartlett Publishers, Inc. (2010)
27. Calder, M., Duguid, A., Gilmore, S., Hillston, J.: Stronger computational modelling of signalling pathways using both continuous and discrete-state methods. In: Priami, C. (ed.) CMSB 2006. LNCS (LNBI), vol. 4210, pp. 63–77. Springer, Heidelberg (2006)
28. Cordero, F., Horvath, A., Manini, D., Napione, L., De Pierro, M., Pavan, S., Picco, A., Veglio, A., Sereno, M., Bussolino, F., Balbo, G.: Simplification of a complex signal transduction model by the application of invariants and flow equivalent server. Theoretical Computer Science 412, 6036–6057 (2011)
29. Younes, H.L.S., Clarke, E.M., Zuliani, P.: Statistical verification of probabilistic properties with unbounded until. In: Davies, J. (ed.) SBMF 2010. LNCS, vol. 6527, pp. 144–160. Springer, Heidelberg (2011)

30. Basu, S., Ghosh, A.P., He, R.: Approximate model checking of PCTL involving unbounded path properties. In: Breitman, K., Cavalcanti, A. (eds.) ICFEM 2009. LNCS, vol. 5885, pp. 326–346. Springer, Heidelberg (2009)
31. Ballarini, P., Forlin, M., Mazza, T., Prandi, D.: Efficient parallel statistical model checking of biochemical networks. In: Proc. PDMC, pp. 47–61 (2009)
32. Ballarini, P., Djafri, H., Duflot, M., Haddad, S., Pekergin, N.: COSMOS: a statistical model checker for the hybrid automata stochastic logic. In: Proceedings of the 8th International Conference on Quantitative Evaluation of Systems (QEST 2011), Aachen, Germany, pp. 143–144. IEEE Computer Society Press (September 2011)
33. El Rabih, D., Pekergin, N.: Statistical model checking using perfect simulation. In: Liu, Z., Ravn, A.P. (eds.) ATVA 2009. LNCS, vol. 5799, pp. 120–134. Springer, Heidelberg (2009)
34. Koh, C.H., Nagasaki, M., Saito, A., Li, C., Wong, L., Miyano, S.: MIRACH: Efficient Model Checker for Quantitative Biological Pathway Models. Bioinformatics 27 (2011)
35. Hucka, M., Finney, A., Sauro, H.M., Bolouri, H., Doyle, J.C., Kitano, H., et al.: The Systems Biology Markup Language (SBML): A Medium for Representation and Exchange of Biochemical Network Models. J. Bioinformatics 19, 524–531 (2003)
36. Zapreev, I.S.: Model checking Markov chains: techniques and tools. PhD thesis, University of Twente, Enschede (March 2008)

Model-Driven Middleware Support
for Team-Oriented Process Management

Matthias Wester-Ebbinghaus and Michael Köhler-Bußmeier

University of Hamburg, Department of Informatics
Theoretical Foundations of Informatics
{wester,koehler}@informatik.uni-hamburg.de
http://www.informatik.uni-hamburg.de/TGI

Abstract. Management of collaborative processes involving multiple parties is one of the dominant topics in contemporary information system research. While the process perspective is quite well understood and supported by a wide range of modeling approaches, it is necessary to go beyond the process perspective alone. We specifically address the following question: If we consider the involved parties of a collaborative process as a *team*, then (1) which are the general *formation rules* for such a team together with the collaborative process it carries out and (2) to which concrete underlying *organizational structure* do these rules apply? To address this question, we present the organizational modeling approach SONAR. The accompanying models are rather high-level and illustrative but at the same time they are rich enough in order to generate executable models and other kinds of code that together form the core of a middleware implementation for team-oriented process management.

1   Introduction

Management of collaborative processes involving multiple parties is one of the most dominant topics in contemporary information system research, especially in the field of business process management (BPM) but also on a smaller scale in the field of computer-supported cooperative work (CSCW) or community support. The process perspective itself is quite well understood and there exists a wide range of more or less similar process modeling approaches (differing in specific aspects), including workflow nets and their descendants [1,2], the Business Process Modeling Notation (BPMN) [19], the Web Service Business Process Execution Language (BPEL) [5], Event-driven Process Chains (EPCs) [14] and the Yet Another Workflow Language (YAWL) [3]. However, there remains the question of organizational structures behind a given set of processes, which is not addressed in a thorough and systematic way by these approaches. We want to formulate this question a bit more vividly in the following way. Given that a collaborative process targets at achieving some high-level *organizational/business task* and if we consider the involved parties of a collaborative process as a *team*, then:

M. Koutny et al. (Eds.): ToPNoC VIII, LNCS 8100, pp. 159–179, 2013.
© Springer-Verlag Berlin Heidelberg 2013

1. Which are the general *formation rules* for such a team together with the collaborative process it carries out?
2. To which concrete underlying *organizational structure* do these rules apply? By an organizational structure we mean a set of organizational positions and relationships between them.

To answer these questions, a more comprehensive modeling approach is necessary, encompassing both a system's processes and structure in an integrated manner. Related work exists in a wide range of disciplines like enterprise architecture management, multi-agent systems and service-oriented computing. In the related work section we elaborate on the positioning of our work in this context. Our main criticism remains, namely that a tight integration of structural and process-oriented aspects is often neglected.

In this context of process and overall organizational modeling, we present the Petri net-based organizational modeling approach SONAR (**S**elf-**O**rganizing **N**et **AR**chitecture). It explicitly addresses the problem statement made so far and especially its manifestation in terms of the concrete questions from above concerning structure and process perspectives in teamwork modeling. We provide a way to capture the whole context of team-oriented process management: from the underlying organizational structure and a given task over team formation up to process execution by the team. From a high-level point of view, one can regard the approach we present as a purely service-oriented one: The team formation mechanism we present is mainly a fine-grained view of a service lookup for accomplishing a high-level business task. Organizations are a quite natural setting for looking at questions of service orchestration and choreography.

We have laid specific emphasis on achieving the following combination: (1) SONAR models are simple enough to be easily understood and analyzed (by means of standard Petri net tools). (2) SONAR models are rich enough to capture the interplay of various organizational concepts in such detail that we can automatically generate executable models and other kinds of code from them. In this context, Figure 1 gives an overview of the results we present in this paper and the sections in the remainder of the paper are linked to the different parts of the figure.

In Section 2, we introduce the SONAR modeling approach, according to which an organizational model basically consists of interwoven structure and process parts. SONAR models initially are high-level models that are devoid of execution-specific details. However, they are Petri net models that inherently come with an operational semantics and thus lead the way to execution. Consequently, in Section 3 we present the SONAR cycle that provides the semantics underlying each SONAR model. This section describes how organizations based on SONAR models operate. The description is still platform-independent and could potentially provide the basis for multiple implementation platforms. In Sections 4 and 5 we present our current implementation approach. In Section 4 we describe how a high-level SONAR model is transformed into software artifacts. Based on this, we present our agent-based middleware platform MULAN4SONAR in Section 5. Feeding the middleware with software artifacts generated from a SONAR model

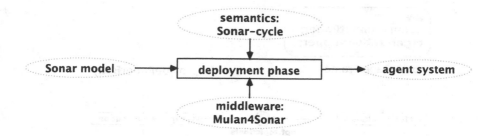

Fig. 1. Model-driven support for teamwork based on SONAR

leads to a multi-agent system that implements the SONAR semantics in terms of the SONAR cycle. We conclude our work in Section 7 and give an outlook to advanced and future topics of our research.

Note that both the SONAR modeling approach and the middleware implementation rest on our previous work (cf. especially [17,18]). Several extensions, simplifications and improvements have been introduced over the years and in this paper, we present the consolidated current state with original contributions concerning both the modeling approach and the middleware support.

2   Organizational Models Based on SONAR

For organized activities two fundamental (and opposing) requirements have to be taken into account, the *division of labour* into various tasks and the *coordination* of carrying out these tasks. For SONAR, this can be rephrased more concretely and with reference to the terminology used in the introduction of the paper. *Coordinated carrying out of tasks* corresponds to a team executing a distributed (multi-party) workflow (DWF). *Division of labor* corresponds to the formation of such a team together with a DWF definition. Formation takes place according to general formation rules and a specific organizational structure to which these rules are applied. Consequently, SONAR models center around the duality of DWF (process) and organizational structure models. Both sides have to be coherently related with one another.

SONAR is based on Petri nets which offer both a graphical representation and formal semantics. In [17] we present SONAR in a formal way with theorems and proofs. However, in this paper we present a new version of SONAR, where the differences concern mainly a more readable and better structured organizational structure model. We will avoid formal specifications and instead give a rather illustrative introduction of the SONAR modeling approach. We just assume a general understanding of Petri nets (cf. [11]).

We will consider a running example throughout the paper. As SONAR models are based around the duality of distributed workflow (DWF) and organizational structure models, we could start with either of them. Here we begin with the workflow perspective. Figure 2 shows a DWF for collaboratively submitting a paper.

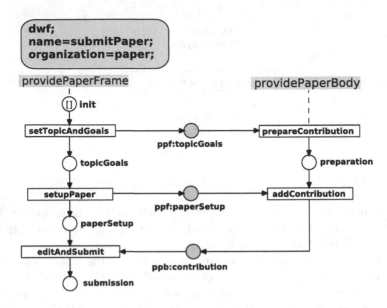

Fig. 2. Workflow with multiple roles for submitting paper

The DWF is distributed in the sense that it encompasses multiple roles, here providePaperFrame and providePaperBody. Each action of the DWF is mapped onto exactly one role. Actions are modeled as transitions. They are connected by places. Places connecting actions belonging to the same role form the *DWF life line* of that role and we arrange such a life line vertically in our models.[1] Places connecting actions of different roles can best be considered as *message transfers between roles* and we draw them as horizontal connections. One can consider the places between the transitions of different roles as the *interface* between these roles.[2] Places and transitions of a DWF model are named. Names of message places are prefixed with a key for the role sending that message (for example ppf: for the role providePaperFrame). Such message place names have to be unique across the whole set of DWF models of an overall SONAR model (see below for the reason). If a DWF model is decomposed into role parts and there exists an interface between two roles, each role part gets its own copy of the corresponding interface places.

---

[1] Of course, we do not rely on graphical arrangements in order to determine the different role parts of a DWF. We are currently working on an action inscription language for DWF transitions. So far, such an inscription does at least contain the name of the role that the transition belongs to. This is even more important when DWF life lines are not just sequences as in the rather simple examples in this paper. They may include forks, joins and concurrency. However, we have omitted the transition inscriptions in the DWF figures of this paper as the different role parts should be easily identified.

[2] Our notions of DWFs and role fragments of DWFs is closely related to the notions of *contracts* and *public views* of parties' shares in contracts from [4].

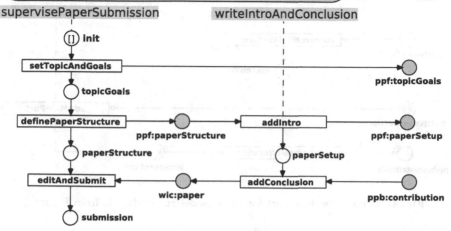

Fig. 3. Refined workflow part for the providePaperFrame role from Figure 2

Figure 3 shows another DWF. More exactly, it shows a DWF fragment.

This fragment consists of two roles supervisePaperSubmission and writeIntroAnd-Conclusion. These two roles can be used to refine the role providePaperFrame from Figure 2. Note that on the right side of Figure 3, the two roles supervisePaperSub-mission and writeIntroAndConclusion *in combination* share the same interface as the role providePaperFrame in Figure 2 in terms of message places (whose names have been carried over and uniquely identify them). In fact, it is possible to sub-stitute the two combined roles supervisePaperSubmission and writeIntroAndConclu-sion for the role providePaperFrame and obtain the same input/output behavior to the outside, i.e. from the viewpoint of the partner role providePaperBody.

Likewise, Figure 4 shows a DWF fragment, where the two roles writeRelat-edWorkSec and writeMainPart can be used to refine/substitute the role provide-PaperBody from Figure 2 while obtaining the same input/output behavior from the viewpoint of the partner role providePaperFrame.

Following this line of thought, it is of course also possible to substitute both roles providePaperFrame and providePaperBody with the combined roles from Fig-ures 3 and 4 respectively as both refinements respect the original input/output behavior of the substituted roles and the overall composition thus fits together. To conclude, we arrive at basically four possible DWFs for jointly submitting a paper. Further models of role refinements would lead to more possibilities of DWF composition. It remains to supplement such a set of DWFs and DWF fragments with a model that determines not only when to compose which DWF parts but also who takes on which roles in a finally composed DWF. This is where SONAR organizational structure models come into play.

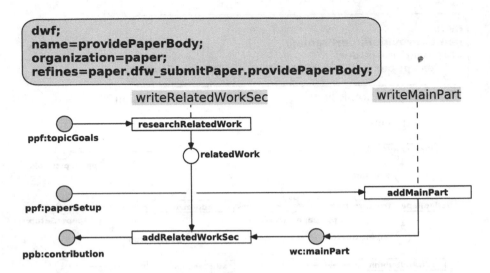

Fig. 4. Refined workflow part for the providePaperBody role from Figure 2

Organizational structures in SONAR are basically modeled as delegation structures, consisting of various organizational positions and task-based relationships between them. Figure 5 shows such a delegation net for the running example of joint paper submission.[3] A SONAR delegation net comprises multiple *positions* that are abstractions of actors (that occupy these positions when a SONAR organization is deployed). Positions are modeled as grey boxes that partition an underlying *task structure*. In Figure 5, we have as positions a *supervisor*, a *phd student* and two *students* that distribute tasks among themselves in order to jointly submit a paper. The underlying task structure is modeled as a Petri net. A place models a *task* and a transition models the *implementation* of a task. For this purpose, each transition has exactly one place in its preset. Task implementation can take on multiple forms and transitions are named accordingly:

1. *Execute:* The task is directly executed.
2. *Delegate:* The task is delegated.
3. *Refine:* Sub-tasks for a task are determined.
4. *Split:* A task is split into (already determined) sub-tasks.

The latter two cases are typically combined. All the implementation cases appear in Figure 5. Delegations are the kind of task implementation that relates two positions while refines, splits and executions are internal to positions.

The intertwining of a SONAR delegation net with DWF (fragment) models lays in the nature of the tasks. Each task in a delegation net corresponds to one

---

[3] Delegation nets have been over-hauled compared to previous publications, cf. [17,18]. The explicit inscription of transitions with the implementation type that they represent leads to slightly larger but much more readable models.

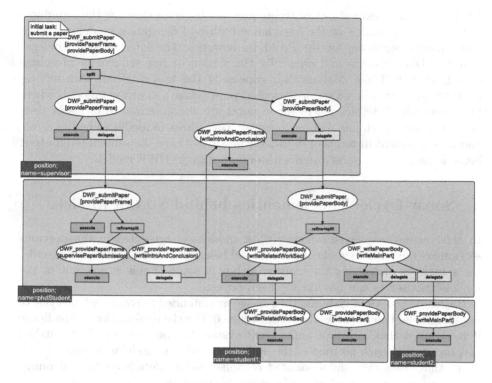

Fig. 5. Delegation model for jointly submitting a paper

or more roles in a DWF. Consequently, the places in Figure 5 are named according to the pattern $DWF_a[role_1, ..., role_n]$, meaning that the task corresponds to implementing the roles $role_1, ..., role_n$ from DWF DWF_a. Combining a delegation model with a set of DWF models leads to a straightforward notion of well-formedness of an overall SONAR model: (1) Delegation has to start with an initial task that corresponds to all roles of a complete DWF model (not a DWF fragment) and (2) task refinements must map onto associated role refinements in the set of DWF (fragment) models. Consequently, Figure 5 shows *one* possible delegation model for the DWF models from Figures 2 – 4 (likewise, other sets of DWF models may fit to the delegation model).

This way, the process perspective represented by DWF modeling is supplemented with an organizational structure perspective that guides both the formation of teams (where positions represent the team members) and the associated team DWFs. For example, the delegation model from Figure 5 allows multiple teams to be formed. An interesting fact is that team formation actually corresponds to the possible firings of the delegation net, its Petri net processes, cf. [12]. Each (maximal) Petri net process of a delegation net model corresponds to a possible team (cf. [17]).

Using Petri nets as the basis for SONAR modeling allows us to to take advantage of well-known analysis techniques. As we rely on simple place/transition

(P/T) nets, there exist standard techniques and tools for checking the soundness of workflow net models or the free-choice nature of delegation models (cf. [1,8] and www.promtools.org for the ProM framework). The interleaving of delegation and DWF models and especially the notion of role refinement of course goes beyond P/T net analysis. But especially the tool set from www.service-technology.org promotes a service-oriented perspective on Petri net models where Petri nets with interface places (open nets) are characterized in terms of their possible partners, cf. [26]. For our purpose, this allows to analyze whether a role and its refinement in terms of multiple roles really have the same input/output behavior and can be substituted with one another in DWF models.

3   Sonar Cycle: The Semantics behind SONAR Models

In this section we describe how SONAR models as presented in the previous section are intended to guide organizational behaviour. In this sense, we describe the semantics underlying the models, although some of this is inherent to the models themselves and has already been covered.

Basically, SONAR models and their usage are intended to cover a whole cycle of organizational behaviour as shown in Figure 6. For the explanation of the figure it is assumed that a SONAR multi-agent system has been set up. In a nutshell this means that each position of the underlying SONAR model is occupied by an agent that takes over the associated responsibilities. Details on SONAR multi-agent systems are covered in the following two sections.

The four parts of the cycle form a complete feedback loop, i.e. the organization *learns* as it adapts to the agent interactions it has stimulated previously. The cycle starts with *team formation* as soon as an organizational task (initial task from the underlying SONAR model) becomes active. This has already been covered in the previous section. A team is formed by successive task implementation steps. As soon as a team is formed, so is the associated team DWF for this particular team.

However, this team DWF possibly encompasses multiple ways to execute it (multiple Petri net processes of the team DWF). Consequently, the team members have to negotiate in order to arrive at a mutually acceptable compromise. This compromise of how to execute a team DWF we call a *team plan*. We will not cover team planning thoroughly in this paper. We have laid the theoretical groundwork for team planning according to our demands in [16], where Petri net unfoldings are used as a data structure for a distributed team planning algorithm.

As soon as a team plan has been negotiated, the plan may be executed by the team. A team plan might be an "ordinary" team plan, where the plan targets at fulfilling a day-to-day business task. In other cases, a team plan might be a *transformation plan*. In this case, the whole team was formed due to an initial task that targets at transforming the organization itself. In this case, steps of the team plan consist for example of adding positions, removing delegation links etc. Consequently, re-organization takes place and this means that the SONAR

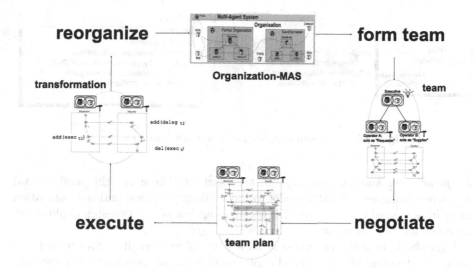

reorganize

form team

transformation

team

add(deleg t1'

add(exec t1)

del(exec t)

Organization-MAS

Operator A: Operator B:
acts as "Requester"   acts as "Supplier"

execute

negotiate

team plan

Fig. 6. The SONAR cycle

model underlying the first step of the cycle is altered. Thus, the cycle is closed. For the same reasons as for team planning, we will not focus on organizational transformations in this paper. The theoretical groundwork has been laid in [15] but the incorporation into our middleware implementation is not yet finished. However, as described in the following section, we have prepared the generation of software artifacts in a way to allow for rather light-weight organizational transformations at run-time.

4   Model Deployment

The models presented so far have been on a relatively high level. They are basically P/T nets, where some naming conventions have to be followed. There are no execution details, except for the fact that Petri nets inherently have an operational semantics. It is not even necessary to model all possible DWFs that can occur during the operation of a SONAR organization. Instead, it is sufficient to model some initial DWF models and then just add models for selective role refinements.

In order to utilize the models in the context of a SONAR-based middleware layer for teamwork, some deployment steps are necessary. The semantics behind SONAR models has been described in the previous section in terms of the SONAR cycle that starts with the occurrence of an initial organizational task (however, a complete cycle is only established in the case, where this initial task is a transformation task). Our current middleware implementation for SONAR does not yet fully support the *negotiate* and *reorganize* steps from Figure 6. We will describe how the requirements for these two steps have already been taken into account for our model deployment approach. Nevertheless, we concentrate on

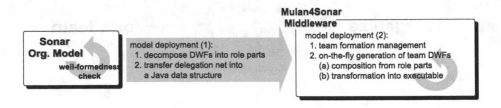

Fig. 7. Model-driven support for teamwork based on SONAR

the *form team* and *execute* steps in this section. These are the fundamental ones when bringing a SONAR model to life while negotiation and reorganization occur in advanced cases. Figure 7 gives an overview of our two-step deployment approach for SONAR models.

After checking well-formedness of all aspects of an overall SONAR model (see Section 2), the first phase of model deployment is pre-processing. One immediate question is whether to use the Petri net models themselves (enriched/extended for deployment)[4] or whether to transfer them into other artifacts. Here, the aspect of re-organization had a strong impact on answering this question. Changing the Petri net models and re-deploying them at run-time can get quite cumbersome and costly. Currently, we have decided to use the DWF models directly in their Petri net form and to transfer the delegation model into a Java data structure.

We treat DWF models and thus *how things are basically done* as rather persistent and we consequently see the DWF role parts as basic behavioral building blocks. Fundamentally changing the DWF models is often better done by starting from scratch. However, instead of changing DWF models, they can always be extended by further role refinements.

The delegation model on the other hand and thus *the context leading to the actual behavior* is in our opinion prone to more frequent and light-weight re-organization efforts: adding/removing positions, adding/removing delegation relationships, adding/removing executions etc. Consequently, we prefer a data structure that handles changes easier. In addition, such a data structure is helpful to share (communicate about) and process knowledge in the context of team formation: determining the eligibility of task implementations, possible delegation partners or whole sub-teams etc.

To conclude, the pre-processing phase of model deployment comprises two parts.

1. All DWF models are decomposed into their singular role parts, which makes it easy to dynamically compose team DWFs later on. It might of course be possible to keep role compositions that always have to appear together in a team DWF, like supervisePaperSubmission and writeIntroAndConclusion from the running example. But as we intend to have dynamic re-organizations of

---

[4] This is what we did for our previous versions of a SONAR middleware layer, cf. [18].

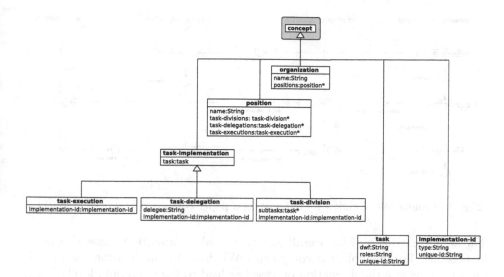

Fig. 8. Concept (or class) diagram for SONAR delegation models

SONAR models, further role refinements might be introduced at run-time. Thus, it is simpler to keep track of each singular role part in the first place.

2. From the delegation model, a Java data structure is generated. Figure 8 shows the according class diagram in UML style. More specifically, it is a *concept diagram* [7] and is supported by the tool suite that we use in the context of our multi-agent framework MULAN that we briefly address in the following section.[5] The class hierarchy resulting from a concept diagram comes with the handy feature that all objects of these classes have FIPA[6]-conform String representations, which allows to directly include them as message contents in agent communication. According to the class hierarchy from Figure 8, each SONAR delegation model is transferred into an *organization object* that contains all other information.

In the second phase of model deployment, the pre-processed models are used by the MULAN4SONAR middleware layer to enable and frame teamwork among members of a SONAR organization. Members are (social or artificial) actors that access the middleware layer and occupy positions of a SONAR delegation model. We will elaborate on the MULAN4SONAR middleware layer and on how to access it in the next section.

Basically, the Java data structure of the delegation model is used to manage task delegation and thus the *form team* step of the SONAR cycle. As soon as a team is formed, there is a unique team DWF associated with it: It is the composed DWF that consists of the role parts that are implemented by *execute* (instead of *refine, split* or *delegate*) transitions during the delegation process.

---

[5] See also http://www.paose.net

[6] http://www.fipa.org

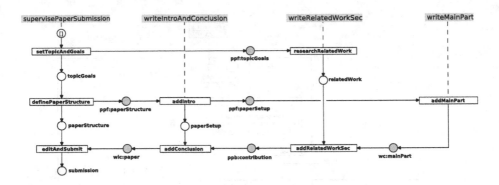

Fig. 9. A multi-role workflow for submitting a paper composed from role fragments

The well-formedness of an overall SONAR model ensures that these role parts fit together. For example, the composed DWF from Figure 9 is the team DWF for a team, where the delegation process has lead to the maximum level of task (and thus role) refinement for the running example of joint paper submission.

Consequently, team formation leads to an on-thy-fly generation of the corresponding team DWF. However, for such a team DWF to be ready for the *execute* step of the SONAR cycle, a further refinement and enrichment has to be carried out. This is also done by automatic generation. Basically, each action transition of a team DWF has to be enriched with execution inscriptions and has to be divided into a *call* and *return* part. Figure 10 exemplifies the substitution rule applied to a DWF transition for the addConclusion action of the team DWF from Figure 9.

The transition is split into two transitions for call and return. The names of places lead to the generation of variable names that are bound to work-item and result objects of the action. The action call is parametrized with the role name, action name and a set of incoming work-items. The surrounding engine for the execution of team DWFs has to take care of forwarding the call to the position holder that implements this role for this team. In addition, the engine generates a unique action ID that can be used to associate action call and return. The action return is parametrized with a result object. We omit details on handling erroneous or aborted execution of DWF actions here.

Figure 11 shows the class diagram for content objects used in the context of executable team DWFs.

More specifically, it shows the generic part. Concrete SONAR models are intended to extend the concept dwf-action-content with customized concepts. In fact, we are working on a high-level action inscription language for SONAR DWF models. Such a language can for example be used to attach pre-conditions, post-conditions and effects for/of DWF actions based on the content objects and their attributes that are involved in the action. For this purpose it is necessary to explicitly define the according custom concepts.

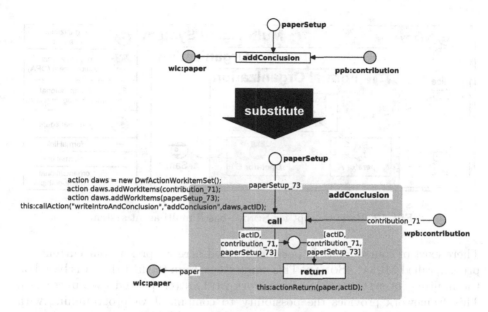

Fig. 10. Substitution rule (by example) for generating executable workflow models

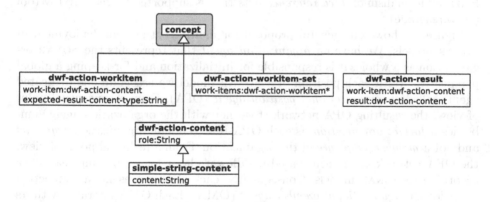

Fig. 11. Concept (or class) diagram for executable team DWF contents

To conclude this section, the illustrative and rather high-level Petri net models that a modeler has to create for a SONAR organization are rich enough to allow the generation of different kinds of executable artifacts for computer-supported teamwork. In the next section, we give an overview of a middleware implementation that utilizes these artifacts.

5 MULAN4SONAR: Agent-Based Teamwork Engine

We present a middleware implementation for teamwork support that is based on SONAR models and their deployment as described in the previous sections.

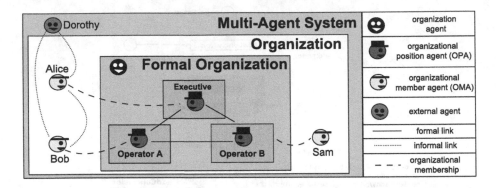

Fig. 12. Basic concept for SONAR-based multi-agent systems

There exist of course multiple possibilities and here we present our current approach, called MULAN4SONAR. This name stems from the fact that it is based on the multi-agent system (MAS) framework MULAN (cf. [7] and www.paose.net). This framework provides the possibility to combine Java programming with Petri net modeling and simulation for realizing MAS and is consequently perfectly suited for our purpose. More concretely, MULAN relies on the high-level Petri net formalism of *Java reference nets* that is supported by the RENEW tool (www.renew.de).[7]

Figure 12 shows our general proposal for multi-agent system deployment of SONAR models. We have an *organization agent* that represents the SONAR organization as a whole. It is responsible for initialization and for keeping a global perspective. With each position of a SONAR model we associate one dedicated agent, called an *organizational position agent* (OPA). From a conceptual point of view, the resulting OPA network (together with the organization agent) embodies a *formal organization* as each OPA represents an organizational *artifact* and not a *member/employee* of the organization. From a technical point of view, the OPA network is an agent-based middleware layer for supporting teamwork according to SONAR models. Consequently, each OPA represents a connection point for an *organizational member agent* (OMA). Each OMA interacts with its associated OPA to carry out organizational tasks and to make decisions, where required. An OPA both enables and constrains organizational behavior of its OMA. The OMA can effect the organization only in a way that is in conformance with the OPA's specification. In return, the OPA relieves its OMA of a considerable amount of organizational overhead by automating coordination and administration. Conceptually speaking, OMAs implement/occupy the formal positions of the organization. Note that an OMA can be an artificial as well as a human agent. OMAs might of course only be partially involved in an

---

[7] An example for using Java inscriptions in the context of a Petri net model was already shown in Figure 10. The other way round is equally possible, namely having Java objects monitoring, triggering or even controlling parts of the execution (simulation) of a Petri net model.

organization and have relationships to multiple other agents than their OPA or even to agents completely external to the organization. From the perspective of the organization, all other ties than the OPA-OPA and OPA-OMA links are considered as informal connections.

Our current implementation of MULAN4SONAR follows this general proposal. However, it does not (yet) feature OPAs as distinct agents. Instead, our current implementation features one central *organization agent* that manages the teamwork processes of a SONAR organization but also utilizes separate *OPA components* for each position. Consequently, we have already prepared the implementation in way to be able to single out the components as OPAs and thus to obtain a more distributed implementation. Figure 13 shows the three-level architecture of the organization agent in its current form. This architecture is actually realized based on the high-level Petri net concept of *nets-within-nets* [24], where Petri nets can have other Petri nets as tokens and cross-net communication is possible. Nets-within-nets modeling and simulation is supported by the RENEW tool and is one of the fundamental features of MAS development with MULAN. The figure only shows a high-level overview of the organization agent's architecture but it represents the actual implementation quite precisely. In the remainder, we describe where the various deployment artifacts from the previous section come into play in order to support the different steps of the SONAR cycle.

On the top level of the *organization agent*, the organization is initialized and the pre-processing of the original SONAR model is carried out, meaning the generation of a Java organization object and the decomposition of DWF models into singular role parts. Afterwards, the *teamwork engine* is initialized with the pre-processed models as input and represents the second level.

The *teamwork engine* sets up *OPA components* for all positions and makes the delegation model in the form of the Java organization object available to them. The generated DWF role parts are stored in a repository. We will not go into detail concerning the manifold responsibilities of the OPA components with respect to their connected OMAs. We just assume that basically, they take care of binding users as members (OMAs) into the organization and manage the inclusion of the OMAs' actions and decisions in conformance to the organizational specifications.

A new *teamwork activity* is started as soon as an OPA (triggered by its OMA) activates an initial task that lies within its position responsibilities. Ongoing teamwork activities and OPA components stay connected via the teamwork engine level (ask OPA transition) as the teamwork activity level constantly requires input by the OPAs to keep the SONAR cycle steps running. The parts of the architecture, where the OPAs are required to make decisions or execute actions are marked by black transitions.

A teamwork activity in its basic form comprises the *form team* and *execute* steps of the Sonar cycle. The *negotiate* and *reorganize* steps are not yet fully integrated into our middleware, but we have already added the channels for organizational transformations as shown in the figure.

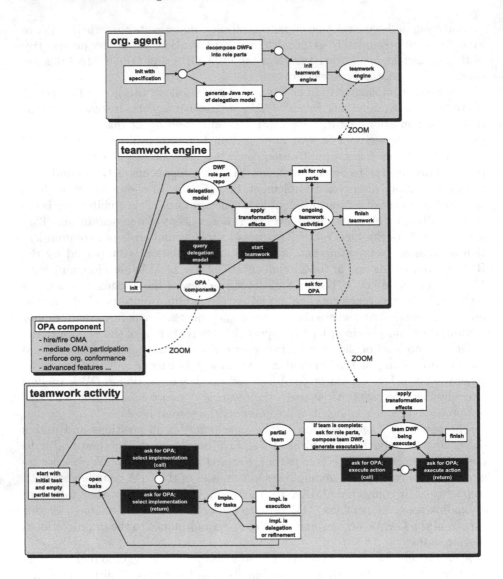

Fig. 13. Three-level architecture of the SONAR teamwork engine agent

Team formation basically comprises the task-for-task delegation process. The result of this is a team together with role parts that need to be implemented. The team activity layer then accesses the DWF role part repository via the teamwork engine layer in order to compose the team DWF from the role parts. From the team DWF, an executable version is generated and the *execute* phase starts. During this phase, the actions of the team DWF are executed. In the case of a reorganization team and team DWF, such actions come with transformation effects on the underlying SONAR model of the organization and thus have feedback on the Java delegation model and/or the DWF role part repository of the teamwork engine layer.

6 Related Work

In the introduction, the central aim of our work was stated as presenting an organizational modeling approach that respects structural and process-related features likewise. It shall be possible to treat both dimensions as distinct but at the same time be able to tightly interweave them. In addition, we aim at a model that immediately leans itself to computer-aided implementation/support. There exists a wide range of related work and in this section we will position our work in relation to it.

While rather comprehensive and multi-dimensional organizational models are to some extent addressed in the field of enterprise architecture management (EAM), EAM is a rather high-level discipline and is at least not necessarily concerned with models whose primary purpose is to be directly transferred into software artifacts (although this may be true for some parts, especially for process models). Contrary to that, the field of organization-oriented multi-agent systems is primarily concerned with quite comprehensive organizational models that exhibit a close gap to software-technical deployment [6,9]. Most of the models that we find here are backed up by a middleware implementation just like we presented for our SONAR approach in this paper. In the MAS field, we find models that encompass multiple integrated organizational perspectives (e.g. structure, function, interactions, norms). But despite this multi-perspective approach, we typically still find approaches where either a structural or a process perspective dominates.

For example, by means of the popular S-$\mathcal{MOISE}^+$ [13] approach, it is possible to build sophisticated structural models. Building upon the two base concepts of roles and groups, complex structural compositions are possible based on various rules for group/role hierarchies and intra- as well as inter-group relationships between roles. However, the process-related dimension plays a much lesser role. While it is possible to define organizational plans in terms of goal and sub-goal relationships and relate groups and roles to them via deontic specifications (obligation, permission), concrete process definitions can only be inferred. Goal relationships like AND, OR, PARALLEL, SEQUENCE allow for some conclusions on processes that lead to the achievement of a top-level goal. But specific and more complex interactions for fulfilling a goal in a cooperative manner that goes beyond the rather limited goal relationships is not possible. The same criticism holds for most of the existing MAS teamwork frameworks, exemplified by the TEAMCORE/KARMA [22] approach. Based on a logical framework of joint commitment and intentions, organization hierarchies and plans in terms of goal hierarchies can be specified. The actual processes for achieving goals have to be inferred from goal relationships and from the peculiarities of the underlying logical framework.

Opposed to such approaches the modeling approach ISLANDER [10] for MAS institutions allows to model complex process arrangements. ISLANDER features the automata-based modeling of interaction *scenes* between participating roles. In addition, multiple scenes are connected via a surrounding so-called *performative structure* that specifies, under which circumstances role-occupants may move from scene to scene (and possibly change roles in doing so). In this case,

an explicit structural modeling dimension is missing and structural relationships between roles can only be inferred from the role responsibilities in the
various scenes and the movement of roles between scenes moves according to the
performative structure.

Contrary to the mentioned MAS approaches, the SONAR model we presented
in this paper aims at a tight integration of structural and process-related features
of an organization. One might argue that due to our Petri net-based approach,
our structural (position delegation) model is actually process-oriented. While
this is certainly true, it still captures the functional and authority-like relationships between positions and thus what traditionally is considered as structure in
organization theory. Of course, real-world organizational scenarios are very complex, comprise a multitude of perspectives and underly many different forces. Our
model intentionally features a restricted set of core organizational features. In
this sense, we believe it is very well suited and applicable for any organizational
setting where the focus lies on the execution of clearly defined and complex
tasks in a shared manner between different parties. It is probably not well suited
for modeling organizational scenarios where clear-cut tasks do not play a dominant role (for example anything from the "natural systems" school of thought in
organizational theory, cf. [23]).

As already mentioned in the introduction, we see the SONAR modeling approach and its underlying semantics to a large part as a detailed view of service
lookups in organizational settings where each role part of a DWF represents its
own service in the context of a larger service cooperation (the whole DWF).
More concretely, our approach lies in the intersection of *service orchestration*
and *service choreography* as described [21]. Service orchestration refers to service cooperation that is largely controlled by a central coordinator. To some
extent, this is true for our approach as there always exists the global perspective
of the whole organization (cf. the organization agent in our middleware implementation). However, our approach is more on the service choreography side,
which means service cooperation between autonomous parties where conversa-
tions and mutual agreement between the parties are key instead of a central
control. There exists a global *choreography model/contract* that the different
parties have to adher to (cf. [20]). The various parties' share of this contract are
described as *behavioral interfaces* and the implementation of these interfaces is
up to the autonomous partners. This maps perfectly onto our notion of DWFs
and DWF fragments that are taken over by position holders. The main feature
that distinguishes our approach from others in this area (as already mentioned
in Section 2, our notions are for example very closely related to the ones in [4])
is the delegation-based mechanism for selecting the various parts for forming
the overall choreography. It is based on a structural model of the organization and consequently poses a natural view on service lookups in organizational
scenarios.

7   Conclusion and Outlook

Starting from the question for an integrated treatment of structure and process perspectives in modeling collaborative systems, we have presented our SONAR approach. It provides a way to capture the whole context of team-oriented process management: from the underlying organizational structure over team formation up to process execution by the team. Put differently, it provides a natural way for task-based organizational scenarios to implement a sophisticated service lookup. The accompanying models are rather high-level and illustrative but at the same time they are rich enough in order to generate executable models and other kinds of code that together form the core of the MULAN4SONAR middleware implementation for team-oriented process management.

Regarding our future research efforts, there is a range of topics that we and other people from our research group are working on.

- *Collaborative Agent Platform (deployment):* Our group has the long-term goal of developing an agent-based platform for computer-supported collaboration. We envision SONAR-based organizational models to be used for specific teamwork applications *on top of the platform* as well as for supporting the infrastructure *of the platform itself*, managing the various platform tasks and processes.
- *Self-organization and team planning:* As explained in Section 3, we have laid the theoretical groundwork to incorporate re-organization and team planning into our approach in [15] and [16] respectively. They are not yet fully incorporated into our middleware implementation.
- *Hierarchy/holism:* While the idea of self-organization introduces multiple management levels in the context of *one* SONAR organization, we also address the concept of having multiple levels of nested SONAR organizations. The basic idea is to have positions being occupied by *organizational units* that are SONAR organizations themselves. This allows to model inter-organizational scenarios and so-called *multi-organization systems*. The refinement concept for roles and tasks inherent to SONAR directly supports such an extension. For a thorough report of our research on modeling organizational units and multi-organization systems (not limited to SONAR), we refer to [25] (in German).
- *Simulation:* We are interested in organizational simulation. We intend to enrich the models with quantitative information and apply routines to evaluate simulation runs with respect to certain criteria. Especially in combination with hierarchic models we are interested in studying the fit of different (types of) organizational units to one another (in terms of nesting relationships as well as in terms of cooperation effectiveness on the same level).

As a test-bed for multi-agent systems our group has implementated a MAS version of the board game "The Settlers of Catan" on top of the MULAN framework. In future work we will re-design this system using the SONAR approach. The intended improvement is an increase of the percentage of *model-generated* code of the whole system, which can easily be compared to the existing implementation.

References

1. van der Aalst, W.: Verification of workflow nets. In: Azéma, P., Balbo, G. (eds.) ICATPN 1997. LNCS, vol. 1248, pp. 407–426. Springer, Heidelberg (1997)
2. van der Aalst, W.: Interorganizational workflows. Systems Analysis - Modelling - Simulation 34(3), 335–367 (1999)
3. van der Aalst, W., ter Hofstede, A.: YAWL: Yet another workflow language. Information Systems 30(4), 245–275 (2005)
4. van der Aalst, W., Lohmann, N., Massuthe, P., Stahl, C., Wolf, K.: Multiparty contracts: Agreeing and implementing interorganizational processes. Computer Journal 53(1), 90–106 (2010)
5. Alves, A., et al.: OASIS web services business process execution language (WS-BPEL) v2.0. OASIS Standard, 11 (April 2007)
6. Boissier, O., Hübner, J.F., Sichman, J.S.: Organization oriented programming: From closed to open organizations. In: O'Hare, G.M.P., Ricci, A., O'Grady, M.J., Dikenelli, O. (eds.) ESAW 2006. LNCS (LNAI), vol. 4457, pp. 86–105. Springer, Heidelberg (2007)
7. Cabac, L.: Modeling Petri Net-Based Multi-Agent Applications. Agent Technology: Theory and Application, Logos, vol. 5 (2010)
8. Desel, J., Esparza, J.: Free Choice Petri Nets. Cambridge Tracks in Theoretical Computer Science, vol. 40. Cambridge University Press (1995)
9. Dignum, V.: The role of organization in agent systems. In: Dignum, V. (ed.) Handbook of Research on Multi-Agent Systems: Semantics and Dynamics of Organizational Models. Information Science Reference, pp. 1–16 (2009)
10. Esteva, M., de la Cruz, D., Sierra, C.: ISLANDER: An electronic institutions editor. In: Proceedings of the First International Joint Conference on Autonomous Agents & Multiagent Systems, AAMAS 2002, pp. 1045–1052. ACM (2002)
11. Girault, C., Valk, R. (eds.): Petri Nets for Systems Engineering: A Guide to Modelling, Verification and Applications. Springer (2003)
12. Goltz, U., Reisig, W.: The non-sequential behaviour of Petri nets. Information and Control 57(2–3), 125–147 (1983)
13. Hübner, J.F., Sichman, J.S., Boissier, O.: Using the $\mathcal{M}oise^+$ for a cooperative framework of MAS reorganisation. In: Bazzan, A.L.C., Labidi, S. (eds.) SBIA 2004. LNCS (LNAI), vol. 3171, pp. 506–515. Springer, Heidelberg (2004)
14. Keller, G., Nüttgens, M., Scheer, A.W.: Semantische Prozessmodellierung auf der Grundlage "Ereignisgesteuerter Prozessketten (EPK)". In: Scheer, A.W. (ed.) Veröffentlichungen des Instituts für Wirtschaftsinformatik (IWi). Universität des Saarlandes, Heft 89 (1992)
15. Köhler-Bußmeier, M.: Analysing SONAR model transformations. In: Accorsi, R., Murata, T., Ranise, S. (eds.) Proceedings of the International Workshop on Petri Net-Based Security (WooPS 2012), pp. 55–70 (2012)
16. Köhler-Bußmeier, M.: Negotiating inter-organisational processes: An approach baaed on unfoldings and workflow nets. In: Proceedings of the International Workshop on Concurrency, Specification and Programming, CS&P 2012 (2012)
17. Köhler-Bußmeier, M., Wester-Ebbinghaus, M., Moldt, D.: A formal model for organisational structures behind process-aware information systems. In: Jensen, K., van der Aalst, W.M.P. (eds.) Transactions on Petri Nets and Other Models of Concurrency II. LNCS, vol. 5460, pp. 98–114. Springer, Heidelberg (2009)
18. Köhler-Bußmeier, M., Wester-Ebbinghaus, M., Moldt, D.: Generating executable multi-agent system prototypes from SONAR specifications. In: De Vos, M., Fornara, N., Pitt, J.V., Vouros, G. (eds.) COIN 2010. LNCS, vol. 6541, pp. 21–38. Springer, Heidelberg (2011)

19. OMG: Business process modeling notation (BPMN) version 1.0. OMG Final Adopted Specification, Object Management Group (2006)
20. Papazoglou, M.: Web Services: Principles and Technology. Pearson Education Limited (2008)
21. Peltz, C.: Web services orchestration and choreography. IEEE Computer 36(10), 46–52 (2003)
22. Pynadath, D., Tambe, M.: An automated teamwork infrastructure for heterogeneous software agents and humans. Autonomous Agents and Multi-Agent Systems 7(1-2), 71–100 (2003)
23. Scott, W.R.: Organizations: Rational, Natural and Open Systems, 5th edn. Prentice Hall (2003)
24. Valk, R.: Object Petri nets: Using the nets-within-nets paradigm. In: Desel, J., Reisig, W., Rozenberg, G. (eds.) Lectures on Concurrency and Petri Nets. LNCS, vol. 3098, pp. 819–848. Springer, Heidelberg (2004)
25. Wester-Ebbinghaus, M.: Von Multiagentensystemen zu Multiorganisationssystemen – Modellierung auf Basis von Petrinetzen. Dissertation, Universität Hamburg, Fachbereich Informatik. Elektronische Veröffentlichung im Bibliothekssystem der Universität Hamburg (2010), http://www.sub.uni-hamburg.de/opus/volltexte/2011/4974/
26. Wolf, K.: Does my service have partners? In: Jensen, K., van der Aalst, W.M.P. (eds.) Transactions on Petri Nets and Other Models of Concurrency II. LNCS, vol. 5460, pp. 152–171. Springer, Heidelberg (2009)

Grade/CPN: A Tool and Temporal Logic for Testing Colored Petri Net Models in Teaching

Michael Westergaard[1,2,*], Dirk Fahland[1], and Christian Stahl[1]

[1] Department of Mathematics and Computer Science,
Eindhoven University of Technology, The Netherlands
{m.westergaard,d.fahland,c.stahl}@tue.nl
[2] National Research University Higher School of Economics,
Moscow, 101000, Russia

Abstract. Grading dozens of Petri net models manually is a tedious and error-prone task. In this paper, we present Grade/CPN, a tool *supporting the grading of Colored Petri nets modeled in CPN Tools*. The tool is extensible, configurable, and can check static and dynamic properties. It automatically handles tedious tasks like checking that good modeling practise is adhered to, and supports tasks that are difficult to automate, such as checking model legibility. We propose and support the *Britney Temporal Logic* which can be used to guide the simulator and to check temporal properties. We provide our experiences with using the tool in a course with 100 participants.

1 Introduction

Colored Petri nets (CPNs) [1] is a formalism useful for modeling a broad range of real-life systems, including complex network protocols [1] and business information systems [2]. It is thus natural to use CPNs or other Petri net formalisms when teaching such subjects. As modeling can only really be learned by doing, hands-on experience is a must. Larger classes can comprise more than one hundred students, and manually checking models created by students is time consuming and error-prone. This is particularly unpleasant because much of the effort is spent on checking trivial things, including whether good modeling standards are adhered to and whether formal requirements to the model are satisfied. In this paper, we aim at *supporting the grading of many models implementing the same specification* by providing with Grade/CPN an *extensible tool* for automatic assessment of such routine properties, allowing teachers to focus on more complicated tasks.

The support required for grading assignments is similar to what is needed for testing or model checking, as we need to check a model against some formal requirements. The models we deal with in our case study have infinite state spaces, so here we focus on the testing perspective, as a model may not be suitable for

---

* The study was implemented in the framework of the Basic Research Program at the National Research University Higher School of Economics (HSE) in 2013.

M. Koutny et al. (Eds.): ToPNoC VIII, LNCS 8100, pp. 180–202, 2013.

model checking due to having a large or even unbounded state space. Thus, parts of the work described here is also applicable to general testing of CPN models, but we present it here in the context in which it was developed. The significant difference to classical testing is that for grading *a possibly large set of different models* is to be checked against *the same specification* in a uniform way.

CPN Tools [3] is a tool for editing, simulating and analysing CPN models. It supports the user during the construction of the model due to incremental syntax checking, which gives immediate feedback about errors, and allows modelers to experiment with incomplete and even only partially correct models. This is a useful feature for inexperienced users and makes CPN Tools suitable in teaching. Furthermore, the Windows version of CPN Tools is downloaded more than 5,000 times a year, indicating that it is broadly used. The broad usage also means that CPN Tools has reached a fairly stable state, which reduces unnecessary frustrations during modeling. Finally, CPN Tools has extensive online help and video tutorials, which means it is easy for students to get started. For these reasons, we think that CPN Tools is a good choice of a tool for teaching.

There are as many ways of using models as there are teachers, so it is important that the requirements for the model can be described easily. This means that the grading tool must be *configurable*, allowing individual teachers to customize what is checked and how adhering to or deviating from each requirement is awarded or punished. In addition, it must be easily possible to *extend* the tool with new requirements. Thus our tool must have a plug-in like architecture allowing new requirements to be added with minimal effort. At the same time, we do not desire a heavy-weight framework with a steep learning curve just to add a simple custom requirement. Of course, such a tool should come with a set of reasonable built-in plug-ins, so it is useful for many scenarios without requiring any programming.

To illustrate our motivation for developing such a tool, assume we want students to model a (simplified) delivery service using CPN Tools. The idea is to model that customers order products from a shop, and the shop uses a delivery service to deliver ordered products to the customers. To this end, we would provide students with a base model as in Fig. 1. The CPN in Fig. 1 models the behavior of the customer and the shop and pro-

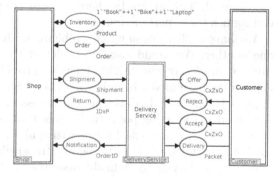

Fig. 1. Base model of a delivery service

vides the interface between customer and delivery service (Reject, Offer, Accept, and Delivery) and the interface between shop and delivery service (Shipment, Return, and Notification). A customer can choose a product from the catalog and place an order via place Order. The shop prepares the ordered product for shipment and sends the resulting packet to the delivery service via Shipment.

The delivery service shall in all tasks try to deliver packets to the respective customers via place Offer. If a customer is not at home, a token is placed on place Reject; otherwise, a token is produced on place Accept and, finally, the delivery service hands over the packet to the customer via place Delivery. Place Return is used to send a packet back to the shop in case the packet could not be delivered. In addition, the delivery service informs the shop via place Notification that a packet has been successfully delivered. The pages Shop and Customer are given but the DeliveryService is empty and intended to be modeled by the student.

When students are given such a base model, they are asked to model the missing part(s) or to change or improve the given model. These changes must adhere to certain constraints. In our example, we would need to be able to check that the given *environment has not been changed* (as the environment constitutes a contract with the external world) and that the *model satisfies the given requirements*, which often means that behavioral properties need to be checked. Our focus on the first version of our tool has therefore been on making it easy to check these requirements.

We have also implemented checks that ensure good modeling practice, including *respecting data hiding* (i.e., student solutions are not allowed to connect to nodes of the environment other than the interface places) and *proper termination* (i.e., ensuring that tokens are not erroneously left behind), and simple *static analysis* (e.g., ensuring that communication channels are used in the correct direction, i.e., no messages are produced on an input channel).

As we cannot check all properties mechanically—for example, whether the model is readable and understandable—we have implemented functionality supporting doing this manually. This includes generating a *view of the model* in which the student-designed parts are highlighted and the given parts from Fig. 1 are dimmed. This allows teachers to focus on the new parts without having to distinguish these parts manually.

We have earlier encountered problems with students copying solutions from one another. We would also like to detect this, so we have *checks that at least make it harder to cheat*. This includes providing each student with a unique copy of the base model from Fig. 1 with a cryptographic signature including the student ID embedded. This makes it impossible for two students to use the same base model as starting point (indicating that one got a copy from the other).

Finally, we want a *report* summarizing all findings; the report should be useful for both teachers, who should be able to grade the model based on the report only, without having to manually open the model in CPN Tools except in special cases, and for students, who should be pointed to flaws in the model, using error traces when applicable. To sum up, we need a tool that

1. Works with CPN Tools models.
2. Provides easy configuration.
3. Is easily extensible.
4. Contains a reasonable base set of capabilities, including:
   (a) Detect changes to a given environment,
   (b) Check dynamic properties using simulation.

    (c) Check good modeling practise, including data hiding, proper termination, and provide simple static analysis.
5. Supports the manual part of the grading process.
6. Detects attempts to defraud.
7. Provides a report that pin-points problems, aids the teacher in grading, and allows students to understand problems.

We have chosen to implement our tool as a vanilla Java application. The language is chosen due to its popularity and platform-independence. We have chosen not to rely on a framework for handling plug-ins, as these frameworks often demand significant overhead due to providing features we do not need (e.g., we do not need dynamic configuration of plug-ins). We have used the library Access/CPN [4] as it provides an easy way to load CPN models and programmatically interact with the simulator.

    We continue with the outline of the architecture of our tool and introduce some simple plug-ins checking basic properties in Sect. 2. In Sect. 3, we introduce a temporal logic which is powerful enough to describe most dynamic requirements while still being easy to use. In Sect. 4, we provide details on automatic attempt to improve coverage and relate our work to automatic testing. In Sect. 5, we provide implementation details and we sum up our experiences using our tool in semi-automatically assessing assignments from close to 100 students. Finally, we discuss related work, conclude the paper, and provide directions for future work.

    A preliminary version of this work has been published in [5]. Compared with [5], we have extended our syntax to handle a global quantifier and variables, and provide a simpler semantics with subtle errors fixed (see Sect. 3). Moreover, the details on coverage and the comparison with automatic testing (see Sect. 4) are new results. We have also implemented some of the future work of the previous paper, including a version of the tool allowing students to get feedback before final grading (see Sect 4), and we report how that has improved the grades of students (see Sect. 5).

2   Architecture

In this section, we outline the architecture of Grade/CPN. We first give the overall architecture and explain how this solves requirements 1, 2, 3, and 7 from the introduction. Then, we provide the details of some of the built-in plug-ins, focusing on requirements 4(a), 4(c), and 6. Requirement 4(b) is handled in detail in the next section, and requirement 5 is handled partly in this section and partly when we report our experiences in Sect. 5.

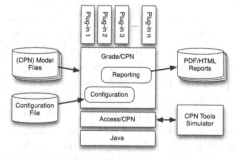

Fig. 2. Overall architecture and environment of Grade/CPN

2.1 Overall Architecture

Figure 2 shows the overall architecture of Grade/CPN. We see that we build on top of Java and Access/CPN [4]. Access/CPN is a Java library making it possible to interact directly with the CPN Tools Simulator, including loading models and translating them to an object structure we can use for static analysis, and send to the simulator process also used by CPN Tools to perform syntax check and simulation of models. Grade/CPN comprises two important components, one for Configuration and one for Reporting, as well as an interface to several Plug-ins. The Configuration component is responsible for loading a configuration file and using it to instantiate and configure the appropriate plug-ins. Each plug-in returns messages useful for the Reporting component, which use this information to generate an on-screen status view showing the overall correctness of the checked models and for generating an individual report for each student. The report can be generated as either an HTML file suitable for reading in a Web-browser or a PDF file suitable for printing or archival.

The central interface of Grade/CPN is PlugIn, shown in Listing 1 (ll. 1–5). Each plug-in must implement this interface. The configure method is a factory method to instantiate the plug-in, and takes how many points should be awarded if the plug-in succeeds and a configuration string. The format of the configuration string is defined by the plug-in, but will typically be a name identifying the plug-in and a list of named parameters. If the plug-in can be instantiated with a given configuration string, it returns a new configured instance and otherwise it returns null. This allows us to create an abstract factory for instantiating plug-ins from a string. Furthermore, a plug-in has a method grade, which is given a student ID, a base model (base), the student solution (model), and a connection to the simulator. The plug-in can use this information to arrive at its conclusion and return a Message, which comprises how many points are awarded and a descriptive message with the reason for the grade.

Reporting. The Reporting component of Fig. 2 is responsible for emitting a report based on the result of the PlugIns. All interfaces pertaining to reporting is shown in Listing 1 (ll. 7–17). The main class is Report (ll. 7–10), which is instantiated for each student ID and contains a set of pairs of PlugIns and Messages (produced by the grade method).

A Message (ll. 11–13) ties together a number of awarded points, a descriptive

Point range	Points	Reason
-100.00 - 0.00	0.00	The interface has not been modified incorrectly.
-5.00 - 0.00	0.00	Declarations were preserved and new ones were added (that is ok).
-5.00 - 0.00	-5.00	generated_Task1b-solution.cpn is not a substring of Task1b-solution.cpn
-5.00 - 0.00	-5.00	Did not match with 0 < 65
0.00 - 0.03	0.03	30 Random Orders was executed successfully 10 times
0.00 - 0.03	0.03	Packet to Depot after Reject was executed successfully 10 times

Fig. 3. Report overview

message and a list of Details providing in-depth reasoning leading to the outcome. Each Detail (ll. 14–17) consists of a descriptive header and either a list of textual details or a single graphical component, which is rendered as an image in the resulting report. For each student a report overview is generated (see Fig. 3 for an example) and supplementary details are added in separate sections.

Listing 1. Plug-in interface and central components

```
1   public interface PlugIn {
2     public PlugIn configure(double maxPoints, String configuration);
3     public Message grade(StudentID id, PetriNet base, PetriNet model,
4                          HighLevelSimulator simulator);
5   }

7   public class Report {
8     public Report(StudentID sid) { ... }
9     void addReport(PlugIn plugin, Message result) { ... }
10  }
11  public class Message {
12    public Message(double points, String message, Detail... details) { ... }
13  }
14  public class Detail {
15    public Detail(String header, String... details) { ... }
16    public Detail(String header, JComponent component) { ... }
17  }

19  public class Tester {
20    public Tester(TestSuite suite, List<StudentID> ids, PetriNet base) { ... }
21    public List<Report> test() { ... }
22  }
23  public abstract class TestSuite {
24    public TestSuite(PlugIn matcher) { ... }
25    public abstract List<PlugIn> getPlugIns();
26  }
27  public class ConfigurationTestSuite extends TestSuite {
28    public ConfigurationTestSuite(File configurationFile) { ... }
29  }
```

Configuration. The Configuration component of Fig. 2 is shown in Listing 1 (ll. 19–29). The main class is a Tester (ll. 19–22), which given a TestSuite, a list of student IDs, and a base model can perform a test (l. 21) and yields a Report for each student. A TestSuite (ll. 23–26) has a distinguished matcher, which is a PlugIn mapping models to student IDs by yielding a high score for a model and student ID pair if the model is created by the student with the given ID and a low score otherwise. A TestSuite can also return a list of PlugIns for the main grading process. One implementation of a TestSuite, the ConfigurationTestSuite (ll. 27–29), is instantiated using a configurationFile which along with an abstract PlugIn factory is used to instantiate the correct PlugIns according to the configuration.

An example configuration file is shown in Listing 2. The file comprises two sections, matcher (ll. 1–2) and test (ll. 4–15), setting up the matcher and the actual tests graded, respectively. The intuition is that each line corresponds to a plug-in; a line starting with a + (ignoring white space) is considered part of the preceding line. Each line starts with a number indicating how many points are awarded for successful execution. If the number is negative, successful execution yields 0 points but a failure yields a punishment. This is followed by a colon and a configuration option recognized by the plug-in and optionally a list of named parameters. For example, in line 5 we see that the plug-in identified by declaration-preservation is instantiated with one named parameter. If the test fails, it yields a punishment of 5 points and if it succeeds, it yields 0 points. Lines 13–14 are merged (as line 14 starts with +). In the following we go into more detail with this example.

2.2   Simple Plug-ins for Interface Preservation

In Listing 2, we use two plug-ins to ensure that the interface to the environment and the environment itself are not modified. The declaration-preservation plug-in (l. 5) makes sure that no declaration in the provided model is removed or

Listing 2. Example configuration file

```
1   [matcher]
2   -5: signature,threshold=65

4   [tests]
5   -5: declaration-preservation
6   -100: interface-preservation,addpages=true,initmark=true,subset=deliveryservice
7   -5: matchfilename
8   0.033: btl,repeats=2,name="Accept 10 Orders",test=
9     + (10 * (--> Order) -> (@(!Order))) &
10    + (10 * (--> Receive) -> (@(!Receive))) &
11    + (@(!Reject)) &
12    + [(--> Handle_Return) => false]
13  0.033: btl,repeats=2,name="Only two cars of capacity 1",test=
14    + [@(|Reject| + |Offer| + |Accept| < 3)]
```

changed. This ensures that it is impossible to change the type of the interface
by redefining color sets. If declarations are removed or changed, this is reported
as an error and if new declarations are added, they are added to the report so it
is easy to see what was added without having to directly compare the student
model with the base model.

The interface-preservation (l. 6) plug-in makes sure that students do not change
the given net structure, but only add new structure. In our example from Fig. 1,
students are only allowed to add new net structure, but not to modify the given
environment. Here, we are given four parameters. The addpages parameter is set
to true, which means that students are allowed to add new pages. The initmark
option is set to true, which means that students are not allowed to change the
initial marking of the model. Finally, the subset parameter contains a list of
pages students are allowed to add structure to. Any page not in this list is not
allowed to be changed at all. Here, we specify that the students are allowed
to alter the DeliveryService page from Fig. 1. Any added page is listed in the
report as is any modified page. If the change is illegal, the error is listed (i.e.,
if a node of the interface is removed or altered, this is highlighted), and if the
model contains no errors, the entire environment is dimmed so only the student
solution is highlighted.

2.3   Fraud Prevention

We have two plug-ins for matching a model to a student ID. In Listing 2, we use
both to award points. We see in line 8 that we instantiate the matchfilename plug-
in. This plug-in simply checks if the student ID is a substring of the filename
(and punishes if it is not). This is fine for honest students; unfortunately, we
have in earlier years encountered students copying models from one another. To
catch that, we instead use the more elaborate signature plug-in as matcher (l. 2).

The signature matcher exploits that all elements of a CPN Tools model have
a unique identifier. This is necessary, e.g., to represent that an arc is connected
to a specific place and transition. While these identifiers must be unique in
the file and match for nodes and arcs, the actual contents of the identifiers
have no semantics. We have developed a simple signer application which, given
a base model, modifies the identifiers in a predictable way. By using a cryptographic random number generator, we can generate a sequence of pseudo-random

numbers using the student ID and a secret passphrase as seed. The idea is that if we know the passphrase and the student ID, we can regenerate the sequence, but using just the sequence (and optionally the student ID), it is not possible to reverse-engineer the passphrase. Now, using the generated sequence of numbers as identifiers of model elements in the file containing the environment, we create a unique signature in the base file for each student.

The signature plug-in can check this signature. It queries for each student ID and student model whether the two match. It regenerates the sequence of random numbers for the student ID and the provided passphrase, and check that the identifiers are present in the file. If they are, the model is considered a match and otherwise not. The plug-in takes a parameter threshold which indicates how many identifiers must be present in the model. As the signing is a one-way process, students are forced to use the appropriate base model and cannot just hand in the same model (even after making cosmetic changes). The teacher only needs to remember the password as the signature key is generated automatically from the password and student ID.

2.4   Model-Checking

Grade/CPN embeds the ASAP model-checker [6], allowing us to check all properties supported by that tool as long as the state-space is finite, including LTL properties using a wide range of reduction techniques. The models we encounter in our case study do not have finite state-spaces, so we have not been focused on this part. The extensible nature of Grade/CPN makes it easy to add this functionality externally, and as a proof-of-concept we have implemented a simple dead-lock checker.

3   Britney Temporal Logic

An important requirement to our tool is to check dynamic properties, requirement 4(b) from the introduction. In the example in Fig. 1, we are for example interested in the behavior when a customer accepts packets ten times in a row and how many packets can be outstanding at any time. As CPN models tend to have huge or even infinite state spaces, we cannot verify such properties in general and especially not for models generated by students who have less experience with modeling. Therefore, we check such properties by guiding the model; that is, we apply a testing-based approach rather than exhaustive state-space exploration, yielding a sound but not necessarily complete checking mechanism.

Guiding the model requires to specify which transition the model should execute. Testing whether some property holds in a state of the model requires a specification of this property. To this end, we introduce the *Britney Temporal Logic* (BTL). This logic is similar to linear-time logic (LTL) [7] but, in addition to checking properties, also allows guiding the model and to specify constraints that should hold in a state. We adopt a syntax more similar to common descriptions of Petri net firing sequences rather than cryptic abbreviations or symbols to make it easier for practitioners to adopt the logic. The choice for an LTL-like logic reflects our wish to have existential counterexamples that can be represented by a simple firing sequence. Other kinds of counterexamples are difficult to find using simulation only and also difficult to present to the user. In the following, we define the syntax of BTL formulae and then their semantics based on Kripke structures [8], and structural operational semantics (SOS) [9] to capture invariant properties and simple rewrite rules to capture the temporal aspects.

3.1 Syntax

A BTL formula is a ⟨*guide*⟩. A guide describes how simulation should be performed; that is, it guides the model to a desired state. The atomic propositions of a guide are described using ⟨*simple*⟩, which is an expression without temporal operators but otherwise allowing full propositional logic on transitions and place invariants. The temporal operators are six arrows emulating the arrows typically used to describe transition steps. Thus *a->b* means that first *a* must hold and subsequently *b* must hold. For example, *a* and *b* can represent transitions, meaning that for the formula to hold, the corresponding transitions are executed one after the other. We lift this operator to *a-->b* meaning that *a* must hold and sometime afterward *b* must hold. Finally, *a--->[b]* means that *a* must hold and when the simulation stops *b* must hold. The brackets indicate that *b* is not used for guiding the simulation anymore (it has terminated after all). We can omit *a*, which is an abbreviation for *true*. For each arrow, we also add a double arrow version indicating that *if a* holds, then *b* holds at the appropriate time.

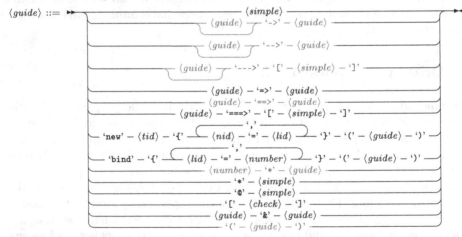

We use operator **new** to define that the firing of a transition initializes one or more variables, and we use operator **bind** to initialize one or more variables with constant values. We also allow bounded and unbounded repetition using a star syntax. In contrary to a regular Kleene star, we put it in front as it improves readability for western readers. Using operator @, a guide can specify an invariant property that should hold in all states. A guide can also include ⟨*check*⟩s, which are not used to guide the model but only to test assertions.

They are therefore allowed to contain disjunctions and negations and general boolean expressions. Finally, a guide can also be the conjunction of two guides.

⟨*check*⟩ ::= ▶━━┳━━━━━━━━━━ ⟨*guide*⟩ ━━━━━━━━━━━━━━━━━━━━━━━━━┳━━◀
         ┣━━━━━━━━ '!' − ⟨*check*⟩ ━━━━━━━┫
         ┣━ ⟨*check*⟩ − '&' − ⟨*check*⟩ ━┫
         ┣━ ⟨*check*⟩ − '|' − ⟨*check*⟩ ━┫
         ┗━ '(' − ⟨*check*⟩ − ')' ━━━━━━┛

In addition to the syntax for guiding, we also allow simple boolean expressions. These are mostly for testing state properties, such as counting the tokens on a place or testing values of the global clock. Attribute *tid* and *pid* in the grammar thereby refer to a transition label and place label, respectively, and *nid* is the name of a CPN variable and *lid* is the name of a local BTL variable. In this definition, constants are only bound to numbers for sake of simplicity, however the extension to arbitrary CPN literals is straight forward. In the syntax, symbol ⟨R⟩ is any of the comparison operators $<, >, \le, \ge, =$. For example, Line 12 in Listing 2 tests that Handle Return is never executed (but does not enforce it like the guides). The formula in line 14 checks that at any point during execution, the three places Reject, Offer, and Accept never contain three or more tokens in total.

⟨*simple*⟩ ::= ▶━━┳━━━━━━━━━━━━━ ⟨*tid*⟩ ━━━━━━━━━━━━━━━━━━━━━━━━━┳━━◀
          ┣━ ⟨*tid*⟩ − '{' ━┳━ ⟨*nid*⟩ ━'='━ ⟨*lid*⟩ ━┳━ '}' ━┫
          ┣━━━ '|' − ⟨*pid*⟩ − '|' − ⟨R⟩ − ⟨*number*⟩ ━━━━┫
          ┣━━━━━━━ 'time' − ⟨R⟩ − ⟨*number*⟩ ━━━━━━━━┫
          ┣━━━━━━━━━━━━━ 'true' ━━━━━━━━━━━━━┫
          ┣━━━━━━━━━━━━ 'false' ━━━━━━━━━━━━┫
          ┣━━━━━━ '!' − ⟨*simple*⟩ ━━━━━━━━┫
          ┣━ ⟨*simple*⟩ − '&' − ⟨*simple*⟩ ━┫
          ┣━ ⟨*simple*⟩ − '|' − ⟨*simple*⟩ ━┫
          ┗━━ '(' − ⟨*simple*⟩ − ')' ━━━━━┛

Our syntax includes a lot of conveniences. We already mentioned that avoiding the precondition for the single arrows is a convenience for a precondition of *true*. Furthermore, all single arrows can be defined from the double arrows by forcing the precondition. The eventuality defined by *a==>b* can be defined in terms of the unbounded repetition and the next operator, and bounded repetition is just a syntactical convenience. Let G, G_1, G_2 be guides, C, C_1, C_2 be checks, and S, S_1, S_2 be simple boolean expressions. In the syntax, we have grayed out all syntactic sugar for which we do not need to explicitly define the semantics.

$$\text{->}G \equiv true\text{->}G$$
$$\text{-->}G \equiv true\text{-->}G$$
$$\text{--->}[C] \equiv true\text{--->}[C] \qquad\qquad (G) \equiv G \qquad\qquad false \equiv !true$$
$$G_1\text{->}G_2 \equiv G_1 \& (G_1\text{=>}G_2) \qquad C_1|C_2 \equiv !(!C_1 \& !C_2) \qquad S_1|S_2 \equiv !(!S_1 \& !S_2)$$
$$G_1\text{-->}G_2 \equiv G_1 \& (G_1\text{==>}G_2) \qquad (C) \equiv C \qquad\qquad (S) \equiv S$$
$$G_1\text{--->}[S] \equiv G_1 \& (G_1\text{===>}[S])$$
$$G_1\text{==>}G_2 \equiv G_1\text{->}(*true\text{->}G_2) \qquad\qquad n * G \equiv \begin{cases} G\text{->}(n-1) * G & \text{if } n \ge 1 \\ true & \text{otherwise.} \end{cases}$$

3.2   Semantics

The semantics of BTL is similar to a standard finite trace semantics for LTL like the one defined in [10]. Intuitively, => corresponds to "next", ==> corresponds to "eventually", @ corresponds to "globally" (in a restricted form), and a formula $[\langle check \rangle]$==>$\langle guide \rangle$ is similar to "until" (in a restricted form). Yet, BTL significantly differs from LTL due to the dual nature of guides (which steer the simulation) and checks (which have to hold).

We interpret BTL formulae over a Kripke structure $K = (Q, \delta, q_0, \Sigma, \lambda)$, where Q is a set of states, $q_0 \in Q$ is the initial state, Σ is a set of transition labels, $\delta \subseteq Q \times \Sigma \times Q$ is the transition relation, and function $\lambda : Q \to 2^{AP}$ maps each state $q \in Q$ to a set of atomic propositions that hold in q. As usual, AP denotes the set of all atomic propositions. In our syntax we have some CPN-specific atomic propositions dealing with places and time, but it obvious that these could be replaced to suit any formalism generating a Kripke structure.

The semantics of a BTL formula is defined over the traces of a Kripke structure K along with an environment, E, which is a function mapping names to values. Normally for a model M, we consider the transition relation $\to_M$ relating two states q_0, q_1 and a transition. What exactly the state and transitions are depends on the concrete formalism. In the case of CPNs, the states are markings and the transitions are pairs consisting of a transition and all variables surrounding it, a *binding element*. We denote by $BE \subseteq T \times 2^{Bindings}$ the set of all possible binding elements for a model, and we write $q_0 \xrightarrow{t\{n_1=v_1,\ldots,n_j=v_j\}}_M q_1$ to denote the model can execute transition t with the binding of variables $n_1 = v_1, \ldots, n_j = v_j$ from state q_0, leading to state q_1. We say that the binding element $t\{n_1 = v_1, \ldots, n_j = v_j\}$ is *enabled* and denote by $name(t\{n_1 = v_1, \ldots, n_j = v_j\}) = t$ the transition name of a binding element.

We first consider how to guide the simulation. This is done by defining a set of allowed transitions for each guide. For simulation, only enabled transitions that are in this set are considered. This in particular means that if the set of allowed transitions is empty, the simulation is considered finished (and not with an error unless the formula is not satisfied). In other words, when considering the truth value of a formula according to a model (without a trace), we only consider the truth value along all traced adhering to the guides. We define the set *guide* over a set of possible binding elements inductively as follows, where S, S_1, S_2 are of type $\langle simple \rangle$, C, C_1, C_2 are of type $\langle check \rangle$, and G, G_1, G_2 are of type $\langle guide \rangle$:

$$guide(tid, q, E) = \{be \in BE \mid name(be) = tid\}$$
$$guide(tid\{n_1 = l_1, \ldots, n_j = l_j\}, q, E) = \{tid\{n_1 = E(l_1), \ldots, n_j = E(l_j)\}\}$$
$$guide(|pid|\ R\ i, q, E) = guide(time\ R\ i, q, E) = BE$$
$$guide(true, q, E) = BE$$
$$guide(!S, q, E) = BE \setminus guide(S, q, E)$$
$$guide(S_1 \& S_2, q, E) = guide(S_1, q, E) \cap guide(S_2, q, E)$$
$$guide(!C, q, E) = BE \setminus guide(C, E)$$
$$guide(C_1 \& C_2, q, E) = guide(C_1, q, E) \cap guide(C_2, q, E)$$

$$guide(G_1 \Rightarrow G_2, q, E) = guide(G ===> [S], q, E) = BE$$
$$guide(\text{new } tid\{n_1 = l_1, \ldots, n_j = l_j\}(G), q, E) = \{tid\{n_1 = v_1, \ldots, n_j = v_j\} \in BE \mid$$
$$tid\{n_1 = v_1, \ldots, n_j = v_j\} \in guide(G, q, E[l_1 \mapsto v_1, \ldots, l_j \mapsto v_j])\}$$
$$guide(\text{bind } \{l_1 = v_1, \ldots, l_j = v_j\}(G), q, E) = guide(G, q, E[l_1 \mapsto v_1, \ldots, l_j \mapsto v_j])$$
$$guide(*S, q, E) = guide([C], q, E) = BE$$
$$guide(@S, q, E) = guide(S, q, E)$$
$$guide(G_1 \wedge G_2, q, E) = guide(G_1, q, E) \cap guide(G_2, q, E)$$

We allow concrete steps if they are needed to satisfy a formula or forbid a step if it would violate it, and otherwise allow anything when we do not care about the outcome.

Next, we define the semantics of $\langle simple \rangle$ over traces $q_0 \xrightarrow{be_1}_M q_1 \xrightarrow{be_2}_M$ $\cdots \xrightarrow{be_k}_M q_k$ of enabled binding elements as follows. Most operators are straightforward with (1) consuming transitions and binding elements for non-empty traces, (2) defining state predicates, and (3) defining propositional connectives.

$$\frac{k \geq 1, \; be_1 \in guide(tid, q_0, E)}{(q_0 \xrightarrow{be_1}_M \cdots q_k), E \models tid} \tag{1}$$

$$\frac{k \geq 1, \; be_1 \in guide(tid\{n_1 = v_1, \ldots, n_j = v_j\}, q_0, E)}{(q_0 \xrightarrow{be_1}_M \cdots q_k), E \models tid\{n_1 = v_1, \ldots, n_j = v_j\}}$$

$$\frac{q_0 \models |pid| \; R \; i}{(q_0 \xrightarrow{be_1}_M \cdots q_k), E \models |pid| \; R \; i} \qquad \frac{q_0 \models time \; R \; i}{(q_0 \xrightarrow{be_1}_M \cdots q_k), E \models time \; R \; i} \tag{2}$$

$$\frac{true}{(q_0 \xrightarrow{be_1}_M \cdots q_k), E \models true} \qquad \frac{(q_0 \xrightarrow{be_1}_M \cdots q_k), E \not\models S}{(q_0 \xrightarrow{be_1}_M \cdots q_k), E \models !S}$$
$$\frac{(q_0 \xrightarrow{be_1}_M \cdots q_k), E \models S_1 \wedge (q_0 \xrightarrow{be_1}_M \cdots q_k), E \models S_2}{(q_0 \xrightarrow{be_1}_M \cdots q_k), E \models S_1 \wedge S_2} \tag{3}$$

The $\langle check \rangle$ is a simple syntactical extension of $\langle guide \rangle$ and treated with them. The operators on $\langle guide \rangle$ are LTL-like. As for $\langle simple \rangle$, we define the syntax over traces $q_0 \xrightarrow{be_1}_M q_1 \xrightarrow{be_2}_M \cdots \xrightarrow{be_k}_M q_k$ of enabled binding elements. Instead of defining the truth value, we need to define a rewrite of a formula to capture the temporal aspects as well as the guiding aspects. We define the *progress* function inductively on the structure of the union of $\langle guide \rangle$ and $\langle check \rangle$, execution trace, and an environment E. We notice that this includes *true* and *false*. A $\langle simple \rangle$ can always be evaluated in the current state or step according to rules (1)-(3).

$$progress(S, q_0 \xrightarrow{be_1}_M \cdots q_k, E) = \begin{cases} true & \text{if } (q_0 \xrightarrow{be_1}_M \cdots q_k, E) \models S \\ false & \text{otherwise} \end{cases} \tag{4}$$

A $\langle guide \rangle$ or a $\langle check \rangle$ may evaluate to *true* or *false* in the current state or step, in which case we return this value. If not, the $\langle guide \rangle$ or $\langle check \rangle$ is rewritten to the formula that has to hold in the next step. Rule (5) shows the rewriting for the conditional next step construct, where G_2 has to hold in the next step if G_1

holds in this step, while the entire formula has to hold in the next step if nothing can be said about G_1 in this step. By (6), conditional "finally" is only evaluated at the end of the trace.

$$progress(G_1\texttt{=>}G_2, q_0 \xrightarrow{be_1}_M \cdots q_k, E) =$$
$$\begin{cases} G_2 & \text{if } progress(G_1, q_0 \xrightarrow{be_1}_M q_1, E) = true \\ true & \text{if } progress(G_1, q_0 \xrightarrow{be_1}_M q_1, E) = false \\ (progress(G_1, q_0 \xrightarrow{be_1}_M \cdots q_k, E)\texttt{=>}G_2) & \text{otherwise} \end{cases} \quad (5)$$

$$progress(G\texttt{===>}[S], q_0 \xrightarrow{be_1}_M \cdots q_k, E) =$$
$$\begin{cases} (q_0, E) \models S & \text{if } G = true, k = 0 \\ true & \text{if } G \neq true, k = 0 \\ (progress(G, q_0 \xrightarrow{b_1}_M \cdots q_k, E))\texttt{===>}[S] & \text{otherwise} \end{cases} \quad (6)$$

Rule (7) replaces the dynamic binding of BTL variables by "new" with the static binding when the concrete values are known and the transition is allowed; the static binding recursively extends the environment for the subformulas (8).

$$progress(\texttt{new } name\{n_1 = l_1, \ldots, n_i = l_i\}(G), q_0 \xrightarrow{be_1}_M \cdots q_k, E) =$$
$$\begin{cases} \psi & \text{if } be_1 = name\{n_1 = v_1, \ldots, n_i = v_i\} \\ false & \text{otherwise} \end{cases} \quad (7)$$

where $\psi = progress(\texttt{bind}\{l_1 = v_1, \ldots, l_i = v_i\}(G), q_0 \xrightarrow{be_1}_M \cdots q_k, E)$.

$$progress(\texttt{bind}\{l_1 = v_1, \ldots, l_i = v_i\}(G), q_0 \xrightarrow{be_1}_M \cdots q_k, E)$$
$$= \begin{cases} true & \text{if } \psi = true \\ \texttt{bind}\{l_1 = v_1, \ldots, l_i = v_i\}(\psi) & \text{otherwise} \end{cases} \quad (8)$$

where $\psi = progress(G, q_0 \xrightarrow{be_1}_M \cdots q_k, E[l_1 \mapsto v_1, \ldots, l_i \mapsto v_i])$.

The "@S" defines a global invariant S that has to hold in each step of the trace until its end (10), the "$*S$" permits the simple S to hold on a prefix of the trace 9.

$$progress(*S, q_0 \xrightarrow{be_1}_M \cdots q_k, E) = \begin{cases} *S & \text{if } k > 0, (q_0 \xrightarrow{be_1}_M q_1), E \models S \\ true & \text{otherwise} \end{cases} \quad (9)$$

$$progress(@S, q_0 \xrightarrow{be_1}_M \cdots q_k, E) = \begin{cases} @S & \text{if } k > 0, (q_0 \xrightarrow{be_1}_M q_1), E \models S \\ true & \text{if } k = 0 \\ false & \text{otherwise} \end{cases} \quad (10)$$

Checks do not restrict the step: they are simply evaluated, or, if they cannot be evaluated, are rewritten according to the current step. We preserve syntactic categories of checks in rules (11) and (12) accordingly.

$$progress([C], q_0 \xrightarrow{be_1}_M \cdots q_k, E)$$
$$= \begin{cases} true & \text{if } progress(C, q_0 \xrightarrow{be_1}_M \cdots q_k, E) = true \\ false & \text{if } progress(C, q_0 \xrightarrow{be_1}_M \cdots q_k, E) = false \\ [progress(C, q_0 \xrightarrow{be_1}_M \cdots q_k, E)] & \text{otherwise} \end{cases} \quad (11)$$

$$progress(!C, q_0 \xrightarrow{be_1}_M \cdots q_k, E)$$

$$= \begin{cases} false & \text{if } progress(C, q_0 \xrightarrow{be_1}_M \cdots q_k, E) = true \\ true & \text{if } progress(C, q_0 \xrightarrow{be_1}_M \cdots q_k, E) = false \\ [!progress(C, q_0 \xrightarrow{be_1}_M \cdots q_k, E)] & \text{otherwise} \end{cases} \tag{12}$$

A satisfied conjunction is rewritten to *true* as in rule (13); this rule equally applies to conjunctions over $\langle check \rangle$s.

$$progress(G_1 \wedge G_2, q_0 \xrightarrow{be_1}_M \cdots q_k, E)$$

$$= \begin{cases} progress(G_1, q_0 \xrightarrow{be_1}_M \cdots q_k, E) & \text{if } progress(G_2, q_0 \xrightarrow{be_1}_M \cdots q_k, E) = true \\ progress(G_2, q_0 \xrightarrow{be_1}_M \cdots q_k, E) & \text{if } progress(G_1, q_0 \xrightarrow{be_1}_M \cdots q_k, E) = true \\ progress(G_1, q_0 \xrightarrow{be_1}_M \cdots q_k, E) \wedge progress(G_2, q_0 \xrightarrow{be_1}_M \cdots q_k, E) & \text{otherwise} \end{cases} \tag{13}$$

The *progress* function determines how to progress the computation for each step. Sometimes the computation cannot progress, however. This can be either because there are no more enabled transitions (the trace is empty) or the guard does not permit progressing. In this case, we need to check that the remaining rewritten formula can terminate, i.e., if it accepts the empty trace. We then lift the computation over traces from individual steps to entire traces. We define an *evaluate* function evaluating the truth value of a formula f over a trace $q_0 \xrightarrow{be_1}_M q_1 \xrightarrow{be_2}_M \cdots \xrightarrow{be_k}_M q_k$ of enabled transitions as follows. The function returns one of three values, *true* meaning the formula holds for the trace, *false* meaning it does not hold, and *unguided* meaning the trace does not follow the guiding function.

$$evaluate(f, q_0 \xrightarrow{be_1} \cdots q_k) =$$

$$\begin{cases} true & \text{if } progress(f, q_0, \emptyset) = true \\ false & \text{if } k = 0, progress(f, q_0, \emptyset) \neq true \\ unguided & \text{if } be_1 \notin guide(q_0, f, \emptyset) \\ evaluate(progress(f, q_0 \xrightarrow{be_1} \cdots q_k), q_1 \xrightarrow{be_2} \cdots q_k) & \text{otherwise} \end{cases} \tag{14}$$

Finally, we say that given a model M and a formula f, M satisfies the formula f, written $M \models f$ if all traces either satisfy the formula or are unguided, formally:

Definition 1 (Satisfaction of BTL). *Given a (CPN) model M and a BTL formula f, we say that M **satisfies** f, written $M \models f$ iff*

$$\forall q_0 \xrightarrow{be_1} \cdots q_k \in M : evaluate(f, q_0 \xrightarrow{be_1} \cdots q_k) \neq false$$

4   Coverage and Choices

Section 3 introduced syntax and semantics of BTL, which allows to specify intended and forbidden behavior of the system. In this section, we discuss how to *test* whether a system model, given as CPN model, satisfies the specification. We first discuss requirements for testing and our approach, including how to get high coverage and how these ideas can be used to handle choices in the form of disjunctions.

4.1   Testing BTL Formulas

Similar to formal verification, testing aims at finding errors in the system model
– that is, finding runs which violate the given specification. In contrast to formal
verification, testing is not exhaustive: Only a fraction of the system's possible
behavior is investigated for whether it violates the specification.

A naive testing algorithm is to randomly walk through the state space of
the system model, until the property tested for is satisfied or violated. This is
repeated several times. If a run violating the specification is found, it is proof that
the system violates the specification. In case no violating run is found, there is
no proof that the system is error free. However, one can compute the probability
by which a specification holds based on the explored behavior in relation to the
complete behavior.

Figure 4 shows a technical example. For evaluating the BTL formula
A-->C, only the *guided traces* of the
execution tree are relevant as unguided traces have no impact on the
satisfaction of a formula. We do not
assign all traces the same probability, as simulation locally decides on
each step regardless of any previous
and future steps. In the first step, the
system is guided to do an A, so all
traces leaving the initial state with an
action different from A are unguided
and not considered. This means the
traces have probability 1 of starting
with an A. The remaining guided tree
is shown in Fig. 4(top right). Edges
correspond choices in the model and
the probabilities show the probability

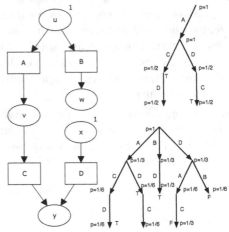

Fig. 4. Example model N, guided execution tree for A-->C, and guided execution
tree for !C-->D

of a random trace having the given prefix. We only consider completed traces,
though we can sometimes make a decision prior to exploring full traces. We
see that after executing A we have a choice between C and D, so each prefix
amounts to half of the probability. The trace ACD satisfies the formula (we can
already see it will after executing just the prefix AC). By just testing the trace
prefix AC, we know that the entire system satisfies A-->C with a probability
of $\frac{1}{2}$, because the probability to see traces with this prefix is $\frac{1}{2}$. By exploring
more alternatives, we see more traces and, in case all explored traces satisfy the
formula, increase the probability that the formula holds, i.e., when also exploring
ADC, which also has probability $1 \cdot \frac{1}{2} \cdot 1 = \frac{1}{2}$, we get that the system satisfies
A-->C with probability 1.

A different situation occurs for the formula !C-->D which has the guided tree
of Fig. 4(bottom right). The guide !C does not prune any (enabled) behavior.
If the test explores the trace DB or DAC, it finds a counterexample for the

formula proving it was violated. By non-exhaustive exploration in testing, we could also end up with just exploring the traces ACD (which has probability $\frac{1}{3} \cdot \frac{1}{2} = \frac{1}{6}$) and BD (which has probability $\frac{1}{3} \cdot 1 = \frac{1}{3}$), and in this case would have a total probability of $\frac{1}{6} + \frac{1}{3} = \frac{1}{2}$ that the formula holds. Once exploring a violating trace, such as DB, that probability drops to 0. Exploring the entire execution tree yields either probability 0 or 1 that the formula holds.

In general, we talk about three different percentages: the coverage, which is the weighted sum of all explored traces; the probability a formula holds, which is the weighted sum of all explored traces if they all satisfy the formula or zero otherwise; and the probability that a random trace satisfies the formula. When we have found no counter-examples these are the same, and obviously the larger the probability that a random trace satisfies the formula, the more difficult it is to find a counter-example. The example shows the main challenge in testing: to explore that fraction of traces that yield a counter-example, or if so such exists, yields a high probability that the formula holds (which increases confidence in the test result).

4.2   Heuristics for Higher Confidence in Test Results

In testing, confidence put into a test result is typically measured in terms of *coverage criteria* [11]. Various coverage criteria have been proposed such as *state coverage* (i.e., the fraction of place that has been marked at least once), *transition coverage* (i.e., the fraction of transitions that occurred at least once, regardless of binding element), or *coverage of all paths* (to a certain length). Coverage criteria are in some sense interchangeable, as one can simulate coverage w.r.t. one criterion by coverage w.r.t. another one [12].

Path Coverage. To improve the naive testing algorithm of repeatedly walking through the system state space in a random way, we leverage two coverage criteria to increase confidence that a CPN model satisfies a given BTL formula: transition coverage and path coverage. Complete coverage for paths is infeasible in the presence of loops or unbounded non-determinism, but covering paths up to a certain length is feasible. To increase path coverage, we essentially explore the guided execution tree of the CPN model by greedily choosing a branch that has the largest probability of falsifying a formula. In the simplest case with no information about the model, this is the one with the largest difference between the probability of a random trace having the prefix represented by the branch and the probability of the formula holding in that subtree. If we consider the example for $!C\text{-->}D$ in Fig. 4, assuming we have explored ACD, starting from an empty trace we would pick either B or D as they both have probability $\frac{1}{3}$ of happening and known probability 0 of the formula holding, whereas the subtree starting with A also has probability $\frac{1}{3}$ of happening and probability $\frac{1}{3}$ of holding.

Transition Coverage. Generating a test for complete coverage of all transitions is an undecidable problem in a CPN model, as for each transition, one would have to find a coloured firing sequence that enables this transition. For this reason, we apply heuristics when exploring the tree of guided executions. We maintain a queue of all transitions of the CPN model. When deciding on the next step in a run, we pick the first enabled transition from the queue and after firing move it to the end of the queue. This way, we increase the chance of firing transitions that were not considered yet. Binding elements are not part of the queue and we also prefer branches giving higher coverage by using the previous heuristic.

More Advanced Criteria. We have assumed that the variables have no impact on the enabled traces. This is of course a simplification, and we could also consider trying to evaluate the guards to drive the model to different states, e.g., using abstraction. We could also use transition invariants (of the uncolored underlying model) to identify loops that are less likely to be interesting, or partially order the transitions according to pre and post places to try and drive a notion of progress in the model.

4.3   Disjunctions

We have avoided adding disjunction to our guides. This is primarily done because adding disjunctions can be very expensive. For example, an expression like $(A\texttt{-->}B)|(B\texttt{-->}D)$ must make a choice when used for guiding if both A and B can be executed. If, in the example in Fig. 4, A is chosen, a D and a C are encountered, and the execution terminated, we cannot conclude that the formula does not hold, as the second part of the disjunction was ignored. We therefore have to back-track and try again to ensure there really is an error, making handling disjunctions as difficult as model-checking.

Furthermore, the semantics of disjunction is not completely obvious as we make truth of formulae relative to the guide. In the formula $((A\texttt{-->}C)|(B\texttt{-->}D))$ $\texttt{-->}D$, must the system be able to respond to both $A\texttt{-->}C$ and $B\texttt{-->}D$ with a D or is it enough that the system responds with a D for one of the environment interpretations? As the truth is relative to the guide, either interpretation becomes unclear; normally we would make the guide of a disjunction the union of the guides for the two elements, but this makes the guide a larger set, which may yield strange results. For example, a system may respond to being guided by $A\texttt{-->}C$ with a D like in Fig. 4 (thus intuitively satisfying the system), but not respond to $B\texttt{-->}D$ with a D. If the system allows this behavior, this would mean that the disjunction is not true, even though one of its sides is; the disjunction inherits similarities to a conjunction (both sides must be satisfiable for the disjunction to be true). This interpretation is counter-intuitive (and contradicts the behavior of disjunction of simple formulae, e.g., $A|B$). The only way to get around that is to change the guide to instead return sets of sets of transitions, one for each branch of a disjunction.

If we split the guide to handle disjunctions, we need to check each set of guides. Each set would partition according to the left side, right side, and intersection of each disjunction all the way through the structure of the guide, causing the number of sets needed to explore to grow exponentially in the number of disjunctions.

Instead of dealing with this, which theoretically is manageable and nice, we have decided that disjunction in guides unnecessarily complicates the semantics and complexity of checking. We can handle multiple environment behaviors by instead checking a formula for each individual environment behavior, and we can already test disjunctions in the simple boolean checks.

5   Practical Experience

In this section, we briefly present our implementation of BTL and Grade/CPN, and practical experiences of using both in a course.

5.1   Implementation

Our implementation of BTL uses simple formula rewriting according to the semantics. Our implementation implements the *guide* set for filtering enabled transitions, pick and execute one that is in the *guide* set and in the set of enabled transitions. We then rewrite the formula according to the previous rules. For efficiency, we have expanded some of the syntactical equivalences, most importantly the future temporal operator (a==>b). When no more transitions are in the intersection, we check if the rewritten formula is satisfied for the empty trace.

We evaluate formulae using a four-valued logic similar to [13]. The idea is that we have two versions of both true and false: The value is definite and can never change and the value is true/false but may change with further execution. For example, if we have a formula a->b and execute c we know for sure that we can never satisfy the formula (we say it is permanently false), whereas for --->b if we execute a c, the formula is only temporarily false (we still have proof obligations but may be able to satisfy them in the future). This allows us to terminate early once a formula is permanently true or false. This has the added advantage of allowing us to provide a rewritten formula after executing a sequence of steps, which often contains hints of shortcomings of the model.

The engine for testing BTL is used in 3 different tools. The grader discussed in Sect. 2 is used by teachers to finally grade assignments. Additionally, we provide two tools for testing BTL formulas (without grading). One is used to help a teacher create BTL specifications by providing immediate feedback on whether a CPN model (created by the teacher as a sample solution or given to the teacher) satisfies a BTL formula. Figure 5 shows a screenshot of testing the formula A-->C for the example in Fig. 4. The

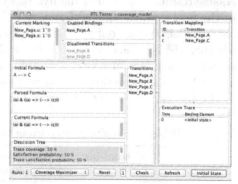

Fig. 5. Screenshot of BTL tester

tool allows to manually create and step through a run of the CPN model, thereby observing how the BTL formula tested for is evaluated step by step. The panel Enabled Bindings shows the list of currently enabled transitions and bindings from which the user can pick one. Disallowed Transitions shows transitions not allowed by the guard function. The panel Current Marking shows the current marking in the run. The panel Current Formula contains the remaining formula that has to be evaluated, whenever a step in the CPN model makes a subformula true or false, the formula in that panel is rewritten according to the BTL semantics of Sect. 3. The panel Execution Trace shows the steps of the run executed so far, including timing information which is valuable for assessing whether time-related guards in the model match time-related conditions in the BTL formula. The tool also reports estimates of the coverage, probability the formula holds, and the probability of a random trace satisfying the formula in the Decision Tree panel.

A simplified version of this tool allows students to check that their models conform to the formulas. Here, the tool is pre-packaged with a set of BTL formulas that the model must satisfy. The students loads their models and the tool automatically tests validity of each formula on the model. In case one formula is not satisfied by the model, the student can manually single-step through the model and watch the formula progress in an interface similar to Fig. 5, aiding in finding and fixing obvious errors before handing in.

5.2 Case Study: Business Information Systems

In this section, we present first experiences we made with Grade/CPN in supporting the evaluation of a CPN assignment in the course Business Information Systems at Eindhoven University of Technology. In this assignment, students were given the base model in Fig. 1 and they had to model the delivery system according to a textual specification. Each of the 94 students had to work on five tasks; for each task, they had to submit one model. We received in total 258 models from 66 students. Table 1 summarizes some statistics. We continue by describing the assessment in more detail and then report on the experiences had.

Assessment. For each of the five tasks, the assessment consisted of two steps. In the first step, we applied Grade/CPN by calling it with a student model, the base model, and a configuration file (see Listing 2). Here, we were interested whether the interface and declaration of the base model have been preserved, whether there is a suspicion of fraud, and whether, depending on the task, six up to fourteen scenarios can be replayed on the model (only two are shown in the Listing). The scenarios were part of the specification of the assignment,

Table 1. Results of supporting the evaluation of 258 CPN models

Task	hand-ins	incorrect models	grader incorrect	full points by grader	full points
1	66	8	0	58	58
2	64	8	0	56	56
3	56	49	7	2	6
4	41	32	4	6	6
5	31	20	2	0	0

and we specified them using BTL. As BTL refers to the interface, it is crucial that students have not changed it. The runtime of the tool was about ten minutes for all students in the case of Task 1 and 2 and about ten minutes for each student model in the case of Tasks 3–5. The reason for the different runtime of Grade/CPN is that Tasks 1 and 2 are simple CPNs with few tests, whereas the remaining tasks performed more thorough tests on more advanced models, including performance analysis, thereby causing a higher analysis effort. Grade/CPN detected two fraud attempts, though they turned out to be caused by students handing in a subsequent assignment using the same base model. In a subsequent run of the course, we caught two students cheating, even though they had tried to conceal that by changing the layout. This attempt would be unlikely to get caught manually, but after singling out the models, we manually inspected them and saw they were clearly the same despite the obfuscation.

In the second step of the assessment, we manually checked each of the generated reports. On average, this took less than five minutes for each report in the case of Task 1 and 2 and about ten minutes in the case of Tasks 3–5. Based on the feedback provided by Grade/CPN, it was easy to check whether a model was actually correct or not, in particular for the untimed CPN models. Basically, the violation of a certain scenario simplified the detection of the cause for this violation drastically. In most cases, we did not even have to look at the counterexample provided by our tool. For Tasks 1 and 2, we had to simulate only five out of 130 student models manually to determine the cause of an error. A similar number of models had to be simulated manually for each of the Tasks 3–5. In those cases, the effort spent on finding the cause of an error was often higher because of the complexity of the models.

The tool automatically detected several subtle errors, such as wrong guards and minor changes to the environment, without having the need to manually open the respective model; it is highly unlikely we would have caught all of these completely manually. We even found subtle errors in our own solutions, yielding better results.

Experiences and Evaluation. Based on experience from previous years, the use of Grade/CPN reduced the amount of time for grading the assignment by a factor of at least two to three. This is factoring in that we used Grade/CPN for the first time and had to both define and understand the defined logic BTL, and also did not place complete confidence in the reported results which probably increased the manual labor as well. Table 1 confirms this observation: For each task, it shows the number of student models received (Col. 2), the number of incorrect models (Col. 3), how many times Grade/CPN gave incorrect results (Col. 4), the number of student models that were graded to be correct according to the tool (Col. 5), and the number student models that were graded to be correct after manually checking them (Col. 6). In fact, whenever the grader assigned full points to a model, then the model was correct. As a result, checking those models manually took almost no time. Given the high number of models for Tasks 1 and 2, we saved a lot of time here. Column 4 shows that only few models were graded incorrectly. In most cases, the cause was a misinterpretation of the specification on the part of the students where we decided that the students should not be punished. Note that we do not show incorrect results of the tool caused by problems specifying a scenario in BTL.

The second column shows that the number of students participating at the assignment decreased from 66 for Task 1 to 31 for Task 5. Moreover, the average number of incorrect student solutions increased from $8/66=12\%$ for Task 1 to $20/31$ $=65\%$ for Task 5. The tasks became more difficult; whereas the first two tasks dealt with untimed CPN models and simple functionality, the remaining three tasks were much more involved. However, for the last two tasks we provided students with a student version of Grade/CPN. The idea was to provide them with a BTL specification that covers the basic functionality of their model. The final BTL specification used by us to grade their assignment contained additional scenarios. We experienced that providing students with Grade/CPN helped them to come up with better models. Whereas only $32/56 = 57\%$ of the students got at least half of the points for the third assignment ($56 - 49 = 7$ correct solutions), this number increased to $28/41 = 68\%$ (11 correct) for Task 4 and $20/31 = 64\%$ (11 correct) for Task 5 even though these were much more involved than the previous tasks. Moreover, we observed that the overall quality of the models increased drastically.

Grading models is a rather monotonous work. Therefore, it is easily possible that one oversees an error or forgets to check some scenario. Using Grade/CPN, this is now impossible and, therefore, we think that we can provide students with a fairer (in the sense of more equal) grading on the one hand and better feedback on the other hand.

Coverage Criteria and Confidence. We also compared the quality of the test result under the 3 different testing strategies (random exploration, increasing coverage of the guided tree, increasing transition coverage) discussed in Sect. 4. We observed that random yields the least confidence in the validity of the formula. Increasing tree coverage raises coverage by factor 4 (compared to random) and increasing transition coverage raises coverage by factor 200 (compared to random). Likewise, increasing the number of runs tested for also raises covarage.

6   Conclusion and Future Work

We have presented Grade/CPN, a tool to semi-automatically grade CPN models. Using Access/CPN, we can support any model created using CPN Tools. The plug-in architecture makes the tool easily extendible: to do so, one must just implement the interface in Listing 1 (ll. 1–5). The pluggable configuration with a very simple base format makes configuration simple. Configuration comprises selecting which plug-ins to use, which weight to assign them, and which parameters to instantiate them. Each plug-in only needs to consider its own options as the overall configuration format is handled by Grade/CPN. Reporting is handled by making all plug-ins return simple messages optionally annotated with more detailed reasoning (Listing 1 ll. 13–15). The information is automatically gathered by Grade/CPN and presented both as an overview in the user interface and as a detailed report. We have presented both simple plug-ins and a very powerful one implementing guided checking of Britney Temporal Logic (BTL). BTL allows us to guide the simulation toward desired scenarios and to check that the environment contracts are adhered to. All plug-ins provide categorized information explaining the score and highlighting any changes made to the model, so teachers processing the reports only have to focus on things that cannot be automatically checked. We have designed and implemented an infrastructure for detecting fraud. We have reported on our experience with the Business Information Systems course where Grade/CPN was used to grade 258 assignments from 94 students. Using Grade/CPN instead of a completely manual approach reduced the manual labor by a factor of two to three. Grade/CPN is being employed again in the same course and results show that the quality of student models has significantly increased after giving them access to the student tester.

The idea of (semi-)automatically grading assignments is not new and closely related to testing. A known testing framework is JUnit [14], which also runs a set of tests and reports the result. The advantage of our tool over JUnit is that JUnit requires programming to get started, whereas we use simple configuration files. From the testing world we also find the tool Jenkins (previously Hudson) [15], which runs tests on a central server and provides near-instantaneous feedback. The main disadvantage of Jenkins in our view is also complexity; while it does not (necessarily) require programming, setup does require complex XML configuration, and extension either requires huge effort or makes it difficult to get consolidated reports. There are many tools for automatically grading programming assignments [16], for example, the tool peach[3] [17], which more focuses on managing hand-ins, but can also run automatic tests. In contrast, we focus on the tests and CPN models directly and assume that models already exist. Our testing approach is similar to runtime LTL [10,13], but our logic also supports guiding. This is similar to hot/cold events in Live-Sequence Charts [18], but our sections are more urgent in that a guide is not only preferred, it is an immediate failure if it is not possible to follow it, making BTL computationally easier to check.

It is very interesting to increase the efficiency of the coverage heuristics for BTL, including expression abstraction, e.g., using a Counter-Example Guided Abstraction Refinement (CEGAR) [19] or similar approach. It is also interesting to employ more static analysis to get even better coverage. Experience says, though, that students often fail to account for particular cases, making it very easy to detect errors in those cases. It would also be interesting to investigate simpler languages. For example, it may be interesting for a teacher simply to see if a given transition is enabled. This is easily expressible in BTL but difficult to check, and employing techniques from directed model-checking [20] may prove beneficial to try more intelligent guiding towards errors. We would also like to extend Grade/CPN with ability to provide simple simulation-based checks of standard safety and liveness properties. We also want to add support for loading models in the PNML standard [21] format to be able to also check models created using other tools.

Acknowledgements. The authors thank Boudewijn van Dongen for fruitful discussions about the requirements for an automatic grader.

References

1. Jensen, K., Kristensen, L.M.: Coloured Petri Nets – Modelling and Validation of Concurrent Systems. Springer (2009)
2. van der Aalst, W.M.P., Stahl, C.: Modeling Business Processes – A Petri Net-Oriented Approach. MIT Press (2011)
3. Online: CPN Tools webpage, http://cpntools.org
4. Westergaard, M., Kristensen, L.M.: The Access/CPN Framework: A Tool for Interacting with the CPN Tools Simulator. In: Franceschinis, G., Wolf, K. (eds.) PETRI NETS 2009. LNCS, vol. 5606, pp. 313–322. Springer, Heidelberg (2009)
5. Westergaard, M., Fahland, D., Stahl, C.: Grade/CPN: Semi-automatic Support for Teaching Petri Nets by Checking Many Petri Nets Against One Specification. In: Proc. of PNSE. CEUR Workshop Proceedings, vol. 851, pp. 32–46. CEUR-WS.org (2012)
6. Westergaard, M., Evangelista, S., Kristensen, L.M.: ASAP: An Extensible Platform for State Space Analysis. In: Franceschinis, G., Wolf, K. (eds.) PETRI NETS 2009. LNCS, vol. 5606, pp. 303–312. Springer, Heidelberg (2009)
7. Pnueli, A.: The Temporal Logic of Programs. In: Proc. of SFCS 1977, pp. 46–57. IEEE Comp. Soc. (1977)
8. Kripke, S.A.: A semantical analysis of modal logic: I. Normal modal propositional calculi. Zeitschrift für Mathematische Logic und Grundlagen der Mathematik 9, 67–96 (1963)
9. Plotkin, G.: A Structural Approach to Operational Semantics. DAIMI-FN 19, Department of Computer Science, University of Aarhus (1981)
10. Giannakopoulou, D., Havelund, K.: Automata-Based Verification of Temporal Properties on Running Programs. In: Proc. ASE, pp. 412–416. IEEE Computer Society (2001)
11. Utting, M., Legeard, B.: Practical Model-Based Testing: A Tools Approach. Morgan Kaufmann Publishers (2006)
12. Weißleder, S.: Simulated satisfaction of coverage criteria on uml state machines. In: ICST 2012, pp. 117–126 (2010)
13. Bauer, A., Leucker, M., Schallhart, C.: Comparing LTL Semantics for Runtime Verification. Logic and Computation 20(3), 651–674 (2010)
14. Online: JUnit webpage, http://junit.org
15. Online: Jenkins Continuous Integration webpage, http://jenkins-ci.org
16. Ihantola, P., Ahoniemi, T., Karavirta, V., Seppälä, O.: Review of Recent Systems for Automatic Assessment of Programming Assignments. In: Proc. International Conference on Computing Education Research, pp. 86–93. ACM (2010)
17. Verhoeff, T.: Programming Task Packages: Peach Exchange Format. Olympiads in Informnatics 2, 192–207 (2008)
18. Damm, W., Harel, D.: LSCs: Breathing Life into Message Sequence Charts. Form. Methods Syst. Des. 19(1), 45–80 (2001)
19. Clarke, E., Grumberg, O., Jha, S., Lu, Y., Veith, H.: Counterexample-Guided Abstraction Refinement for Symbolic Model Checking. J. ACM 50, 752–794 (2003)
20. Edelkamp, S., Lluch Lafuente, A., Leue, S.: Directed Explicit Model Checking with HFS-SPIN. In: Dwyer, M.B. (ed.) SPIN 2001. LNCS, vol. 2057, pp. 57–79. Springer, Heidelberg (2001)
21. ISO/IEC: Software and system engineering – High-level Petri nets – Part 2: Transfer format. ISO/IEC 15909-2:2011

Author Index

Baldan, Paolo   1
Ben Maissa, Yann   24
Bernardinello, Luca   48

Cocco, Nicoletta   1

Dedova, Anna   71

Fahland, Dirk   180

Giummolè, Federica   1

Heiner, Monika   123
Herajy, Mostafa   123

Janowska, Agata   89

Köhler-Bußmeier, Michael   159
Kordon, Fabrice   24

Mangioni, Elisabetta   48
Mouline, Salma   24

Penczek, Wojciech   89
Petrucci, Laure   71
Półrola, Agata   89
Pomello, Lucia   48

Rohr, Christian   142

Schwarick, Martin   123
Sidorova, Natalia   106
Simeoni, Marta   1
Stahl, Christian   180

Thierry-Mieg, Yann   24

van der Werf, Jan Martijn E.M.   106
van Hee, Kees M.   106

Wester-Ebbinghaus, Matthias   159
Westergaard, Michael   180

Zbrzezny, Andrzej   89